ROCKY& BULLWINKLE™

CLASSICS
VOLUME 2

WITHDRAWN

ROCKY & BULLWINKLE™
CLASSICS
VOLUME 2

Though credited to **Al Kilgore**, research has shown that artists **Fred Fredericks**, **Jerry Robinson**, and **Mel Crawford** likely contributed artwork to stories written by **Jack Mendelsohn**, **Dave Berg**, and others.

Cover by **Roger Langridge** • Cover Colors by **Jeremy Colwell** • Collection Edits by **Justin Eisinger** & **Alonzo Simon** • Collection Design by **Gilberto Lazcano**

ISBN: 978-1-63140-019-3

17 16 15 14   1 2 3 4

IDW®

www.IDWPUBLISHING.com
IDW founded by Ted Adams, Alex Garner, Kris Oprisko, and Robbie Robbins

Ted Adams, CEO & Publisher
Greg Goldstein, President & COO
Robbie Robbins, EVP/Sr. Graphic Artist
Chris Ryall, Chief Creative Officer/Editor-in-Chief
Matthew Ruzicka, CPA, Chief Financial Officer
Alan Payne, VP of Sales
Dirk Wood, VP of Marketing
Lorelei Bunjes, VP of Digital Services
Jeff Webber, VP of Digital Publishing & Business Development

Facebook: **facebook.com/idwpublishing**
Twitter: **@idwpublishing**
YouTube: **youtube.com/idwpublishing**
Instagram: **instagram.com/idwpublishing**
deviantART: **idwpublishing.deviantart.com**
Pinterest: **pinterest.com/idwpublishing/idw-staff-faves**

BULLWINKLE and ROCKY

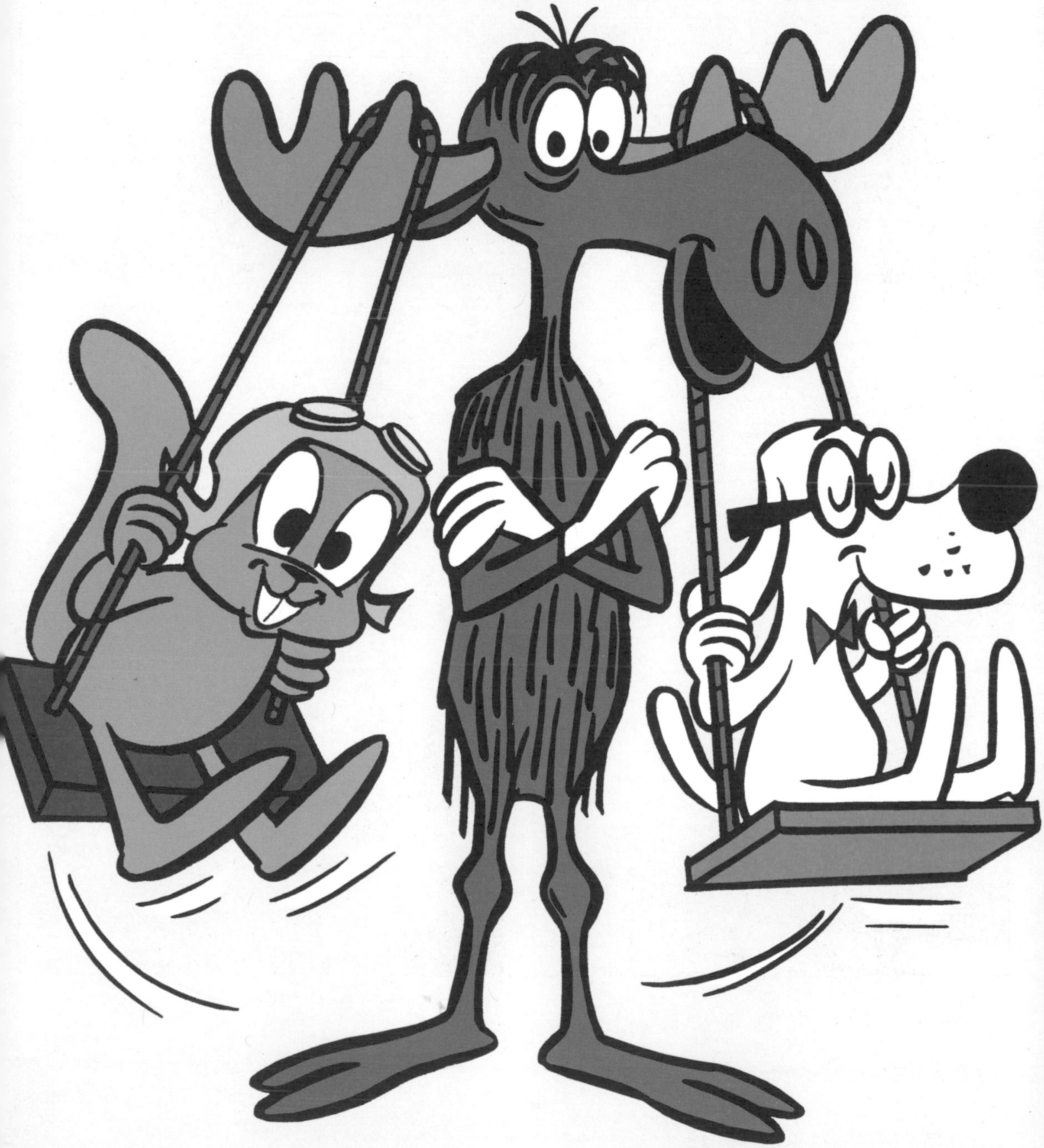

ISSUE #5 · GOLD KEY · SEPTEMBER 1972

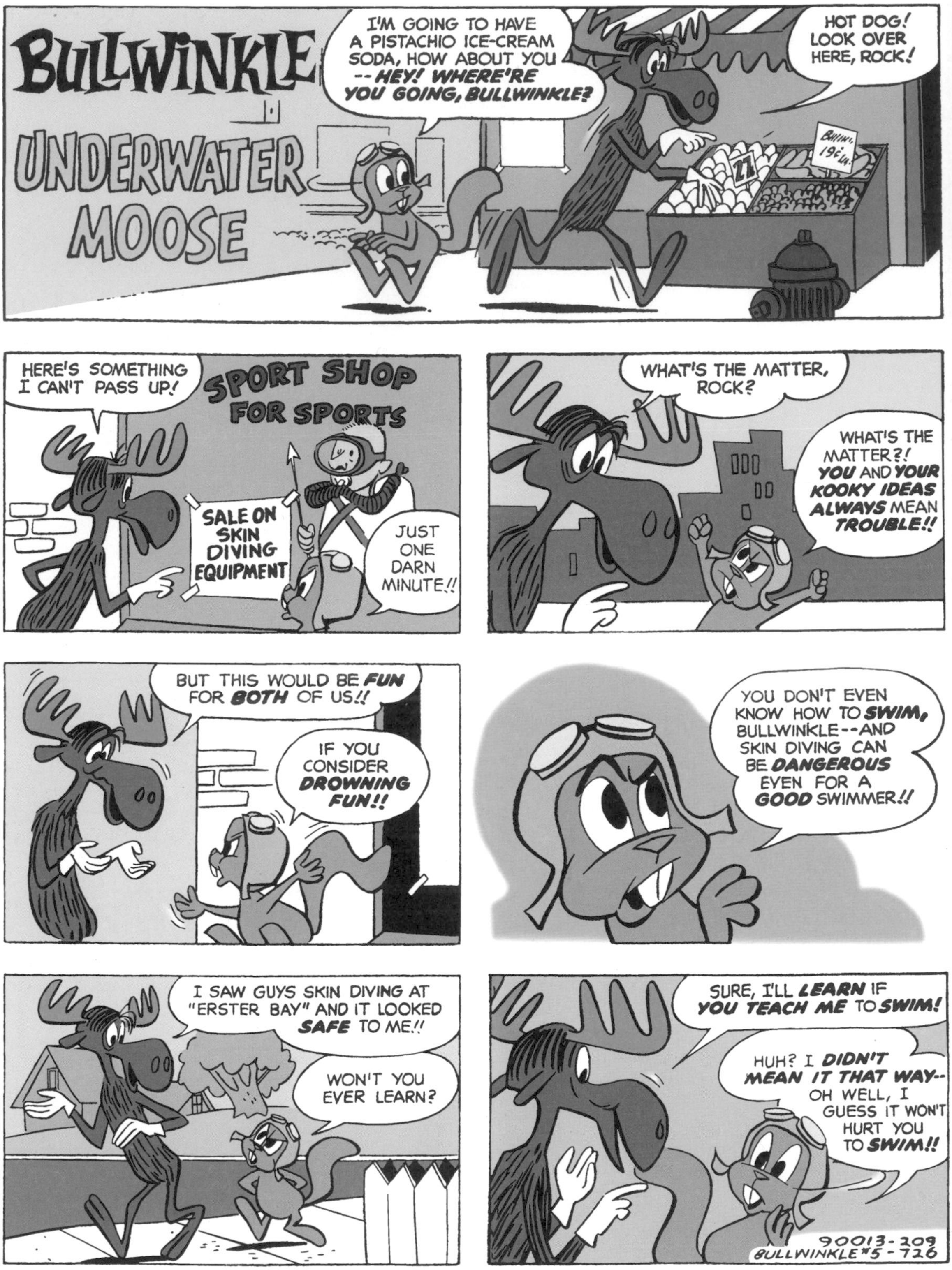
BULLWINKLE
UNDERWATER MOOSE
I'M GOING TO HAVE A PISTACHIO ICE-CREAM SODA, HOW ABOUT YOU --HEY! WHERE'RE YOU GOING, BULLWINKLE?
HOT DOG! LOOK OVER HERE, ROCK!
HERE'S SOMETHING I CAN'T PASS UP!
SPORT SHOP FOR SPORTS
SALE ON SKIN DIVING EQUIPMENT
JUST ONE DARN MINUTE!!
WHAT'S THE MATTER, ROCK?
WHAT'S THE MATTER?! YOU AND YOUR KOOKY IDEAS ALWAYS MEAN TROUBLE!!
BUT THIS WOULD BE FUN FOR BOTH OF US!!
IF YOU CONSIDER DROWNING FUN!!
YOU DON'T EVEN KNOW HOW TO SWIM, BULLWINKLE--AND SKIN DIVING CAN BE DANGEROUS EVEN FOR A GOOD SWIMMER!!
I SAW GUYS SKIN DIVING AT "ERSTER BAY" AND IT LOOKED SAFE TO ME!!
WON'T YOU EVER LEARN?
SURE, I'LL LEARN IF YOU TEACH ME TO SWIM!
HUH? I DIDN'T MEAN IT THAT WAY--OH WELL, I GUESS IT WON'T HURT YOU TO SWIM!!
90013-209
BULLWINKLE #5 - 726

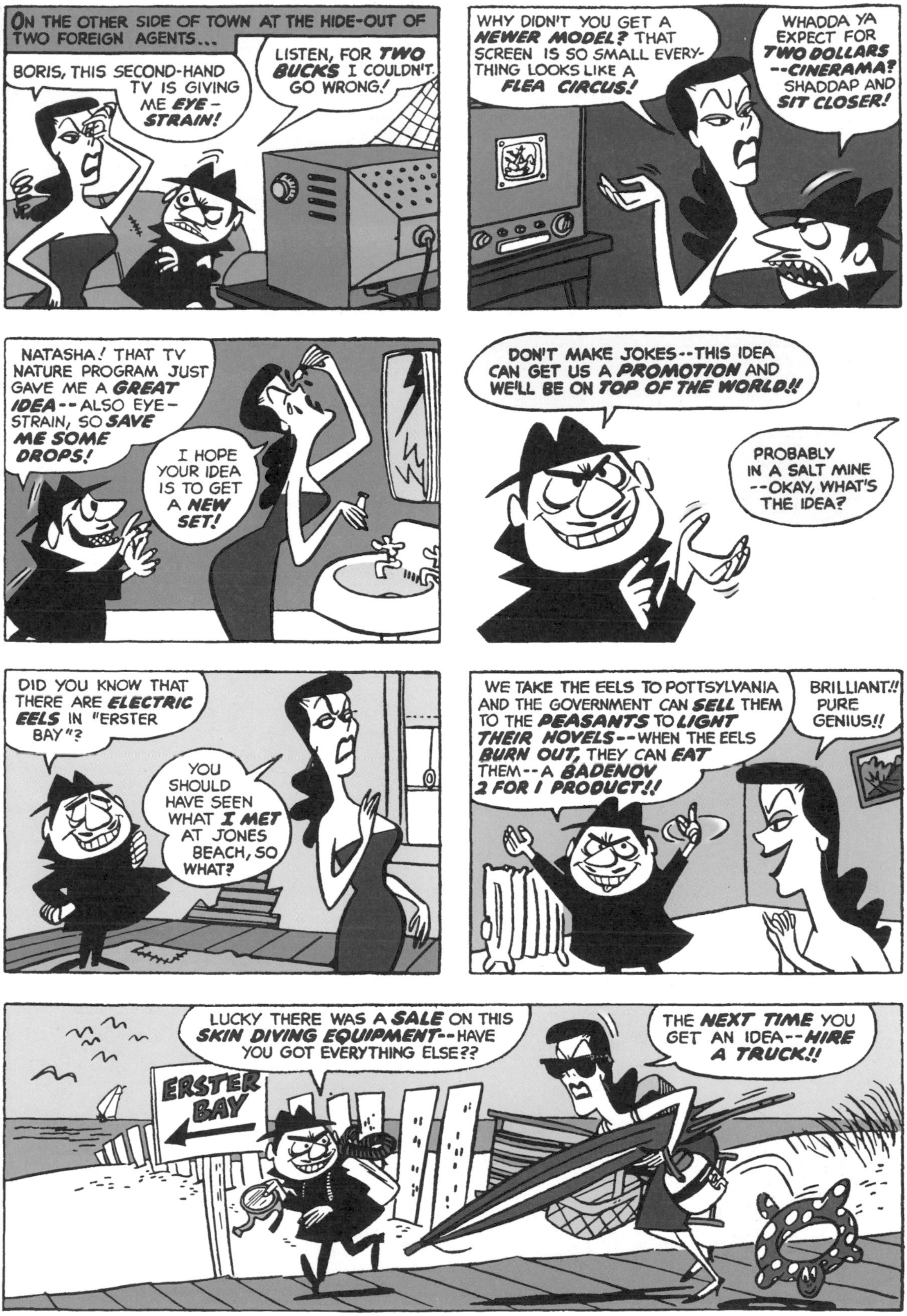
ON THE OTHER SIDE OF TOWN AT THE HIDE-OUT OF TWO FOREIGN AGENTS...
BORIS, THIS SECOND-HAND TV IS GIVING ME EYE-STRAIN!
LISTEN, FOR TWO BUCKS I COULDN'T GO WRONG!
WHY DIDN'T YOU GET A NEWER MODEL? THAT SCREEN IS SO SMALL EVERYTHING LOOKS LIKE A FLEA CIRCUS!
WHADDA YA EXPECT FOR TWO DOLLARS --CINERAMA? SHADDAP AND SIT CLOSER!
NATASHA! THAT TV NATURE PROGRAM JUST GAVE ME A GREAT IDEA-- ALSO EYE-STRAIN, SO SAVE ME SOME DROPS!
I HOPE YOUR IDEA IS TO GET A NEW SET!
DON'T MAKE JOKES--THIS IDEA CAN GET US A PROMOTION AND WE'LL BE ON TOP OF THE WORLD!!
PROBABLY IN A SALT MINE --OKAY, WHAT'S THE IDEA?
DID YOU KNOW THAT THERE ARE ELECTRIC EELS IN "ERSTER BAY"?
YOU SHOULD HAVE SEEN WHAT I MET AT JONES BEACH, SO WHAT?
WE TAKE THE EELS TO POTTSYLVANIA AND THE GOVERNMENT CAN SELL THEM TO THE PEASANTS TO LIGHT THEIR HOVELS--WHEN THE EELS BURN OUT, THEY CAN EAT THEM--A BADENOV 2 FOR 1 PRODUCT!!
BRILLIANT!! PURE GENIUS!!
LUCKY THERE WAS A SALE ON THIS SKIN DIVING EQUIPMENT--HAVE YOU GOT EVERYTHING ELSE??
THE NEXT TIME YOU GET AN IDEA--HIRE A TRUCK!!
ERSTER BAY

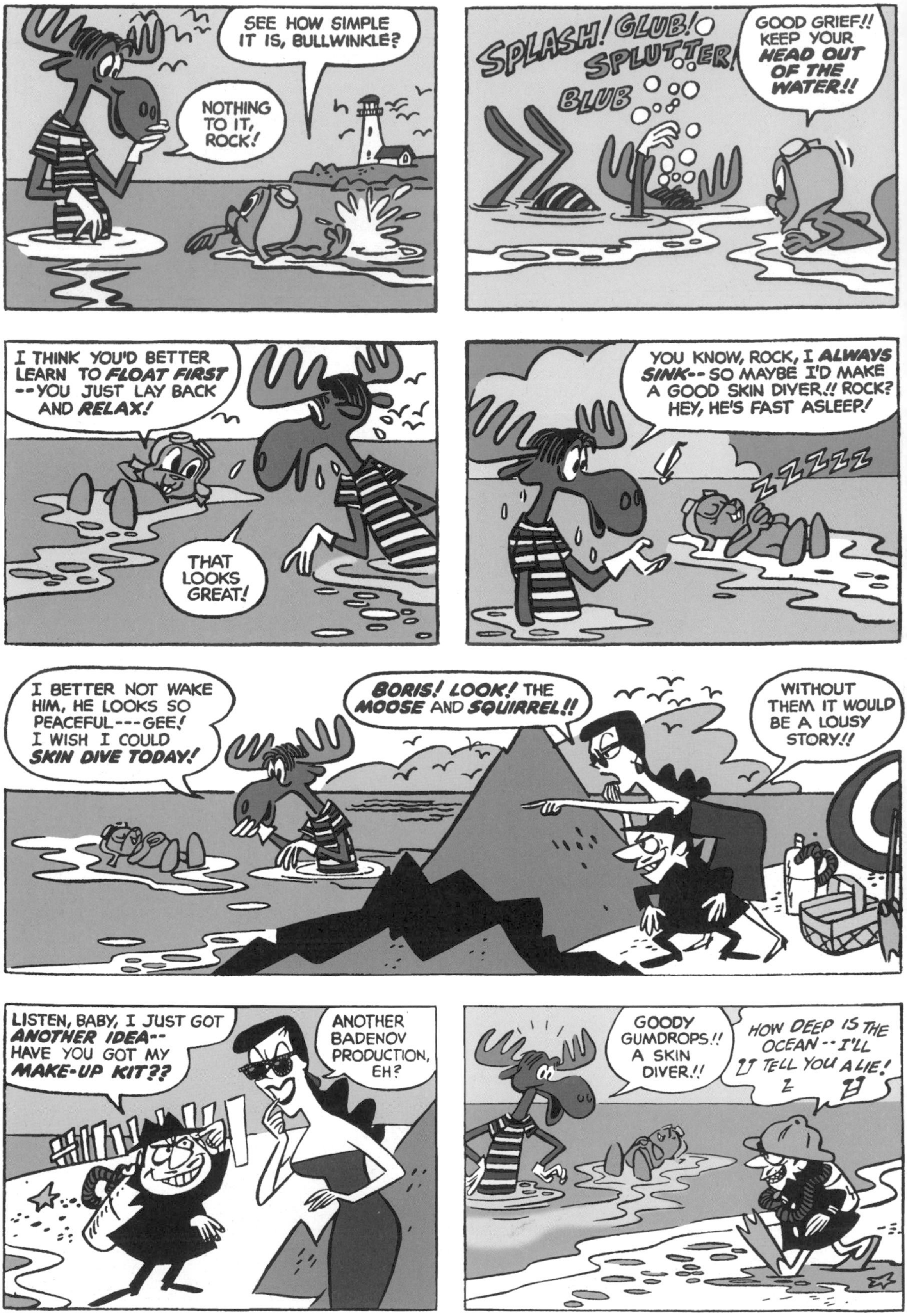
SEE HOW SIMPLE IT IS, BULLWINKLE?
NOTHING TO IT, ROCK!
SPLASH! GLUB! SPLUTTER! BLUB
GOOD GRIEF!! KEEP YOUR HEAD OUT OF THE WATER!!
I THINK YOU'D BETTER LEARN TO FLOAT FIRST --YOU JUST LAY BACK AND RELAX!
THAT LOOKS GREAT!
YOU KNOW, ROCK, I ALWAYS SINK-- SO MAYBE I'D MAKE A GOOD SKIN DIVER!! ROCK? HEY, HE'S FAST ASLEEP!
ZZZZZZ
I BETTER NOT WAKE HIM, HE LOOKS SO PEACEFUL---GEE! I WISH I COULD SKIN DIVE TODAY!
BORIS! LOOK! THE MOOSE AND SQUIRREL!!
WITHOUT THEM IT WOULD BE A LOUSY STORY!!
LISTEN, BABY, I JUST GOT ANOTHER IDEA-- HAVE YOU GOT MY MAKE-UP KIT??
ANOTHER BADENOV PRODUCTION, EH?
GOODY GUMDROPS!! A SKIN DIVER!!
HOW DEEP IS THE OCEAN --I'LL TELL YOU A LIE!

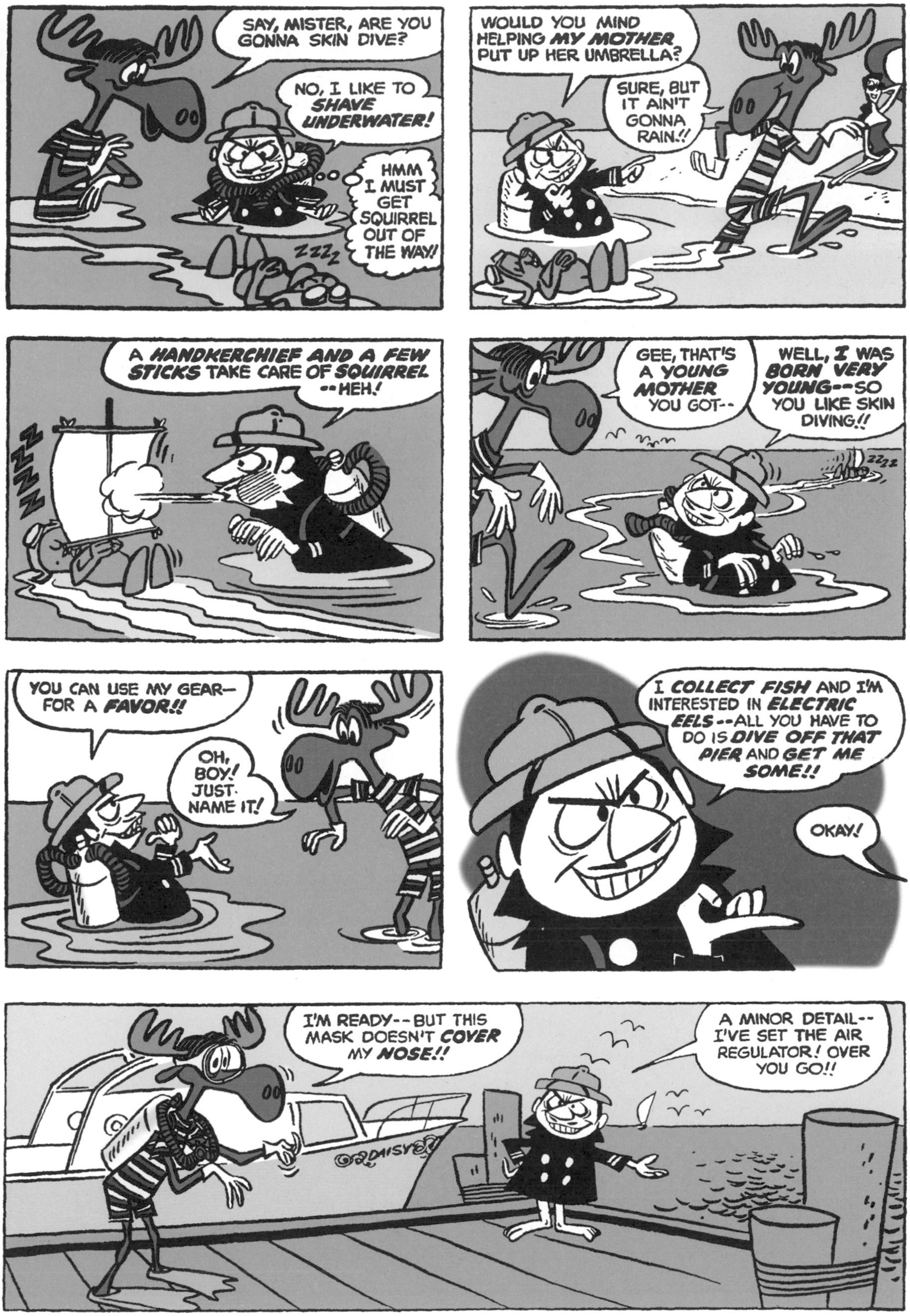
SAY, MISTER, ARE YOU GONNA SKIN DIVE?
NO, I LIKE TO SHAVE UNDERWATER!
HMM I MUST GET SQUIRREL OUT OF THE WAY!
ZZZZ
WOULD YOU MIND HELPING MY MOTHER PUT UP HER UMBRELLA?
SURE, BUT IT AIN'T GONNA RAIN!!
A HANDKERCHIEF AND A FEW STICKS TAKE CARE OF SQUIRREL --HEH!
ZZZZ
GEE, THAT'S A YOUNG MOTHER YOU GOT--
WELL, I WAS BORN VERY YOUNG--SO YOU LIKE SKIN DIVING!!
ZZZZ
YOU CAN USE MY GEAR— FOR A FAVOR!!
OH, BOY! JUST NAME IT!
I COLLECT FISH AND I'M INTERESTED IN ELECTRIC EELS--ALL YOU HAVE TO DO IS DIVE OFF THAT PIER AND GET ME SOME!!
OKAY!
I'M READY--BUT THIS MASK DOESN'T COVER MY NOSE!!
A MINOR DETAIL-- I'VE SET THE AIR REGULATOR! OVER YOU GO!!
DAISY

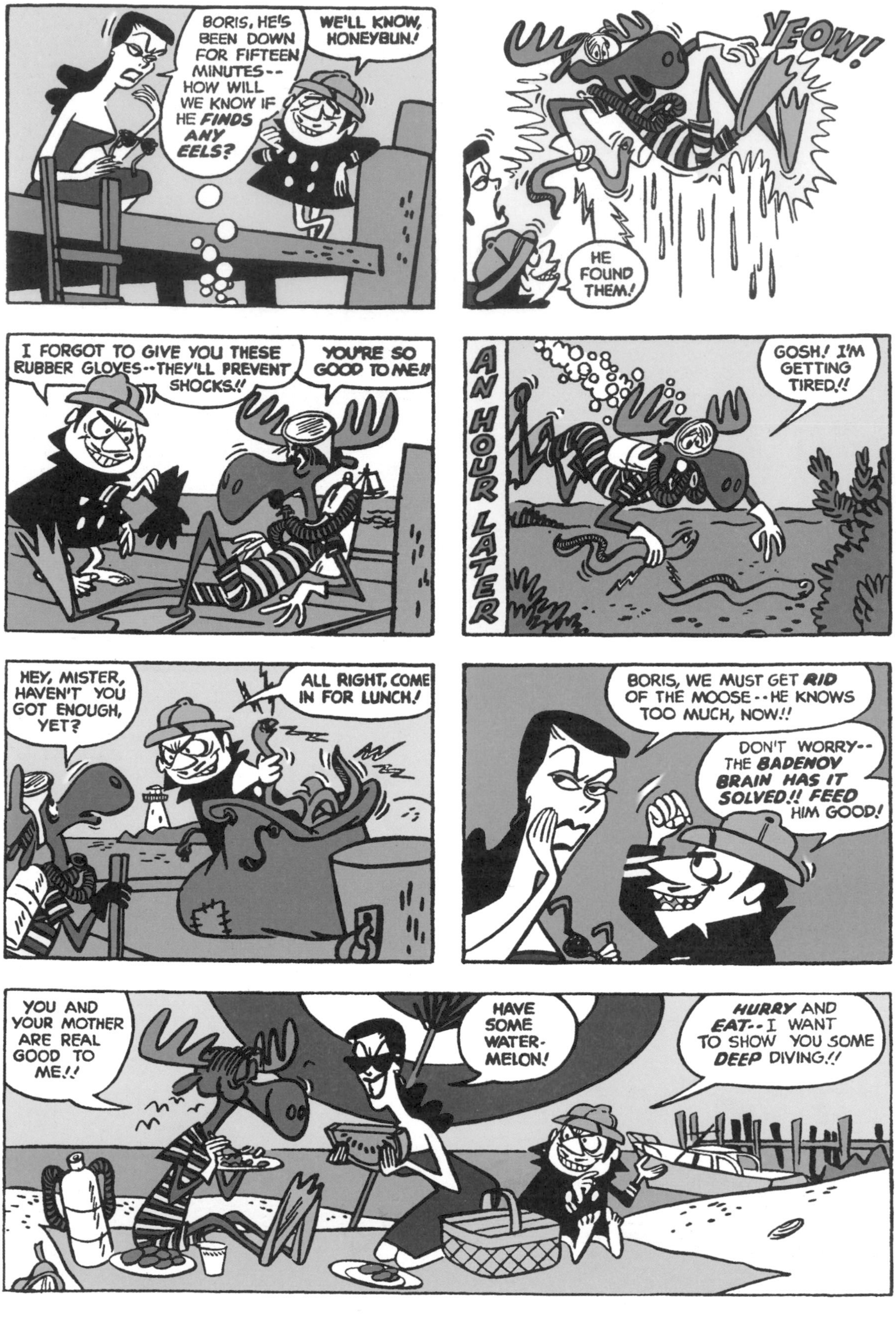
BORIS, HE'S BEEN DOWN FOR FIFTEEN MINUTES-- HOW WILL WE KNOW IF HE FINDS ANY EELS?
WE'LL KNOW, HONEYBUN!
YEOW!
HE FOUND THEM!
I FORGOT TO GIVE YOU THESE RUBBER GLOVES--THEY'LL PREVENT SHOCKS!!
YOU'RE SO GOOD TO ME!!
AN HOUR LATER
GOSH! I'M GETTING TIRED!!
HEY, MISTER, HAVEN'T YOU GOT ENOUGH, YET?
ALL RIGHT, COME IN FOR LUNCH!
BORIS, WE MUST GET RID OF THE MOOSE--HE KNOWS TOO MUCH, NOW!!
DON'T WORRY-- THE BADENOV BRAIN HAS IT SOLVED!! FEED HIM GOOD!
YOU AND YOUR MOTHER ARE REAL GOOD TO ME!!
HAVE SOME WATER-MELON!
HURRY AND EAT--I WANT TO SHOW YOU SOME DEEP DIVING!!

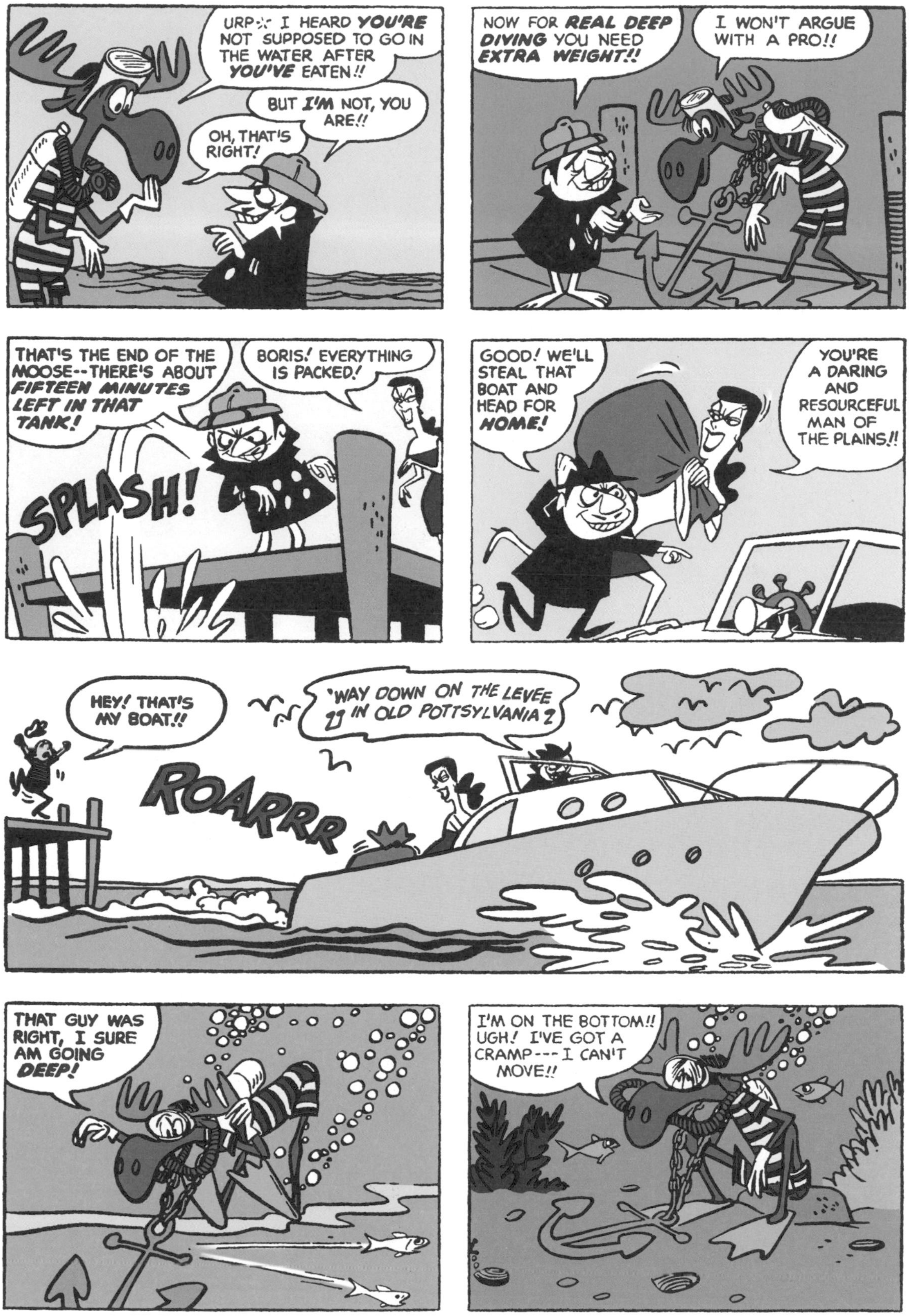
URP* I HEARD YOU'RE NOT SUPPOSED TO GO IN THE WATER AFTER YOU'VE EATEN!!
BUT I'M NOT, YOU ARE!!
OH, THAT'S RIGHT!
NOW FOR REAL DEEP DIVING YOU NEED EXTRA WEIGHT!!
I WON'T ARGUE WITH A PRO!!
THAT'S THE END OF THE MOOSE--THERE'S ABOUT FIFTEEN MINUTES LEFT IN THAT TANK!
BORIS! EVERYTHING IS PACKED!
SPLASH!
GOOD! WE'LL STEAL THAT BOAT AND HEAD FOR HOME!
YOU'RE A DARING AND RESOURCEFUL MAN OF THE PLAINS!!
HEY! THAT'S MY BOAT!!
'WAY DOWN ON THE LEVEE ♪ IN OLD POTTSYLVANIA ♪
ROARRRR
THAT GUY WAS RIGHT, I SURE AM GOING DEEP!
I'M ON THE BOTTOM!! UGH! I'VE GOT A CRAMP---I CAN'T MOVE!!

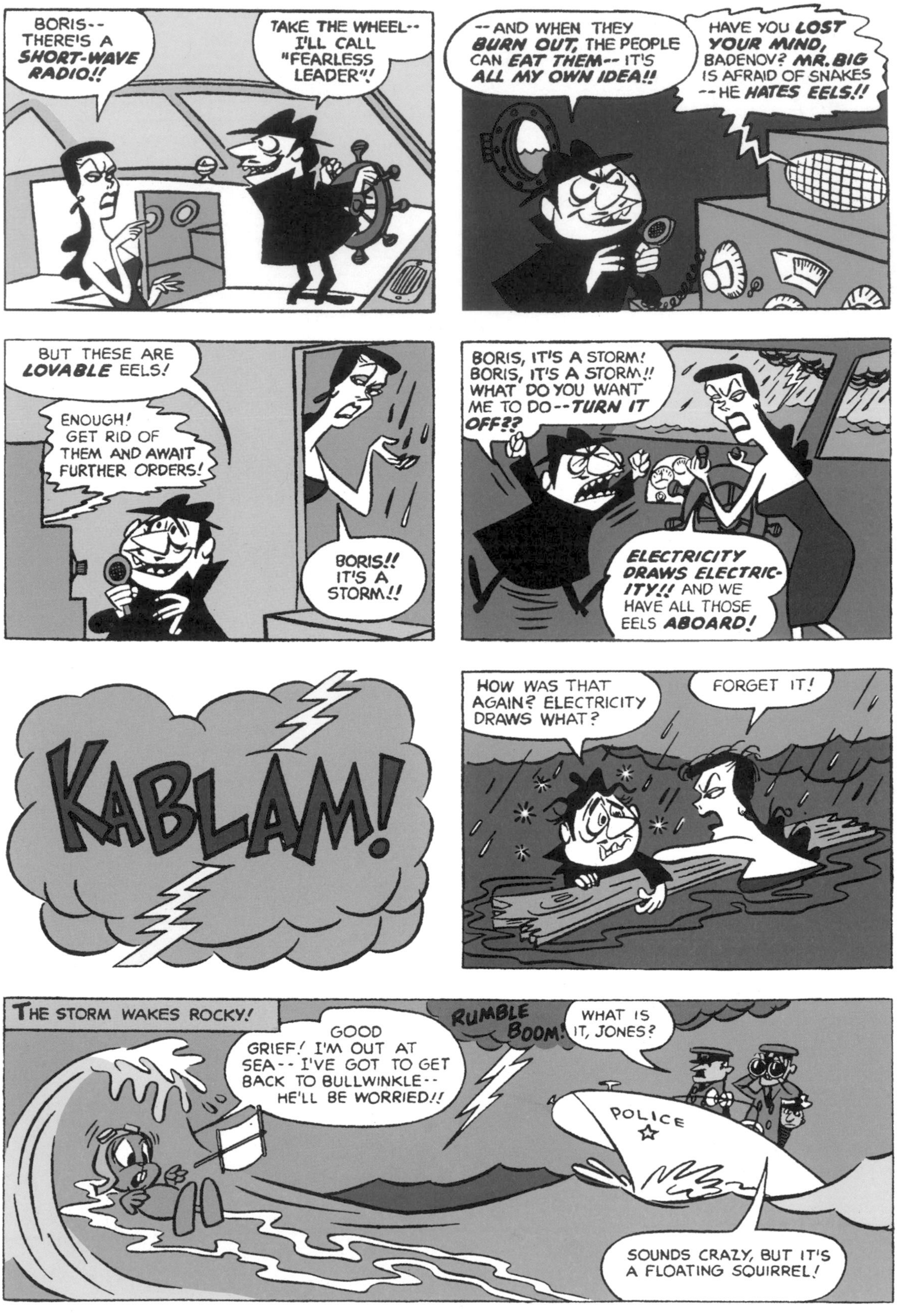
BORIS-- THERE'S A SHORT-WAVE RADIO!!
TAKE THE WHEEL-- I'LL CALL "FEARLESS LEADER"!
--AND WHEN THEY BURN OUT, THE PEOPLE CAN EAT THEM-- IT'S ALL MY OWN IDEA!!
HAVE YOU LOST YOUR MIND, BADENOV? MR. BIG IS AFRAID OF SNAKES --HE HATES EELS!!
BUT THESE ARE LOVABLE EELS!
ENOUGH! GET RID OF THEM AND AWAIT FURTHER ORDERS!
BORIS!! IT'S A STORM!!
BORIS, IT'S A STORM! BORIS, IT'S A STORM!! WHAT DO YOU WANT ME TO DO--TURN IT OFF??
ELECTRICITY DRAWS ELECTRICITY!! AND WE HAVE ALL THOSE EELS ABOARD!
KABLAM!
HOW WAS THAT AGAIN? ELECTRICITY DRAWS WHAT?
FORGET IT!
THE STORM WAKES ROCKY!
GOOD GRIEF! I'M OUT AT SEA-- I'VE GOT TO GET BACK TO BULLWINKLE-- HE'LL BE WORRIED!!
RUMBLE BOOM!
WHAT IS IT, JONES?
POLICE
SOUNDS CRAZY, BUT IT'S A FLOATING SQUIRREL!

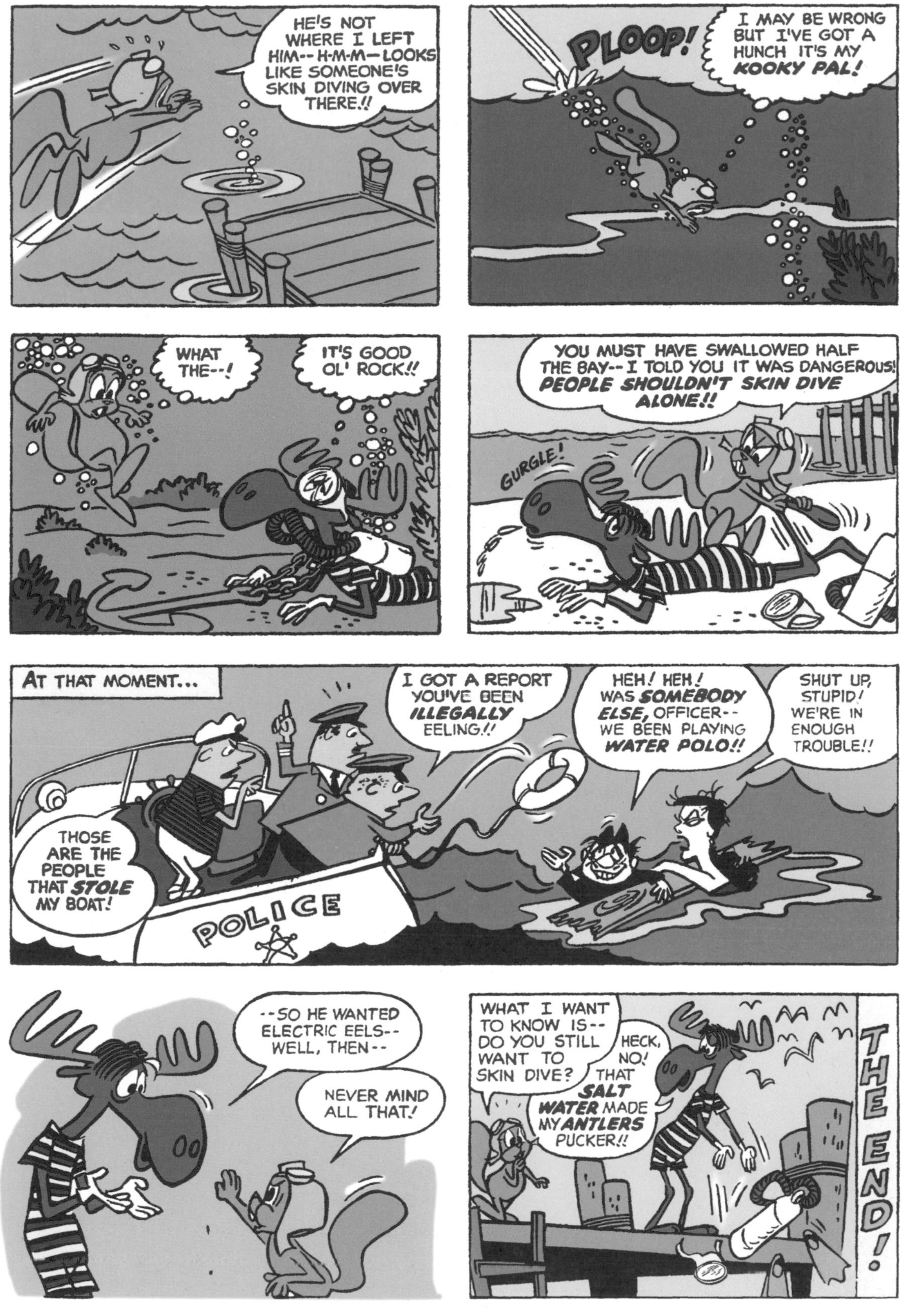
HE'S NOT WHERE I LEFT HIM-- H-M-M-- LOOKS LIKE SOMEONE'S SKIN DIVING OVER THERE.!!
PLOOP!
I MAY BE WRONG BUT I'VE GOT A HUNCH IT'S MY KOOKY PAL!
WHAT THE--!
IT'S GOOD OL' ROCK!!
YOU MUST HAVE SWALLOWED HALF THE BAY-- I TOLD YOU IT WAS DANGEROUS! PEOPLE SHOULDN'T SKIN DIVE ALONE!!
GURGLE!
AT THAT MOMENT...
THOSE ARE THE PEOPLE THAT STOLE MY BOAT!
I GOT A REPORT YOU'VE BEEN ILLEGALLY EELING!!
HEH! HEH! WAS SOMEBODY ELSE, OFFICER-- WE BEEN PLAYING WATER POLO!!
SHUT UP, STUPID! WE'RE IN ENOUGH TROUBLE!!
POLICE
--SO HE WANTED ELECTRIC EELS-- WELL, THEN--
NEVER MIND ALL THAT!
WHAT I WANT TO KNOW IS-- DO YOU STILL WANT TO SKIN DIVE?
HECK, NO! THAT SALT WATER MADE MY ANTLERS PUCKER!!
THE END!

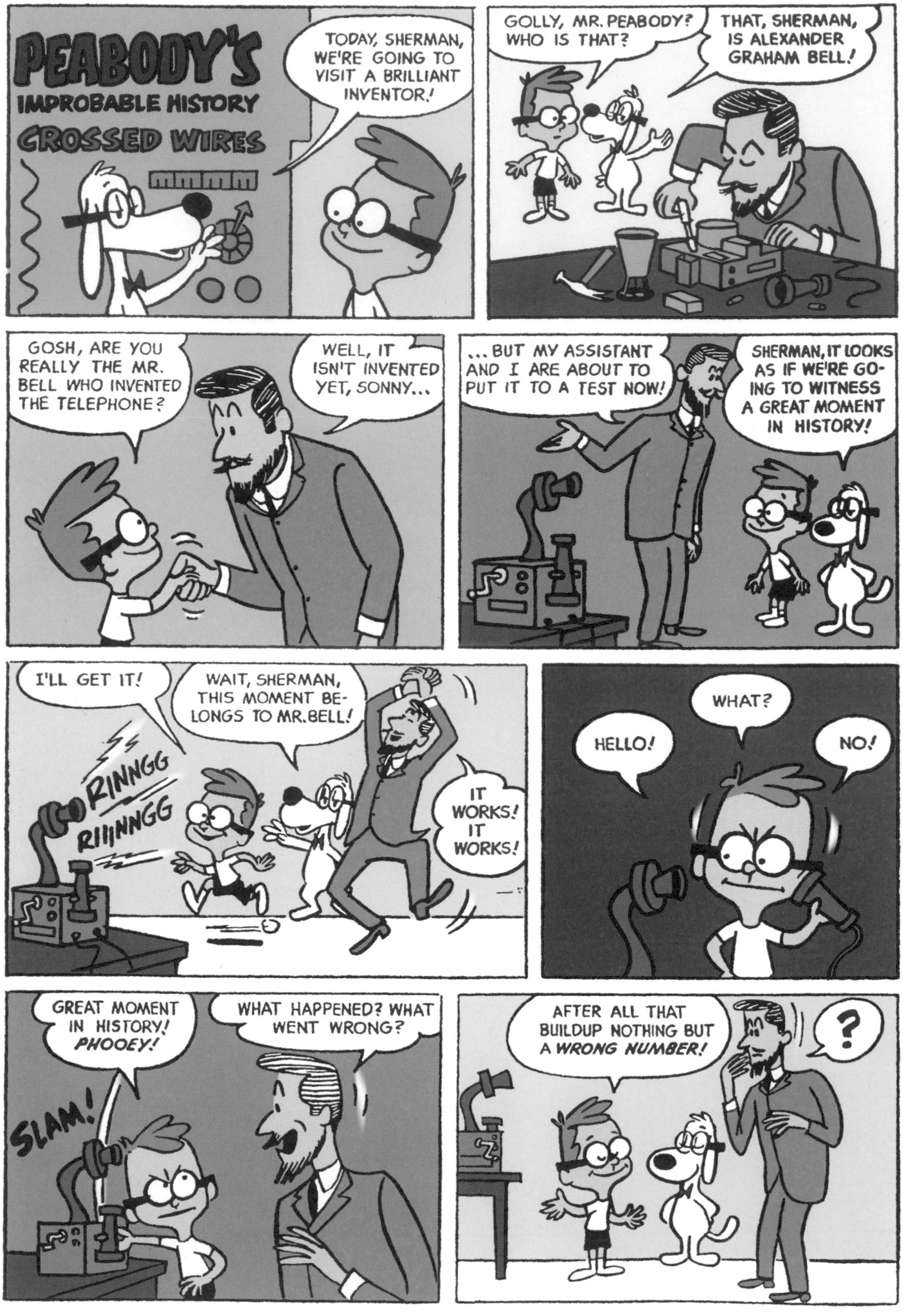
PEABODY'S
IMPROBABLE HISTORY
CROSSED WIRES
TODAY, SHERMAN, WE'RE GOING TO VISIT A BRILLIANT INVENTOR!
GOLLY, MR. PEABODY? WHO IS THAT?
THAT, SHERMAN, IS ALEXANDER GRAHAM BELL!
GOSH, ARE YOU REALLY THE MR. BELL WHO INVENTED THE TELEPHONE?
WELL, IT ISN'T INVENTED YET, SONNY...
...BUT MY ASSISTANT AND I ARE ABOUT TO PUT IT TO A TEST NOW!
SHERMAN, IT LOOKS AS IF WE'RE GOING TO WITNESS A GREAT MOMENT IN HISTORY!
I'LL GET IT!
WAIT, SHERMAN, THIS MOMENT BELONGS TO MR. BELL!
RINNGG
RIIINNGG
IT WORKS! IT WORKS!
HELLO!
WHAT?
NO!
GREAT MOMENT IN HISTORY! PHOOEY!
WHAT HAPPENED? WHAT WENT WRONG?
SLAM!
AFTER ALL THAT BUILDUP NOTHING BUT A WRONG NUMBER!
?

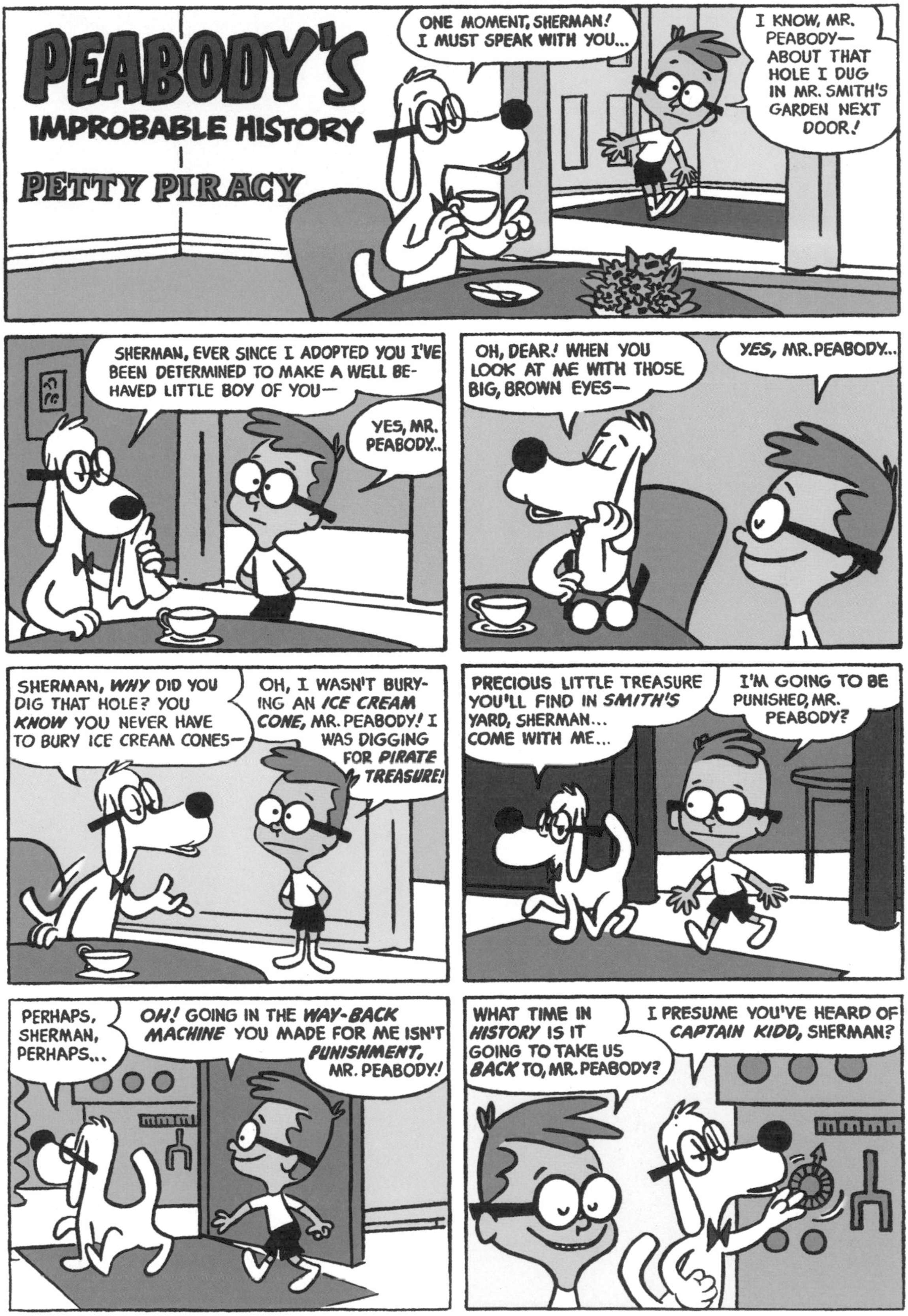
PEABODY'S
IMPROBABLE HISTORY
PETTY PIRACY
ONE MOMENT, SHERMAN! I MUST SPEAK WITH YOU...
I KNOW, MR. PEABODY— ABOUT THAT HOLE I DUG IN MR. SMITH'S GARDEN NEXT DOOR!
SHERMAN, EVER SINCE I ADOPTED YOU I'VE BEEN DETERMINED TO MAKE A WELL BE-HAVED LITTLE BOY OF YOU—
YES, MR. PEABODY...
OH, DEAR! WHEN YOU LOOK AT ME WITH THOSE BIG, BROWN EYES—
YES, MR. PEABODY...
SHERMAN, WHY DID YOU DIG THAT HOLE? YOU KNOW YOU NEVER HAVE TO BURY ICE CREAM CONES—
OH, I WASN'T BURY-ING AN ICE CREAM CONE, MR. PEABODY! I WAS DIGGING FOR PIRATE TREASURE!
PRECIOUS LITTLE TREASURE YOU'LL FIND IN SMITH'S YARD, SHERMAN... COME WITH ME...
I'M GOING TO BE PUNISHED, MR. PEABODY?
PERHAPS, SHERMAN, PERHAPS...
OH! GOING IN THE WAY-BACK MACHINE YOU MADE FOR ME ISN'T PUNISHMENT, MR. PEABODY!
WHAT TIME IN HISTORY IS IT GOING TO TAKE US BACK TO, MR. PEABODY?
I PRESUME YOU'VE HEARD OF CAPTAIN KIDD, SHERMAN?

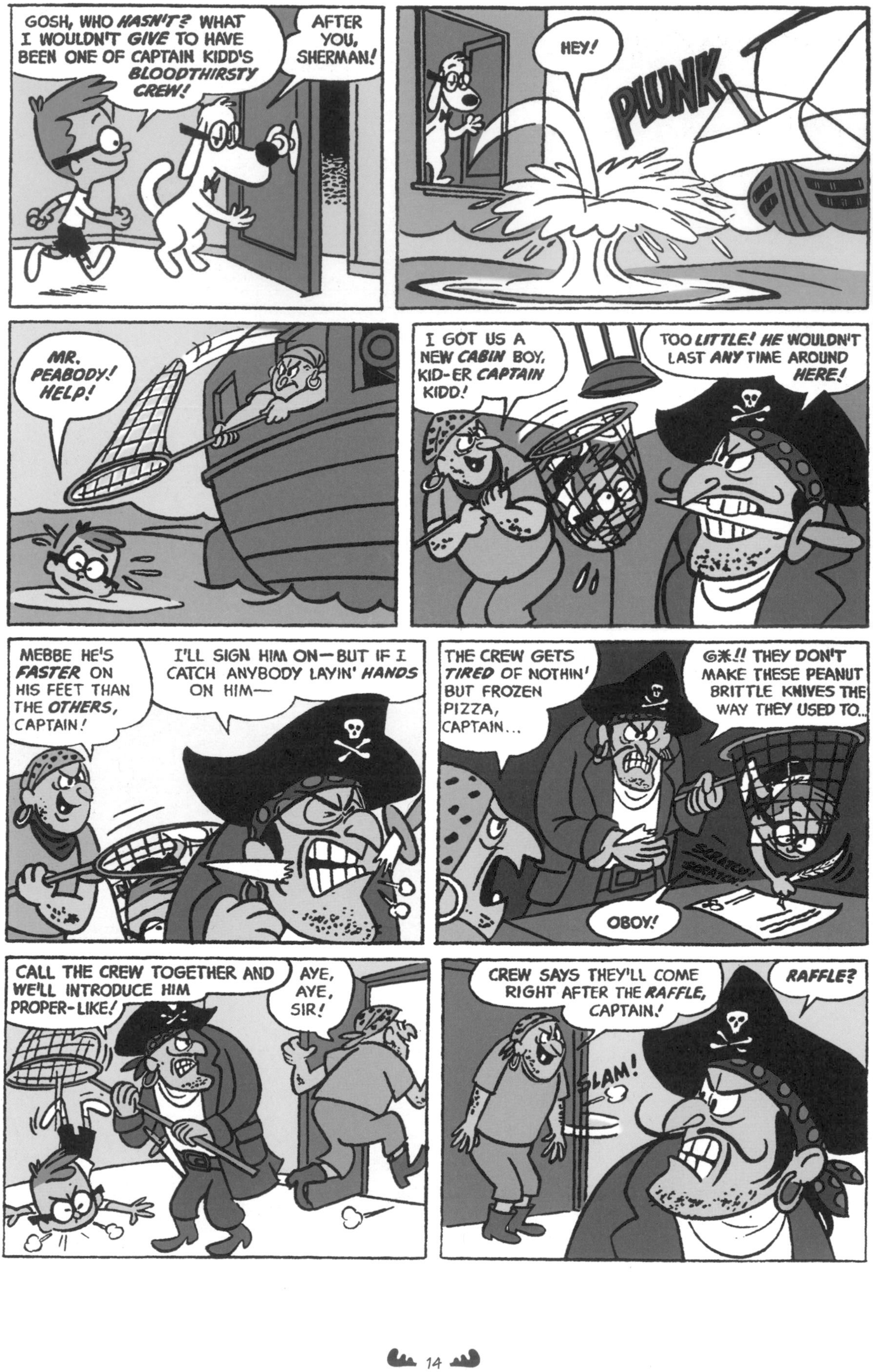

GOSH, WHO HASN'T? WHAT I WOULDN'T GIVE TO HAVE BEEN ONE OF CAPTAIN KIDD'S BLOODTHIRSTY CREW!
AFTER YOU, SHERMAN!
HEY!
PLUNK
MR. PEABODY! HELP!
I GOT US A NEW CABIN BOY, KID-ER CAPTAIN KIDD!
TOO LITTLE! HE WOULDN'T LAST ANY TIME AROUND HERE!
MEBBE HE'S FASTER ON HIS FEET THAN THE OTHERS, CAPTAIN!
I'LL SIGN HIM ON—BUT IF I CATCH ANYBODY LAYIN' HANDS ON HIM—
THE CREW GETS TIRED OF NOTHIN' BUT FROZEN PIZZA, CAPTAIN...
G✱!! THEY DON'T MAKE THESE PEANUT BRITTLE KNIVES THE WAY THEY USED TO...
SCRATCH! SCRATCH!
OBOY!
CALL THE CREW TOGETHER AND WE'LL INTRODUCE HIM PROPER-LIKE!
AYE, AYE, SIR!
CREW SAYS THEY'LL COME RIGHT AFTER THE RAFFLE, CAPTAIN!
SLAM!
RAFFLE?

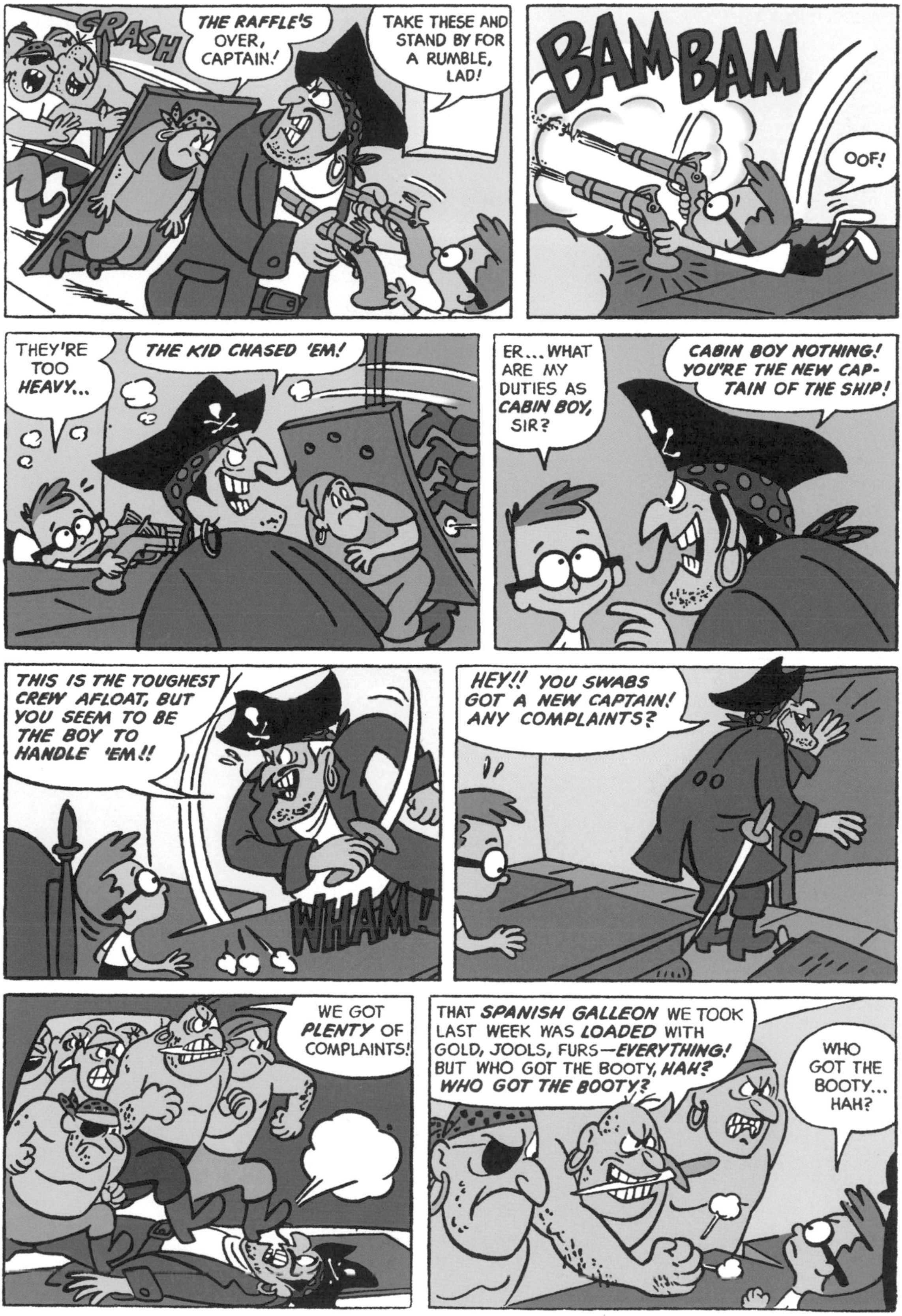
CRASH
THE RAFFLE'S OVER, CAPTAIN!
TAKE THESE AND STAND BY FOR A RUMBLE, LAD!
BAM BAM
OOF!
THEY'RE TOO HEAVY...
THE KID CHASED 'EM!
ER... WHAT ARE MY DUTIES AS CABIN BOY, SIR?
CABIN BOY NOTHING! YOU'RE THE NEW CAPTAIN OF THE SHIP!
THIS IS THE TOUGHEST CREW AFLOAT, BUT YOU SEEM TO BE THE BOY TO HANDLE 'EM!!
WHAM!
HEY!! YOU SWABS GOT A NEW CAPTAIN! ANY COMPLAINTS?
WE GOT PLENTY OF COMPLAINTS!
THAT SPANISH GALLEON WE TOOK LAST WEEK WAS LOADED WITH GOLD, JOOLS, FURS—EVERYTHING! BUT WHO GOT THE BOOTY, HAH? WHO GOT THE BOOTY?
WHO GOT THE BOOTY... HAH?

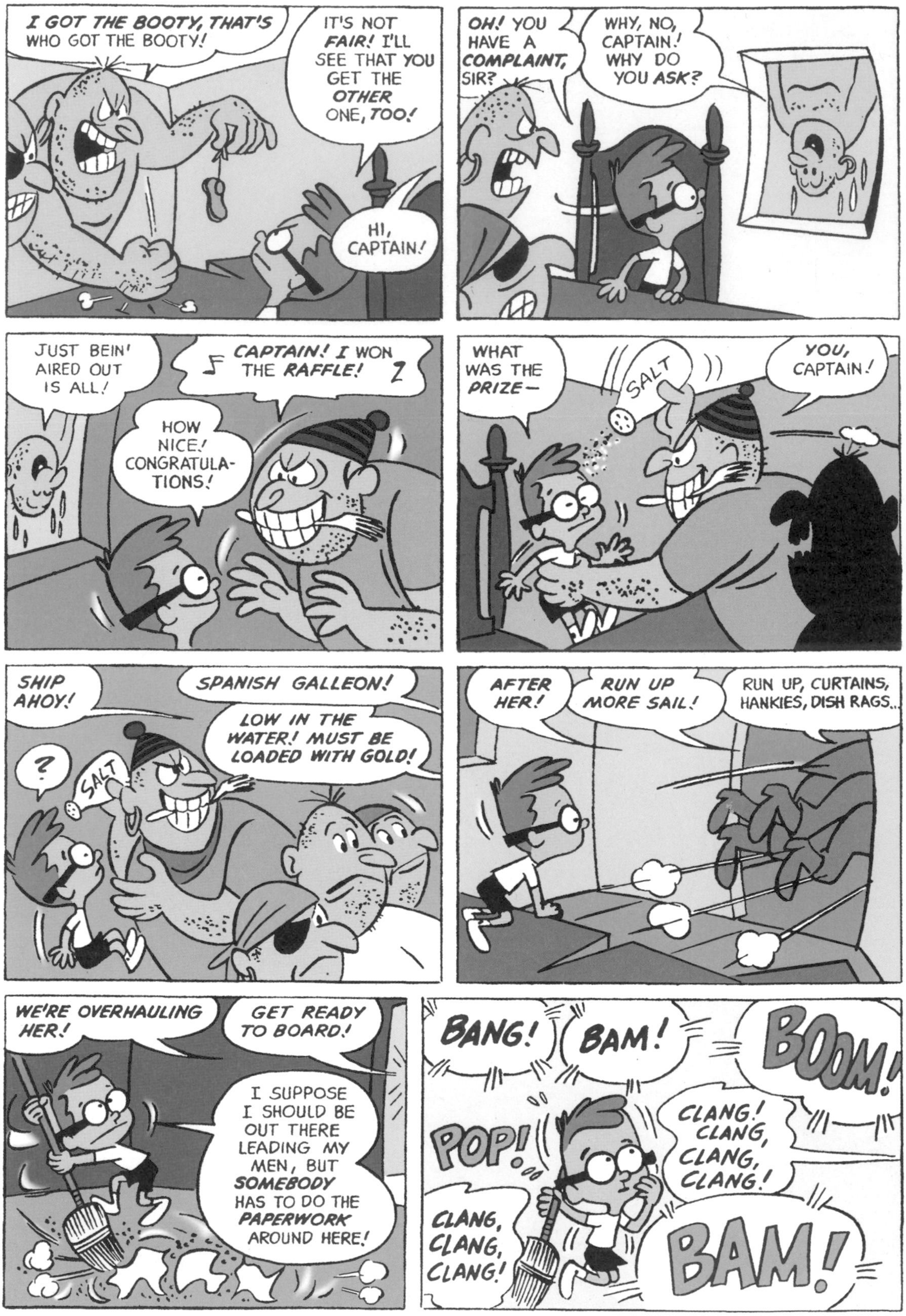
I GOT THE BOOTY, THAT'S WHO GOT THE BOOTY!
IT'S NOT FAIR! I'LL SEE THAT YOU GET THE OTHER ONE, TOO!
HI, CAPTAIN!
OH! YOU HAVE A COMPLAINT, SIR?
WHY, NO, CAPTAIN! WHY DO YOU ASK?
JUST BEIN' AIRED OUT IS ALL!
CAPTAIN! I WON THE RAFFLE!
HOW NICE! CONGRATULA-TIONS!
WHAT WAS THE PRIZE—
SALT
YOU, CAPTAIN!
SHIP AHOY!
SPANISH GALLEON!
LOW IN THE WATER! MUST BE LOADED WITH GOLD!
?
SALT
AFTER HER!
RUN UP MORE SAIL!
RUN UP, CURTAINS, HANKIES, DISH RAGS...
WE'RE OVERHAULING HER!
GET READY TO BOARD!
I SUPPOSE I SHOULD BE OUT THERE LEADING MY MEN, BUT SOMEBODY HAS TO DO THE PAPERWORK AROUND HERE!
BANG!
BAM!
BOOM!
POP!
CLANG! CLANG, CLANG, CLANG!
CLANG, CLANG, CLANG!
BAM!

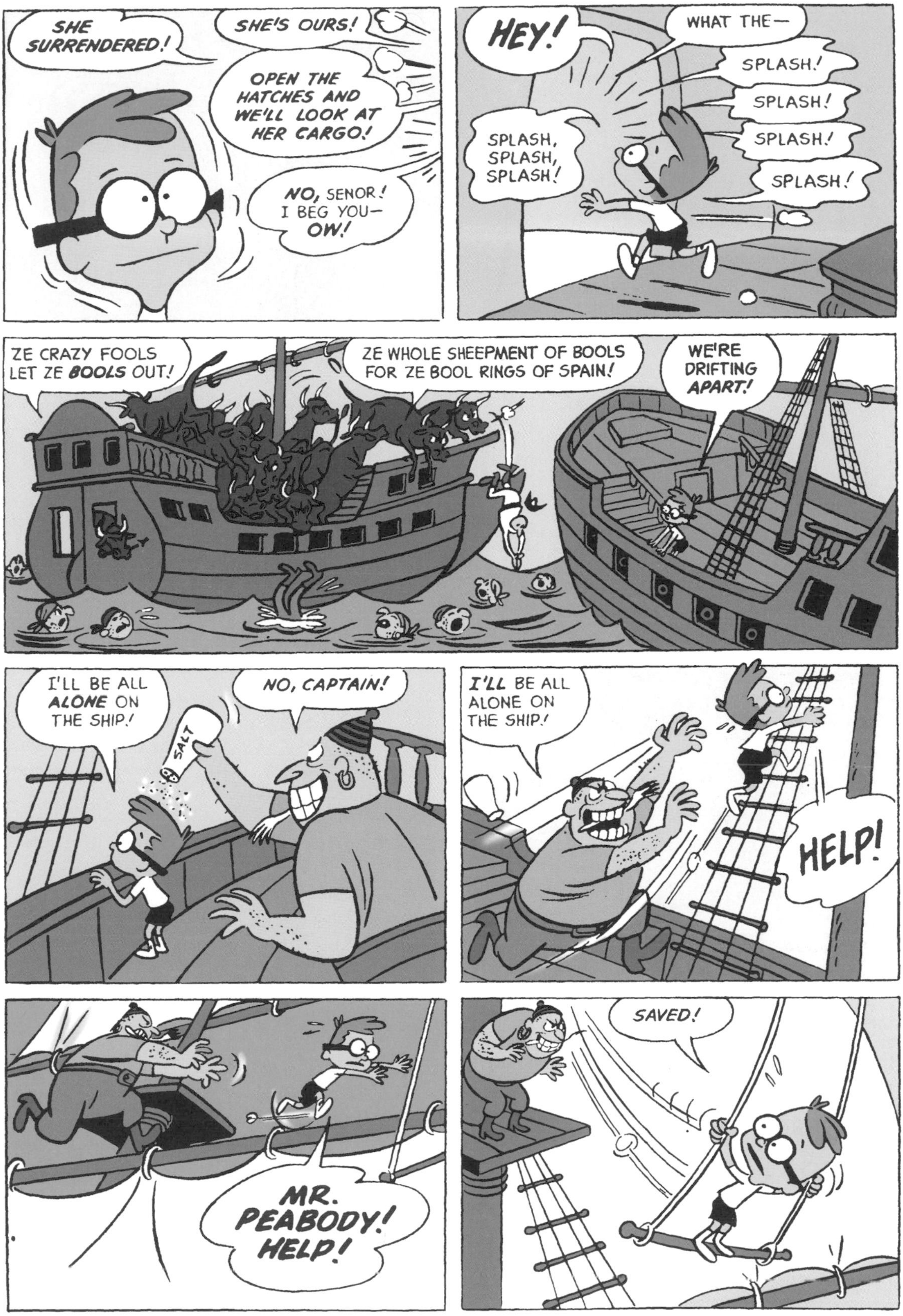

SHE SURRENDERED!
SHE'S OURS!
OPEN THE HATCHES AND WE'LL LOOK AT HER CARGO!
NO, SENOR! I BEG YOU— OW!
HEY!
WHAT THE—
SPLASH!
SPLASH!
SPLASH!
SPLASH, SPLASH, SPLASH!
SPLASH!
ZE CRAZY FOOLS LET ZE BOOLS OUT!
ZE WHOLE SHEEPMENT OF BOOLS FOR ZE BOOL RINGS OF SPAIN!
WE'RE DRIFTING APART!
I'LL BE ALL ALONE ON THE SHIP!
NO, CAPTAIN!
SALT
I'LL BE ALL ALONE ON THE SHIP!
HELP!
MR. PEABODY! HELP!
SAVED!

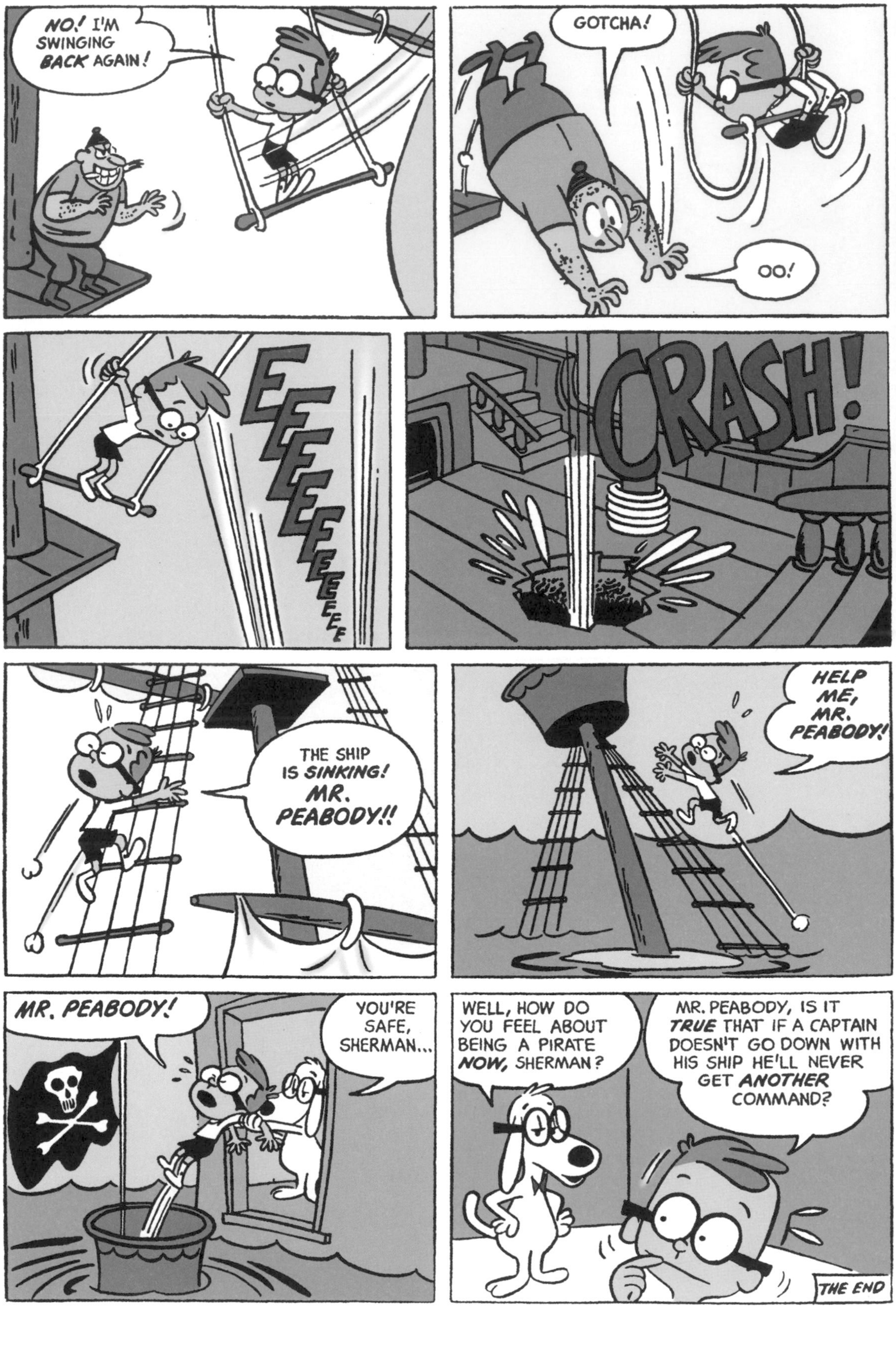
NO! I'M SWINGING BACK AGAIN!
GOTCHA!
OO!
EEEEEEEEEEE
CRASH!
THE SHIP IS SINKING! MR. PEABODY!!
HELP ME, MR. PEABODY!
MR. PEABODY!
YOU'RE SAFE, SHERMAN...
WELL, HOW DO YOU FEEL ABOUT BEING A PIRATE NOW, SHERMAN?
MR. PEABODY, IS IT TRUE THAT IF A CAPTAIN DOESN'T GO DOWN WITH HIS SHIP HE'LL NEVER GET ANOTHER COMMAND?
THE END

Frivolous Facts

In Portugal they have an electronic machine that plays Tic-Tac-Toe. It chuckles when it wins and growls when it loses.

A college student has just finished a study of the best way to cool a cup of coffee. He's written a 78 page report complete with formulas and graphs.

In New Zealand a horse named Brampton tripped as he was finishing the race and rolled across the finish line. This was the first time a horse ever won a race on his back.

They're selling a bed which wakes you automatically, sits you up, turns on your radio, TV set, and coffee percolator.

The smallest book ever printed was a volume of poetry. Fifteen copies could be laid side by side on a postage stamp.

Latvian fishermen catch twice as many herring with nets dyed green as with nets dyed blue.

An Arizona sportsman has had his automobile lined with mink.

A Tennessee scientist has developed a hog feed made from chopped chicken feathers.

You can take a course in panning for gold at the University of Alaska.

When newspapermen rushed to photograph a huge sea-serpent off Nantucket they found it to be a giant rubber balloon designed for a Thanksgiving Day parade.

A rubbish collecting company on Long Island sprays all its cans with the scent of lavender.

A chicken pie must contain at least one and one eighth ounces of chicken for each pound of pie, according to the law in California.

A late model British ocean liner not only moves forward and backward, but can go sideways as well.

They say that in Tokyo subways you'll often see a woman get up to offer a seat to a man.

A canning firm has designed a pea-pinching machine which squeezes a pea and records its exact degree of tenderness.

In Florida fishermen have used strips of orange peel as a lure for mackerel.

A Japanese doctor has collected tape recordings of forty kinds of snores.

They've developed a synthetic skunk perfume that is used to repel rattlesnakes.

A hosiery firm in Britain made socks that were so long-wearing that the plant had to shut down. No re-orders.

Among the paintings displayed at an art show was an original created by worms dipped in oil colors and encouraged to roam across the canvas.

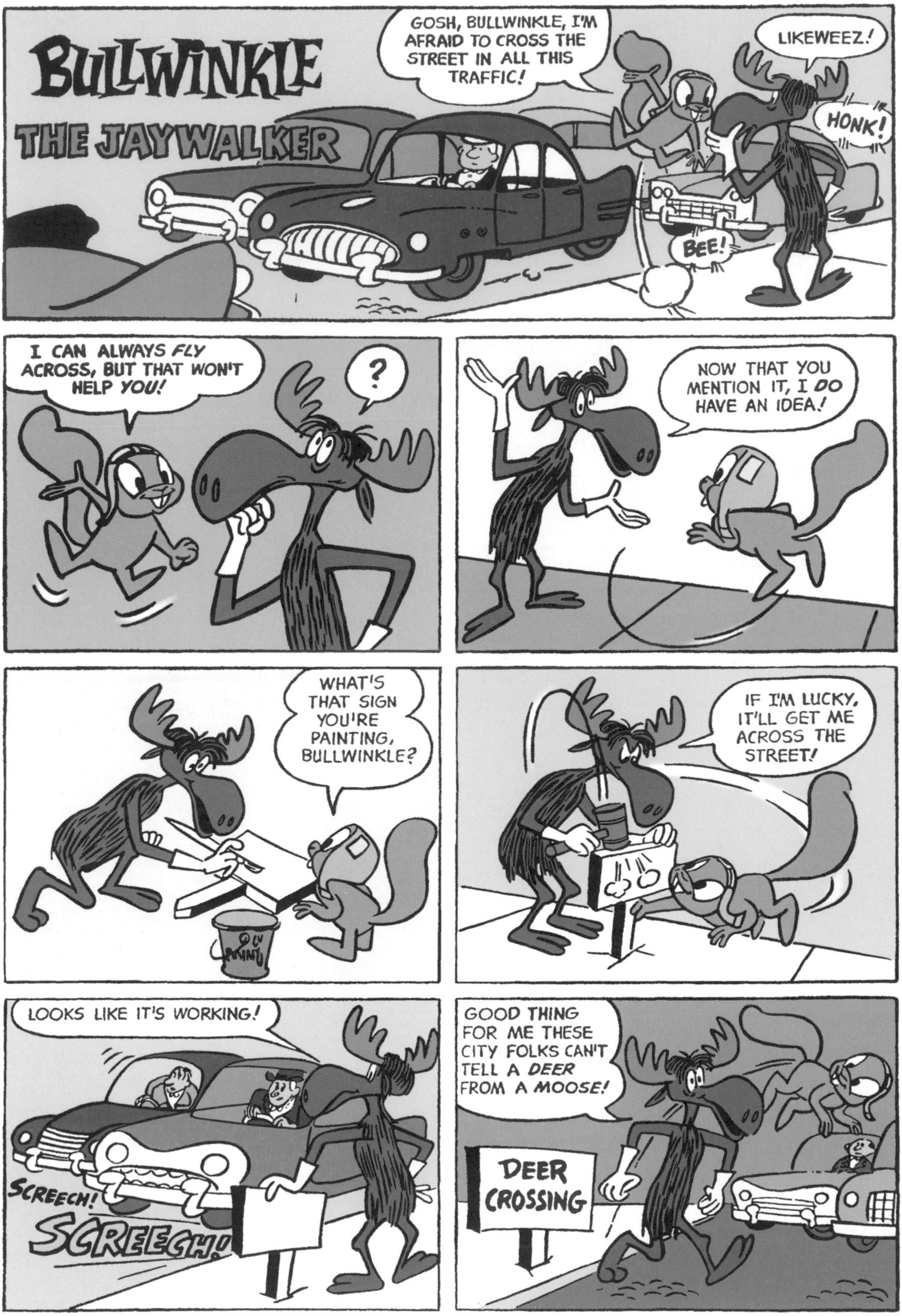
BULLWINKLE
THE JAYWALKER
GOSH, BULLWINKLE, I'M AFRAID TO CROSS THE STREET IN ALL THIS TRAFFIC!
LIKEWEEZ!
HONK!
BEE!
I CAN ALWAYS FLY ACROSS, BUT THAT WON'T HELP YOU!
?
NOW THAT YOU MENTION IT, I DO HAVE AN IDEA!
WHAT'S THAT SIGN YOU'RE PAINTING, BULLWINKLE?
IF I'M LUCKY, IT'LL GET ME ACROSS THE STREET!
LOOKS LIKE IT'S WORKING!
SCREECH!
SCREECH!
GOOD THING FOR ME THESE CITY FOLKS CAN'T TELL A DEER FROM A MOOSE!
DEER CROSSING

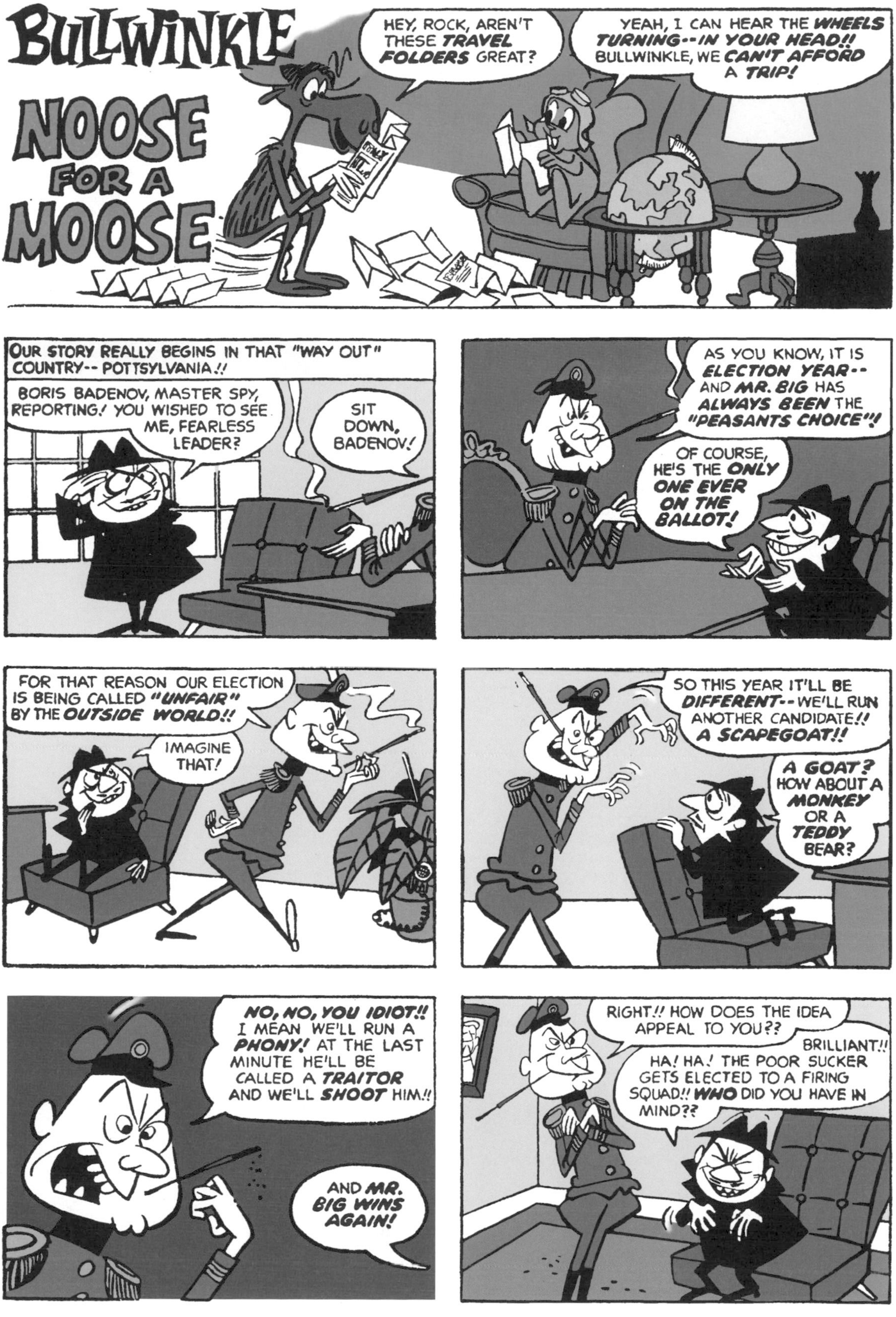
BULLWINKLE
NOOSE FOR A MOOSE
HEY, ROCK, AREN'T THESE TRAVEL FOLDERS GREAT?
YEAH, I CAN HEAR THE WHEELS TURNING--IN YOUR HEAD!! BULLWINKLE, WE CAN'T AFFORD A TRIP!
OUR STORY REALLY BEGINS IN THAT "WAY OUT" COUNTRY-- POTTSYLVANIA!!
BORIS BADENOV, MASTER SPY, REPORTING! YOU WISHED TO SEE ME, FEARLESS LEADER?
SIT DOWN, BADENOV!
AS YOU KNOW, IT IS ELECTION YEAR-- AND MR. BIG HAS ALWAYS BEEN THE "PEASANTS CHOICE"!!
OF COURSE, HE'S THE ONLY ONE EVER ON THE BALLOT!
FOR THAT REASON OUR ELECTION IS BEING CALLED "UNFAIR" BY THE OUTSIDE WORLD!!
IMAGINE THAT!
SO THIS YEAR IT'LL BE DIFFERENT--WE'LL RUN ANOTHER CANDIDATE!! A SCAPEGOAT!!
A GOAT? HOW ABOUT A MONKEY OR A TEDDY BEAR?
NO, NO, YOU IDIOT!! I MEAN WE'LL RUN A PHONY! AT THE LAST MINUTE HE'LL BE CALLED A TRAITOR AND WE'LL SHOOT HIM!!
AND MR. BIG WINS AGAIN!
RIGHT!! HOW DOES THE IDEA APPEAL TO YOU??
BRILLIANT!! HA! HA! THE POOR SUCKER GETS ELECTED TO A FIRING SQUAD!! WHO DID YOU HAVE IN MIND??

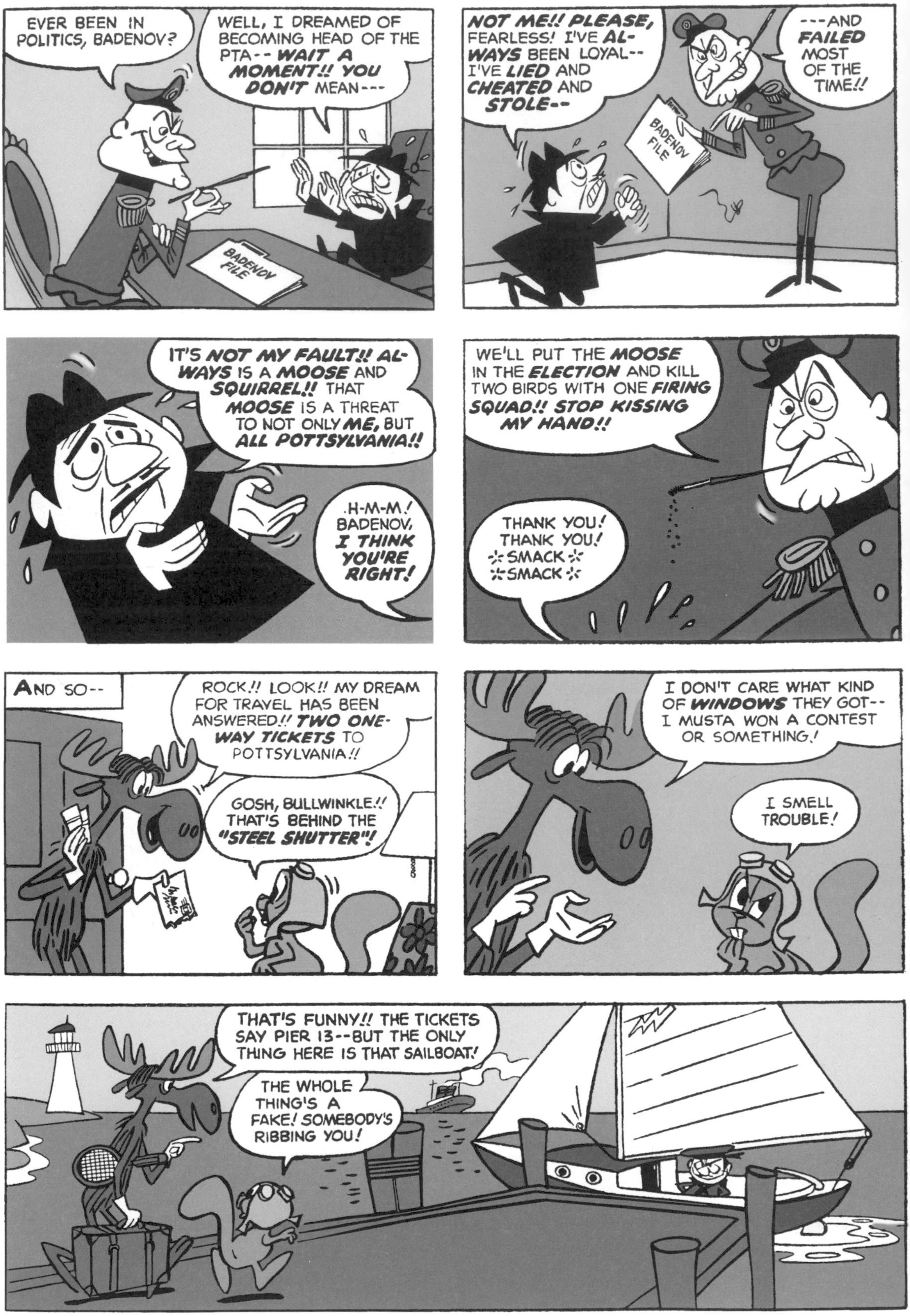
EVER BEEN IN POLITICS, BADENOV?
WELL, I DREAMED OF BECOMING HEAD OF THE PTA-- WAIT A MOMENT!! YOU DON'T MEAN---
BADENOV FILE
NOT ME!! PLEASE, FEARLESS! I'VE ALWAYS BEEN LOYAL-- I'VE LIED AND CHEATED AND STOLE--
---AND FAILED MOST OF THE TIME!!
BADENOV FILE
IT'S NOT MY FAULT!! ALWAYS IS A MOOSE AND SQUIRREL!! THAT MOOSE IS A THREAT TO NOT ONLY ME, BUT ALL POTTSYLVANIA!!
H-M-M! BADENOV, I THINK YOU'RE RIGHT!
WE'LL PUT THE MOOSE IN THE ELECTION AND KILL TWO BIRDS WITH ONE FIRING SQUAD!! STOP KISSING MY HAND!!
THANK YOU! THANK YOU! SMACK SMACK
AND SO--
ROCK!! LOOK!! MY DREAM FOR TRAVEL HAS BEEN ANSWERED!! TWO ONE-WAY TICKETS TO POTTSYLVANIA!!
GOSH, BULLWINKLE!! THAT'S BEHIND THE "STEEL SHUTTER"!
I DON'T CARE WHAT KIND OF WINDOWS THEY GOT-- I MUSTA WON A CONTEST OR SOMETHING!
I SMELL TROUBLE!
THAT'S FUNNY!! THE TICKETS SAY PIER 13--BUT THE ONLY THING HERE IS THAT SAILBOAT!
THE WHOLE THING'S A FAKE! SOMEBODY'S RIBBING YOU!

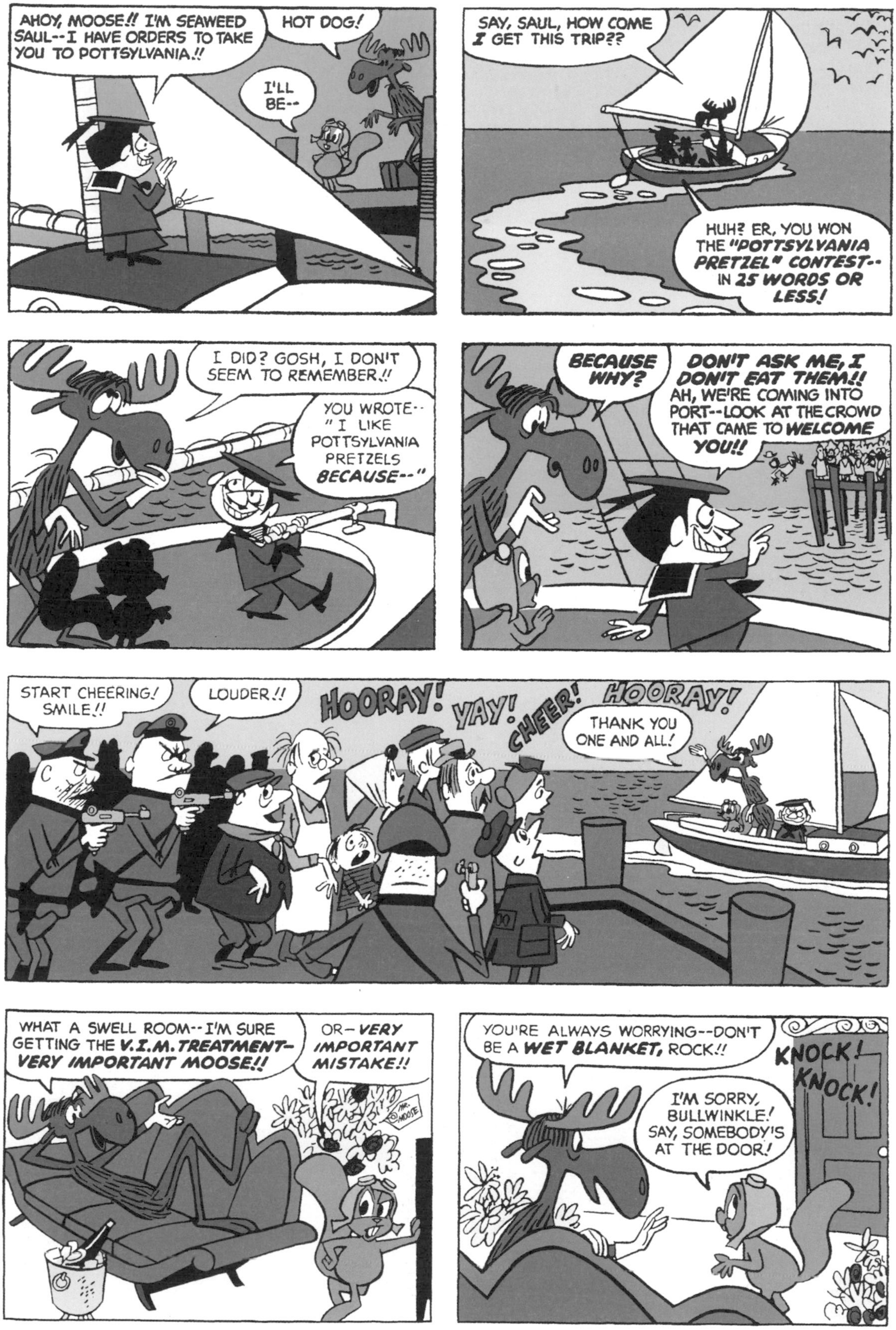
AHOY, MOOSE!! I'M SEAWEED SAUL--I HAVE ORDERS TO TAKE YOU TO POTTSYLVANIA!!
HOT DOG!
I'LL BE--
SAY, SAUL, HOW COME I GET THIS TRIP??
HUH? ER, YOU WON THE "POTTSYLVANIA PRETZEL" CONTEST--IN 25 WORDS OR LESS!
I DID? GOSH, I DON'T SEEM TO REMEMBER!!
YOU WROTE--"I LIKE POTTSYLVANIA PRETZELS BECAUSE--"
BECAUSE WHY?
DON'T ASK ME, I DON'T EAT THEM!! AH, WE'RE COMING INTO PORT--LOOK AT THE CROWD THAT CAME TO WELCOME YOU!!
START CHEERING! SMILE!!
LOUDER!!
HOORAY!
YAY!
CHEER!
HOORAY!
THANK YOU ONE AND ALL!
WHAT A SWELL ROOM--I'M SURE GETTING THE V.I.M. TREATMENT-VERY IMPORTANT MOOSE!!
OR--VERY IMPORTANT MISTAKE!!
YOU'RE ALWAYS WORRYING--DON'T BE A WET BLANKET, ROCK!!
KNOCK! KNOCK!
I'M SORRY, BULLWINKLE! SAY, SOMEBODY'S AT THE DOOR!

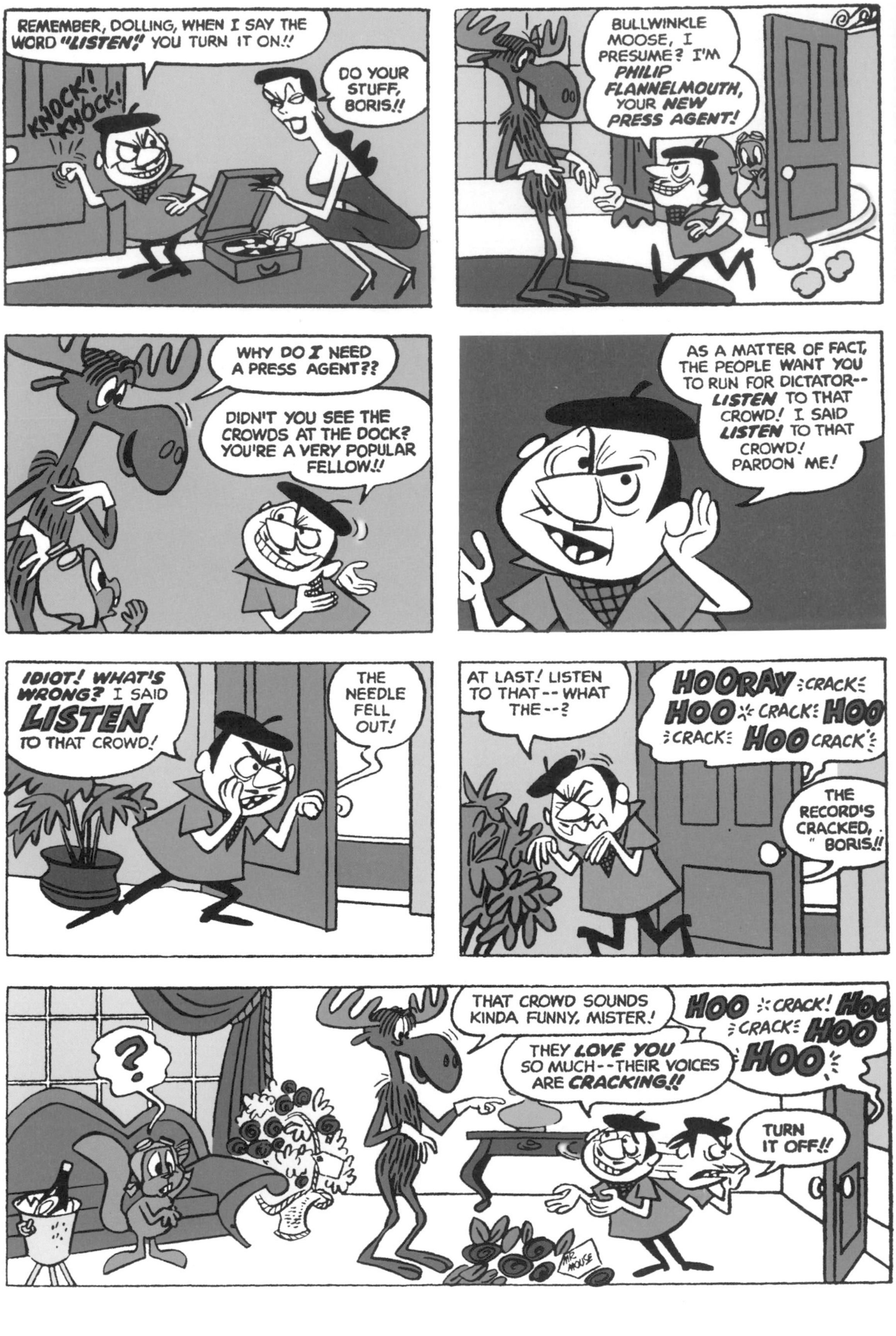

REMEMBER, DOLLING, WHEN I SAY THE WORD "LISTEN," YOU TURN IT ON!!
KNOCK! KNOCK!
DO YOUR STUFF, BORIS!!
BULLWINKLE MOOSE, I PRESUME? I'M PHILIP FLANNELMOUTH, YOUR NEW PRESS AGENT!
WHY DO I NEED A PRESS AGENT??
DIDN'T YOU SEE THE CROWDS AT THE DOCK? YOU'RE A VERY POPULAR FELLOW!!
AS A MATTER OF FACT, THE PEOPLE WANT YOU TO RUN FOR DICTATOR-- LISTEN TO THAT CROWD! I SAID LISTEN TO THAT CROWD! PARDON ME!
IDIOT! WHAT'S WRONG? I SAID LISTEN TO THAT CROWD!
THE NEEDLE FELL OUT!
AT LAST! LISTEN TO THAT -- WHAT THE --?
HOORAY CRACK HOO CRACK HOO CRACK HOO CRACK
THE RECORD'S CRACKED, BORIS!!
THAT CROWD SOUNDS KINDA FUNNY, MISTER!
THEY LOVE YOU SO MUCH--THEIR VOICES ARE CRACKING!!
HOO CRACK! HOO CRACK HOO HOO
TURN IT OFF!!
?
MR. MOUSE

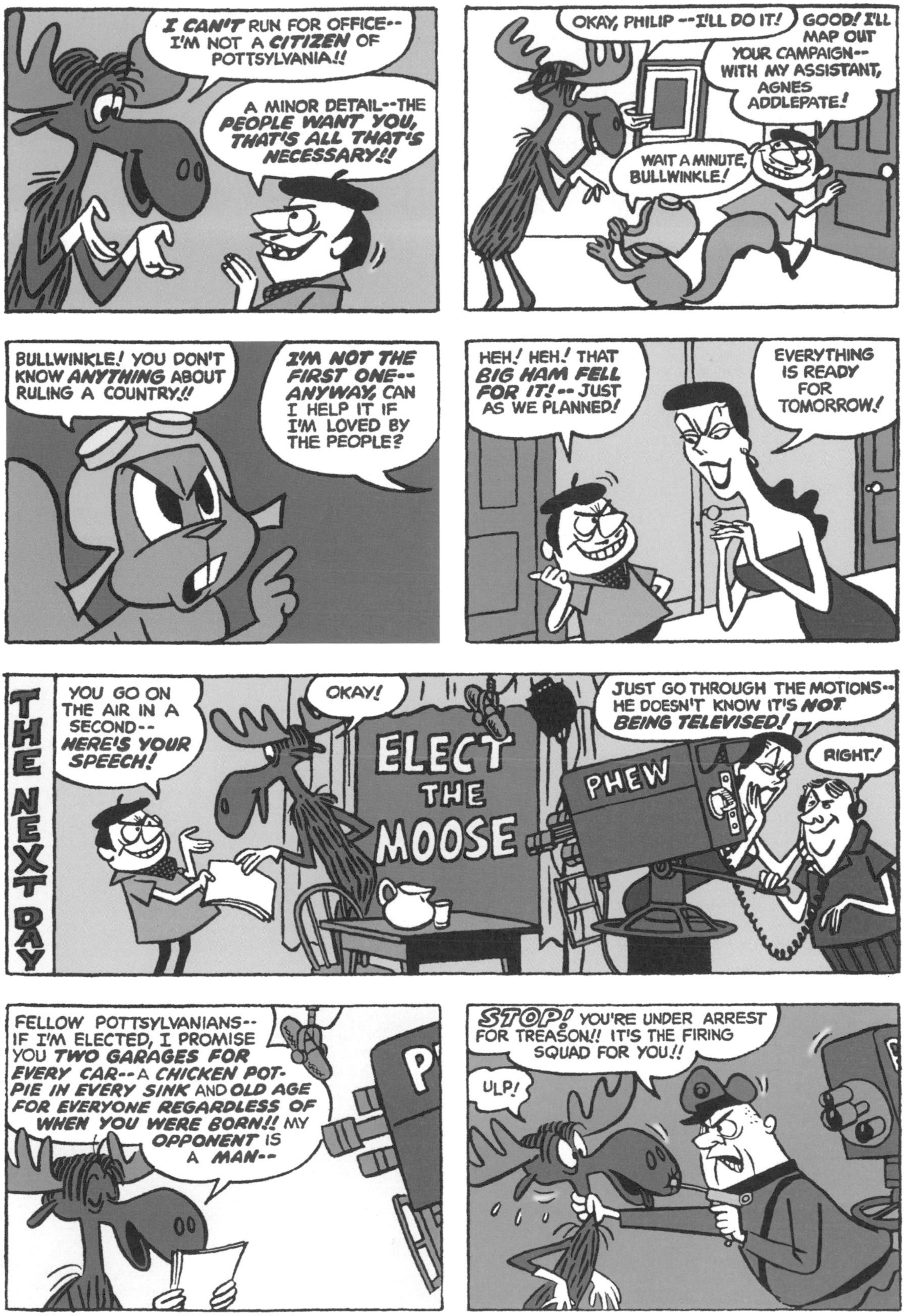

I CAN'T RUN FOR OFFICE-- I'M NOT A CITIZEN OF POTTSYLVANIA!!
A MINOR DETAIL--THE PEOPLE WANT YOU, THAT'S ALL THAT'S NECESSARY!!
OKAY, PHILIP --I'LL DO IT!
GOOD! I'LL MAP OUT YOUR CAMPAIGN-- WITH MY ASSISTANT, AGNES ADDLEPATE!
WAIT A MINUTE, BULLWINKLE!
BULLWINKLE! YOU DON'T KNOW ANYTHING ABOUT RULING A COUNTRY!!
I'M NOT THE FIRST ONE-- ANYWAY, CAN I HELP IT IF I'M LOVED BY THE PEOPLE?
HEH! HEH! THAT BIG HAM FELL FOR IT!-- JUST AS WE PLANNED!
EVERYTHING IS READY FOR TOMORROW!
THE NEXT DAY
YOU GO ON THE AIR IN A SECOND-- HERE'S YOUR SPEECH!
OKAY!
ELECT THE MOOSE
JUST GO THROUGH THE MOTIONS-- HE DOESN'T KNOW IT'S NOT BEING TELEVISED!
PHEW
RIGHT!
FELLOW POTTSYLVANIANS-- IF I'M ELECTED, I PROMISE YOU TWO GARAGES FOR EVERY CAR-- A CHICKEN POT-PIE IN EVERY SINK AND OLD AGE FOR EVERYONE REGARDLESS OF WHEN YOU WERE BORN!! MY OPPONENT IS A MAN--
STOP! YOU'RE UNDER ARREST FOR TREASON!! IT'S THE FIRING SQUAD FOR YOU!!
ULP!

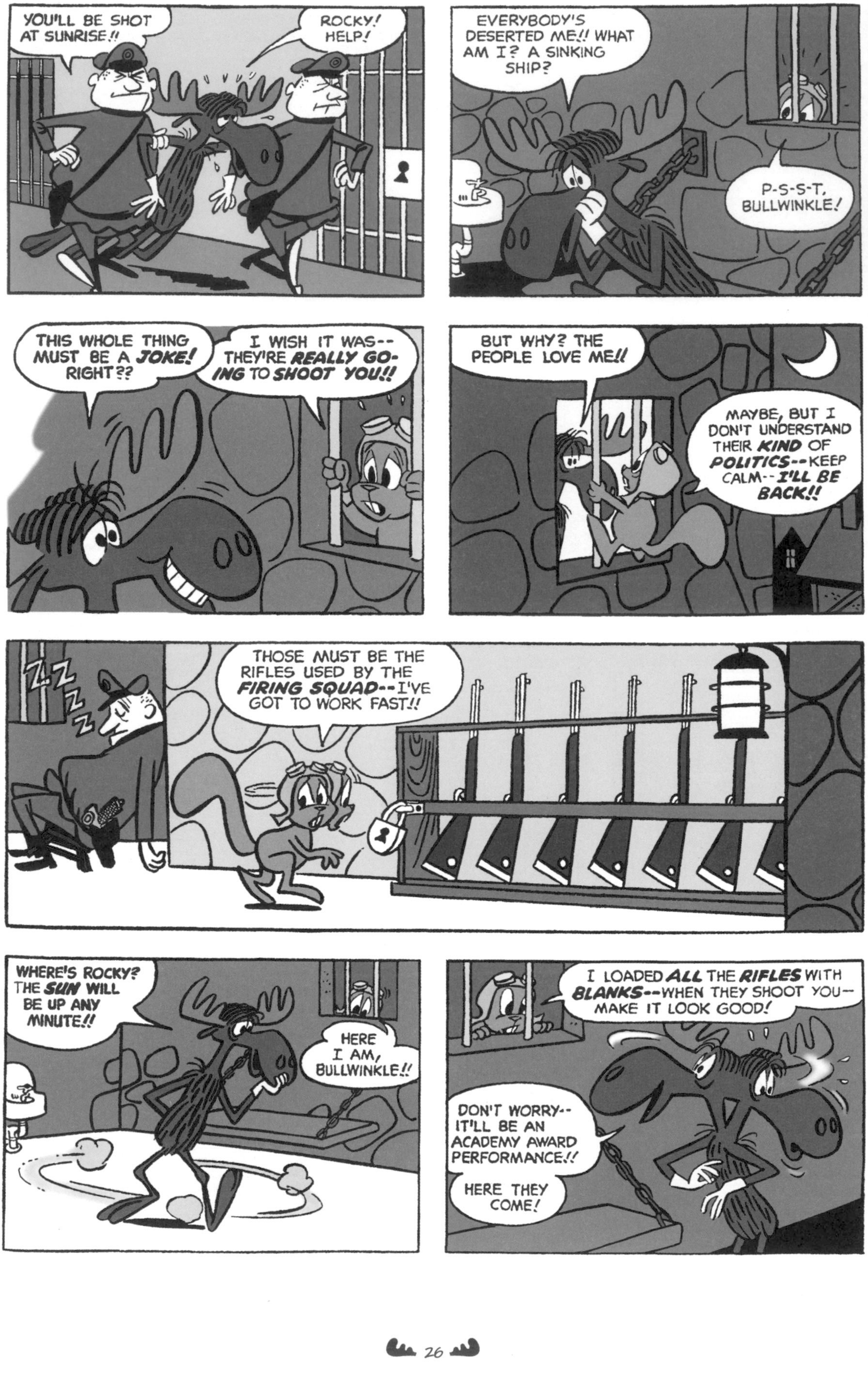
YOU'LL BE SHOT AT SUNRISE!!
ROCKY! HELP!
EVERYBODY'S DESERTED ME!! WHAT AM I? A SINKING SHIP?
P-S-S-T, BULLWINKLE!
THIS WHOLE THING MUST BE A JOKE! RIGHT??
I WISH IT WAS-- THEY'RE REALLY GOING TO SHOOT YOU!!
BUT WHY? THE PEOPLE LOVE ME!!
MAYBE, BUT I DON'T UNDERSTAND THEIR KIND OF POLITICS--KEEP CALM--I'LL BE BACK!!
ZZZZ
THOSE MUST BE THE RIFLES USED BY THE FIRING SQUAD--I'VE GOT TO WORK FAST!!
WHERE'S ROCKY? THE SUN WILL BE UP ANY MINUTE!!
HERE I AM, BULLWINKLE!!
I LOADED ALL THE RIFLES WITH BLANKS--WHEN THEY SHOOT YOU--MAKE IT LOOK GOOD!
DON'T WORRY--IT'LL BE AN ACADEMY AWARD PERFORMANCE!!
HERE THEY COME!

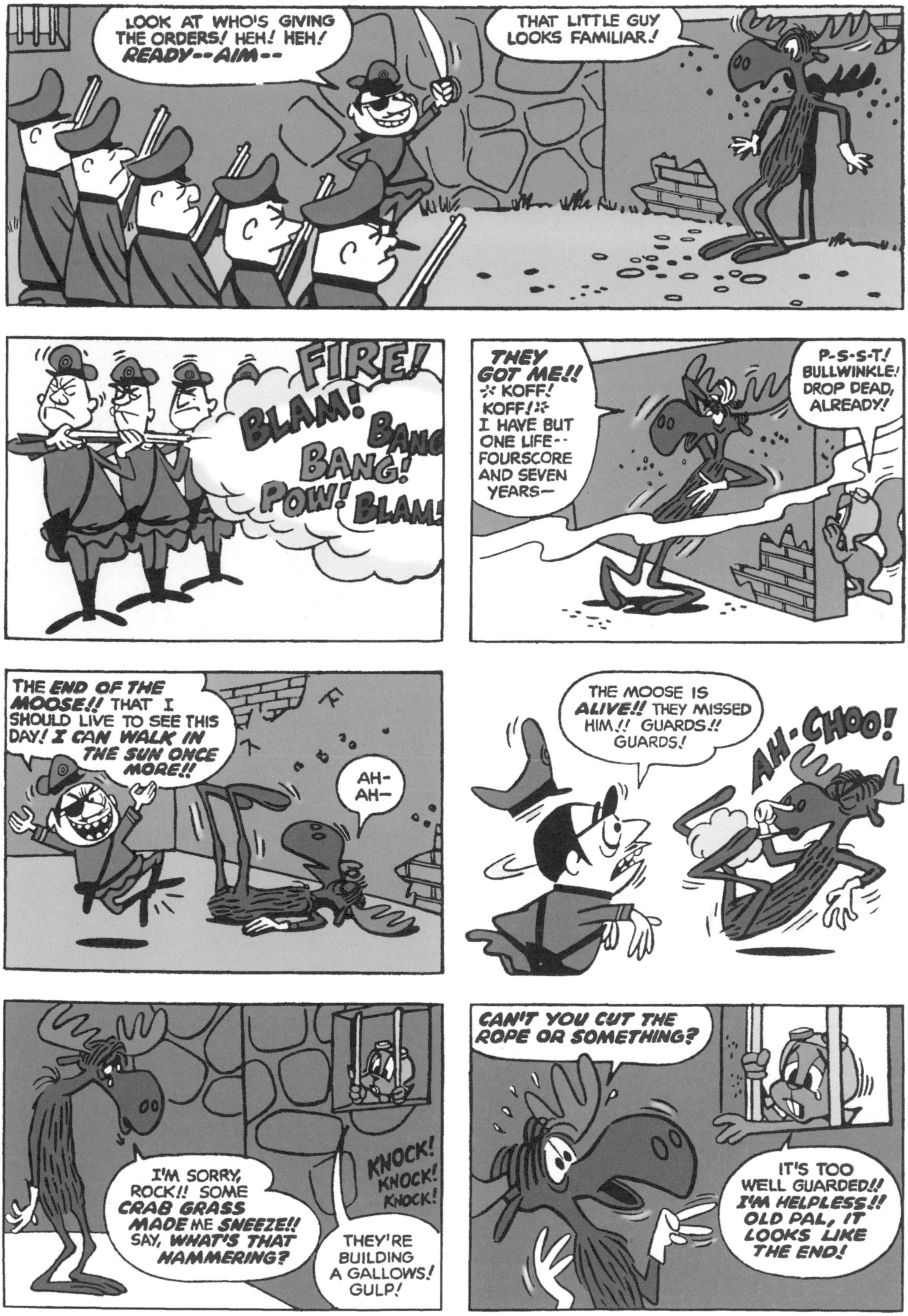
LOOK AT WHO'S GIVING THE ORDERS! HEH! HEH! READY--AIM--
THAT LITTLE GUY LOOKS FAMILIAR!
FIRE!
BLAM! BANG BANG! POW! BLAM!
THEY GOT ME!! KOFF! KOFF! I HAVE BUT ONE LIFE-- FOURSCORE AND SEVEN YEARS—
P-S-S-T! BULLWINKLE! DROP DEAD, ALREADY!
THE END OF THE MOOSE!! THAT I SHOULD LIVE TO SEE THIS DAY! I CAN WALK IN THE SUN ONCE MORE!!
AH- AH-
THE MOOSE IS ALIVE!! THEY MISSED HIM!! GUARDS!! GUARDS!
AH-CHOO!
I'M SORRY, ROCK!! SOME CRAB GRASS MADE ME SNEEZE!! SAY, WHAT'S THAT HAMMERING?
KNOCK! KNOCK! KNOCK!
THEY'RE BUILDING A GALLOWS! GULP!
CAN'T YOU CUT THE ROPE OR SOMETHING?
IT'S TOO WELL GUARDED!! I'M HELPLESS!! OLD PAL, IT LOOKS LIKE THE END!

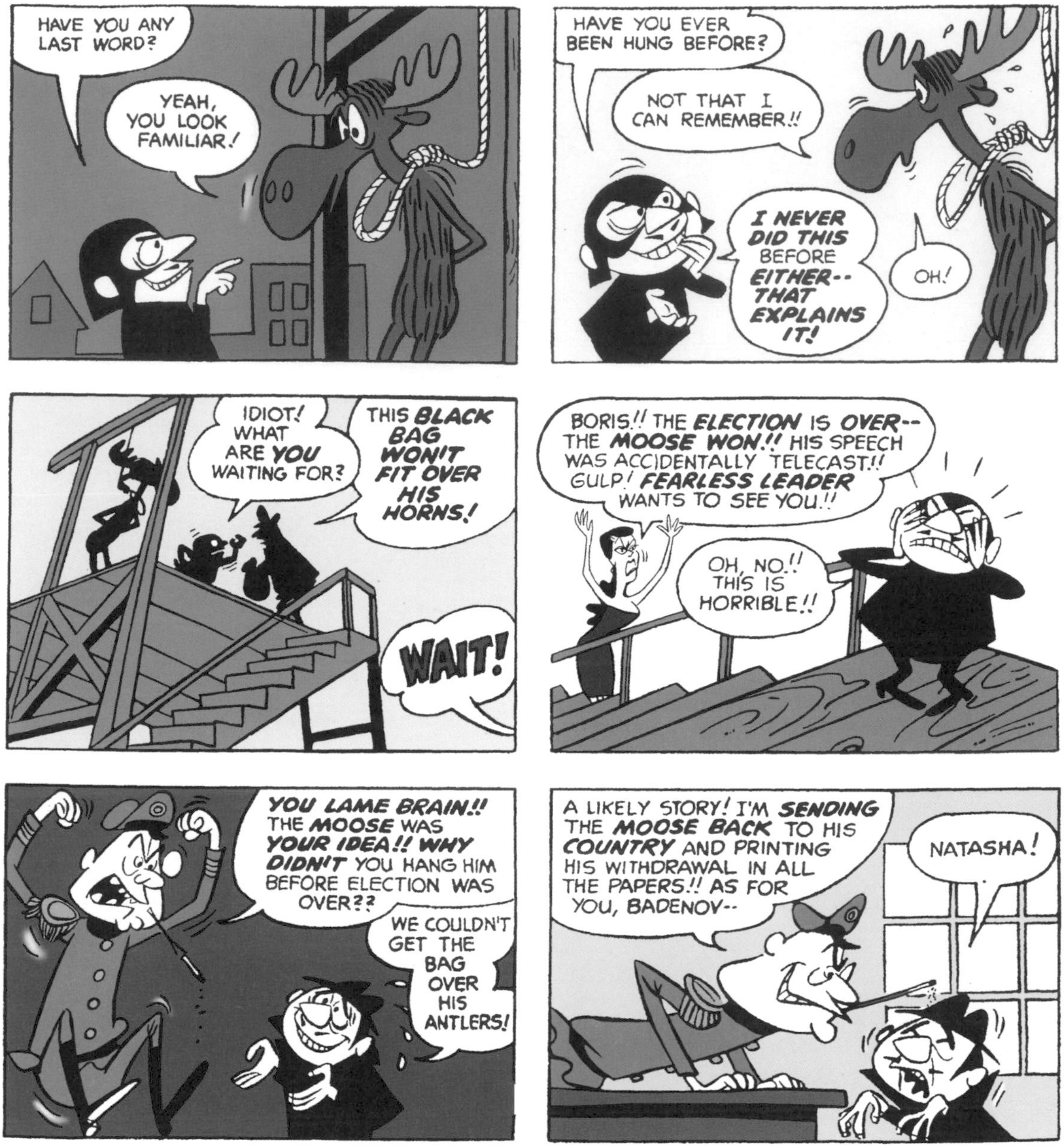
HAVE YOU ANY LAST WORD?
YEAH, YOU LOOK FAMILIAR!
HAVE YOU EVER BEEN HUNG BEFORE?
NOT THAT I CAN REMEMBER!!
I NEVER DID THIS BEFORE EITHER-- THAT EXPLAINS IT!
OH!
IDIOT! WHAT ARE YOU WAITING FOR?
THIS BLACK BAG WON'T FIT OVER HIS HORNS!
WAIT!
BORIS!! THE ELECTION IS OVER-- THE MOOSE WON!! HIS SPEECH WAS ACCIDENTALLY TELECAST!! GULP! FEARLESS LEADER WANTS TO SEE YOU!!
OH, NO!! THIS IS HORRIBLE!!
YOU LAME BRAIN!! THE MOOSE WAS YOUR IDEA!! WHY DIDN'T YOU HANG HIM BEFORE ELECTION WAS OVER??
WE COULDN'T GET THE BAG OVER HIS ANTLERS!
A LIKELY STORY! I'M SENDING THE MOOSE BACK TO HIS COUNTRY AND PRINTING HIS WITHDRAWAL IN ALL THE PAPERS!! AS FOR YOU, BADENOV--
NATASHA!

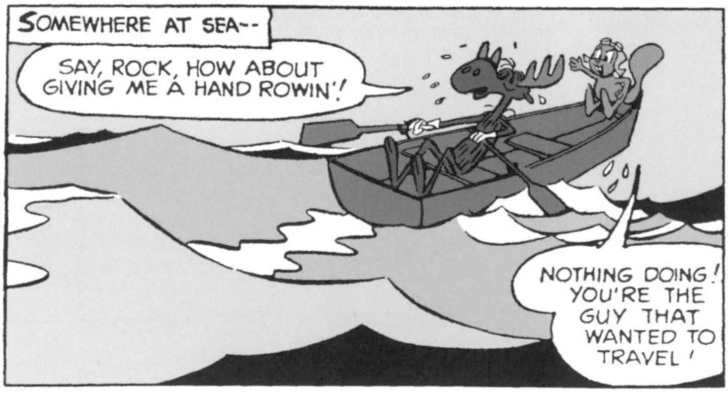
SOMEWHERE AT SEA--
SAY, ROCK, HOW ABOUT GIVING ME A HAND ROWIN'!
NOTHING DOING! YOU'RE THE GUY THAT WANTED TO TRAVEL!

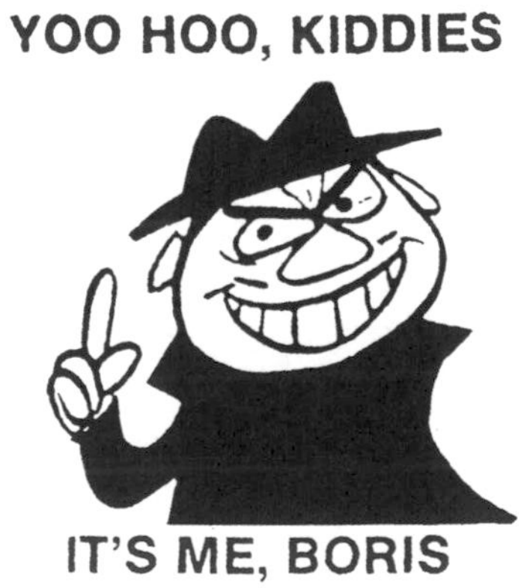
YOO HOO, KIDDIES
IT'S ME, BORIS

BULLWINKLE and ROCKY

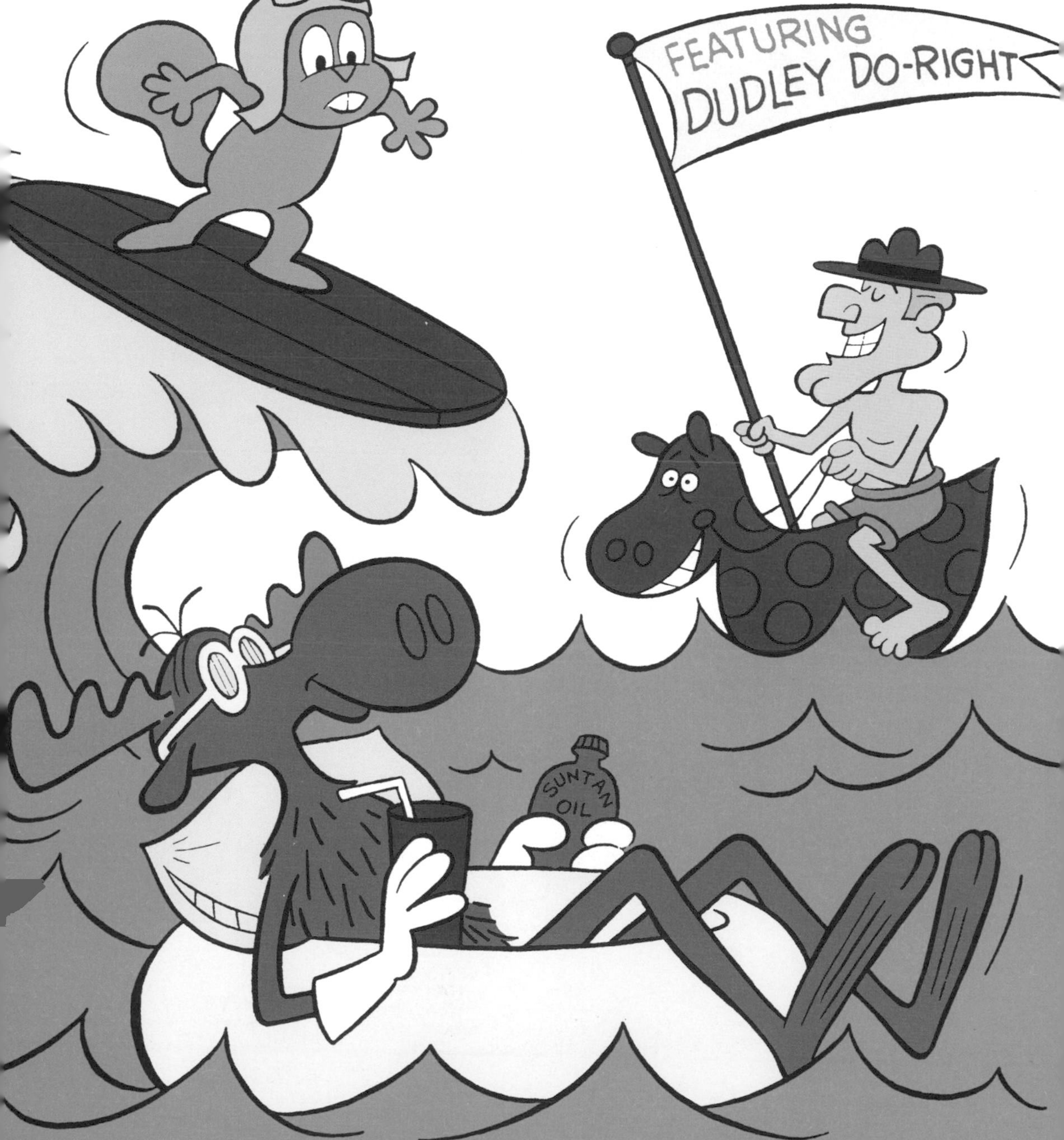
FEATURING DUDLEY DO-RIGHT
SUNTAN OIL

ISSUE #6 · GOLD KEY · JANUARY 1973

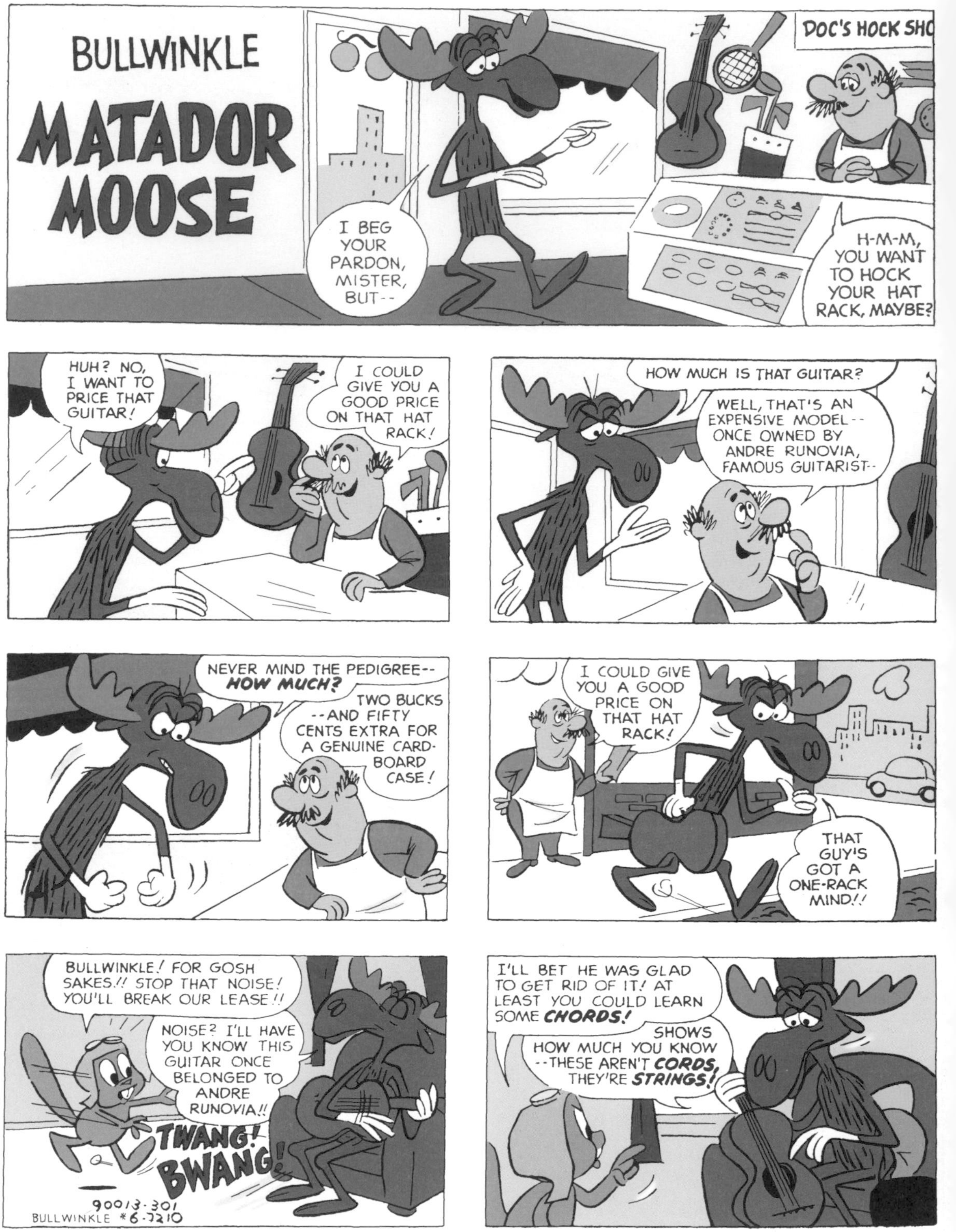
BULLWINKLE
MATADOR MOOSE
DOC'S HOCK SHO
I BEG YOUR PARDON, MISTER, BUT--
H-M-M, YOU WANT TO HOCK YOUR HAT RACK, MAYBE?
HUH? NO, I WANT TO PRICE THAT GUITAR!
I COULD GIVE YOU A GOOD PRICE ON THAT HAT RACK!
HOW MUCH IS THAT GUITAR?
WELL, THAT'S AN EXPENSIVE MODEL-- ONCE OWNED BY ANDRE RUNOVIA, FAMOUS GUITARIST--
NEVER MIND THE PEDIGREE-- **HOW MUCH?**
TWO BUCKS --AND FIFTY CENTS EXTRA FOR A GENUINE CARD-BOARD CASE!
I COULD GIVE YOU A GOOD PRICE ON THAT HAT RACK!
THAT GUY'S GOT A ONE-RACK MIND!!
BULLWINKLE! FOR GOSH SAKES!! STOP THAT NOISE! YOU'LL BREAK OUR LEASE!!
NOISE? I'LL HAVE YOU KNOW THIS GUITAR ONCE BELONGED TO ANDRE RUNOVIA!!
TWANG! BWANG!
90013-301
BULLWINKLE *6-7210
I'LL BET HE WAS GLAD TO GET RID OF IT! AT LEAST YOU COULD LEARN SOME **CHORDS!**
SHOWS HOW MUCH YOU KNOW --THESE AREN'T **CORDS,** THEY'RE **STRINGS!**

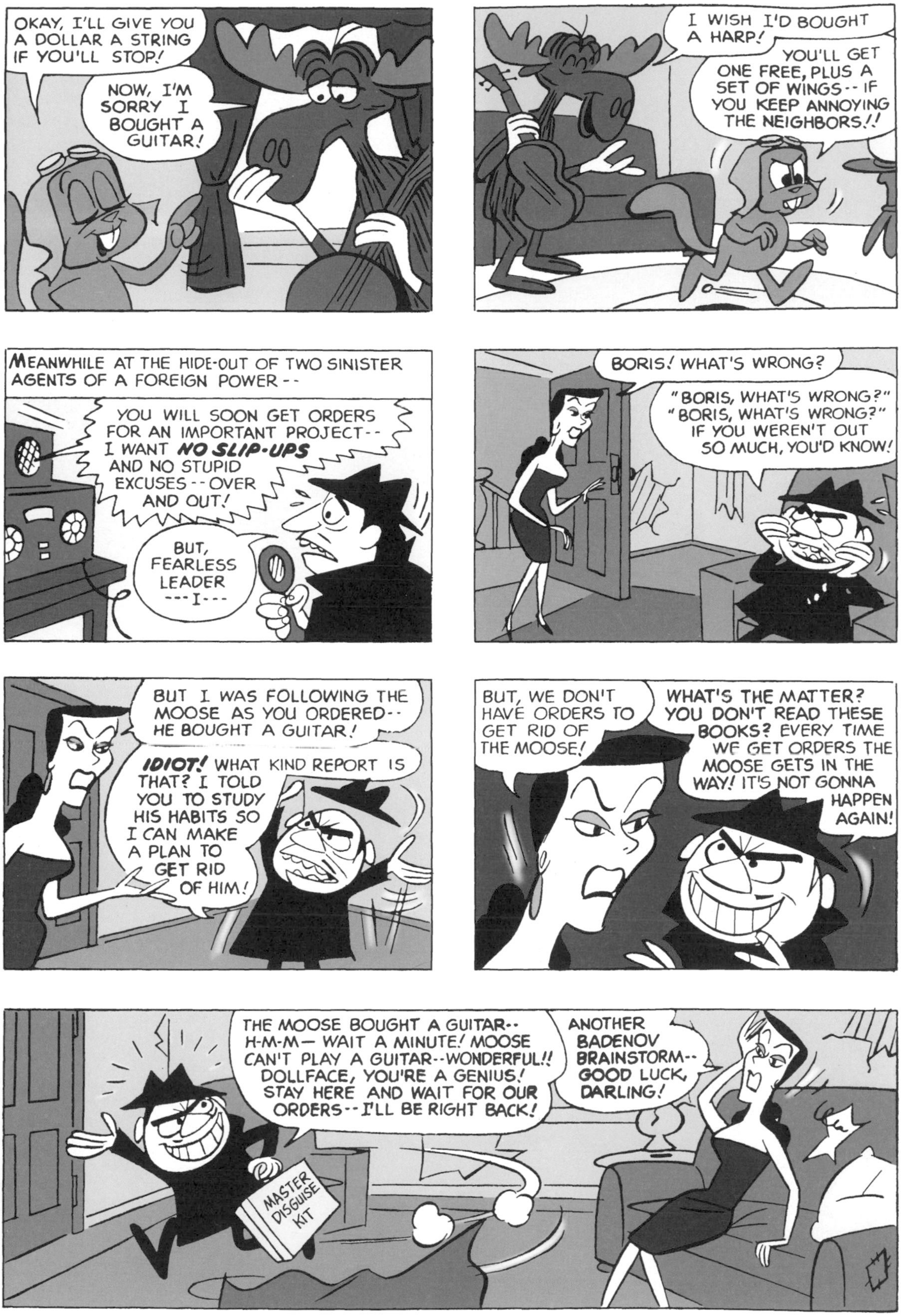
OKAY, I'LL GIVE YOU A DOLLAR A STRING IF YOU'LL STOP!
NOW, I'M SORRY I BOUGHT A GUITAR!
I WISH I'D BOUGHT A HARP!
YOU'LL GET ONE FREE, PLUS A SET OF WINGS-- IF YOU KEEP ANNOYING THE NEIGHBORS!!
MEANWHILE AT THE HIDE-OUT OF TWO SINISTER AGENTS OF A FOREIGN POWER--
YOU WILL SOON GET ORDERS FOR AN IMPORTANT PROJECT-- I WANT NO SLIP-UPS AND NO STUPID EXCUSES--OVER AND OUT!
BUT, FEARLESS LEADER ---I---
BORIS! WHAT'S WRONG?
"BORIS, WHAT'S WRONG?" "BORIS, WHAT'S WRONG?" IF YOU WEREN'T OUT SO MUCH, YOU'D KNOW!
BUT I WAS FOLLOWING THE MOOSE AS YOU ORDERED-- HE BOUGHT A GUITAR!
IDIOT! WHAT KIND REPORT IS THAT? I TOLD YOU TO STUDY HIS HABITS SO I CAN MAKE A PLAN TO GET RID OF HIM!
BUT, WE DON'T HAVE ORDERS TO GET RID OF THE MOOSE!
WHAT'S THE MATTER? YOU DON'T READ THESE BOOKS? EVERY TIME WE GET ORDERS THE MOOSE GETS IN THE WAY! IT'S NOT GONNA HAPPEN AGAIN!
THE MOOSE BOUGHT A GUITAR-- H-M-M— WAIT A MINUTE! MOOSE CAN'T PLAY A GUITAR--WONDERFUL!! DOLLFACE, YOU'RE A GENIUS! STAY HERE AND WAIT FOR OUR ORDERS--I'LL BE RIGHT BACK!
ANOTHER BADENOV BRAINSTORM-- GOOD LUCK, DARLING!
MASTER DISGUISE KIT

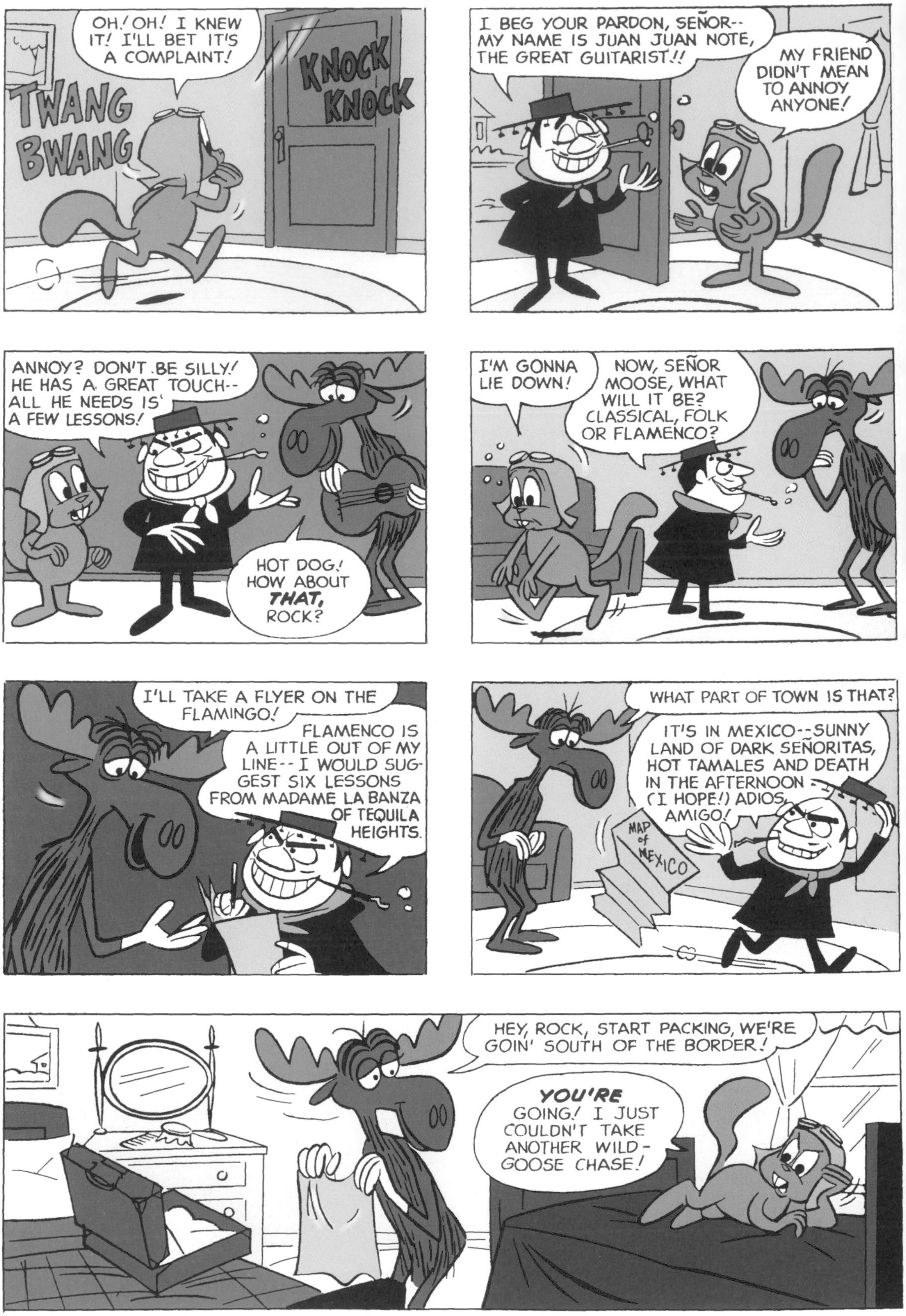
OH! OH! I KNEW IT! I'LL BET IT'S A COMPLAINT!
TWANG BWANG
KNOCK KNOCK
I BEG YOUR PARDON, SEÑOR--MY NAME IS JUAN JUAN NOTE, THE GREAT GUITARIST!!
MY FRIEND DIDN'T MEAN TO ANNOY ANYONE!
ANNOY? DON'T BE SILLY! HE HAS A GREAT TOUCH--ALL HE NEEDS IS A FEW LESSONS!
HOT DOG! HOW ABOUT **THAT,** ROCK?
I'M GONNA LIE DOWN!
NOW, SEÑOR MOOSE, WHAT WILL IT BE? CLASSICAL, FOLK OR FLAMENCO?
I'LL TAKE A FLYER ON THE FLAMINGO!
FLAMENCO IS A LITTLE OUT OF MY LINE--I WOULD SUGGEST SIX LESSONS FROM MADAME LA BANZA OF TEQUILA HEIGHTS.
WHAT PART OF TOWN IS THAT?
IT'S IN MEXICO--SUNNY LAND OF DARK SEÑORITAS, HOT TAMALES AND DEATH IN THE AFTERNOON (I HOPE!) ADIOS, AMIGO!
MAP of MEXICO
HEY, ROCK, START PACKING, WE'RE GOIN' SOUTH OF THE BORDER!
YOU'RE GOING! I JUST COULDN'T TAKE ANOTHER WILD-GOOSE CHASE!

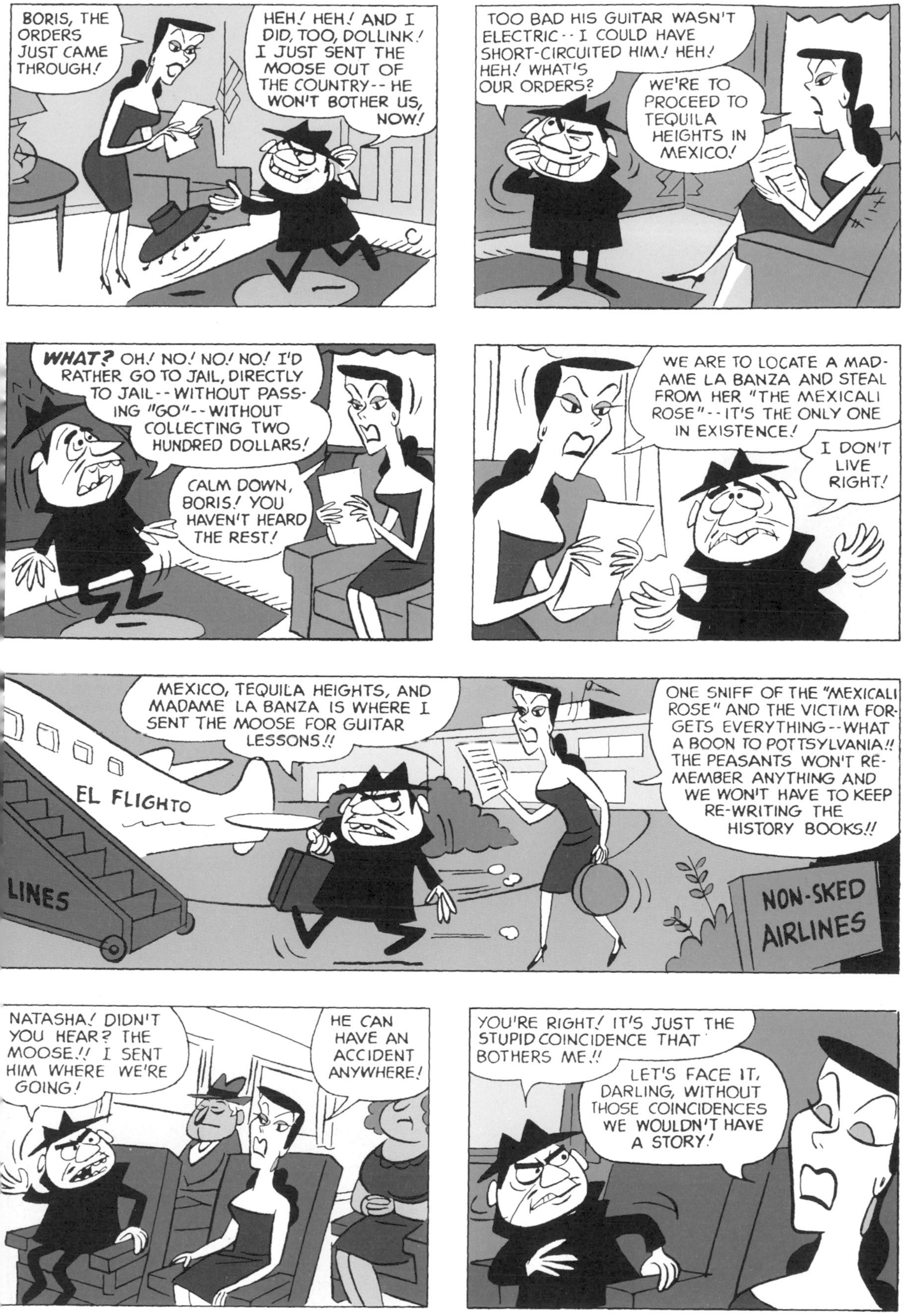
BORIS, THE ORDERS JUST CAME THROUGH!
HEH! HEH! AND I DID, TOO, DOLLINK! I JUST SENT THE MOOSE OUT OF THE COUNTRY-- HE WON'T BOTHER US, NOW!
TOO BAD HIS GUITAR WASN'T ELECTRIC-- I COULD HAVE SHORT-CIRCUITED HIM! HEH! HEH! WHAT'S OUR ORDERS?
WE'RE TO PROCEED TO TEQUILA HEIGHTS IN MEXICO!
WHAT? OH! NO! NO! NO! I'D RATHER GO TO JAIL, DIRECTLY TO JAIL-- WITHOUT PASSING "GO"-- WITHOUT COLLECTING TWO HUNDRED DOLLARS!
CALM DOWN, BORIS! YOU HAVEN'T HEARD THE REST!
WE ARE TO LOCATE A MADAME LA BANZA AND STEAL FROM HER "THE MEXICALI ROSE"-- IT'S THE ONLY ONE IN EXISTENCE!
I DON'T LIVE RIGHT!
MEXICO, TEQUILA HEIGHTS, AND MADAME LA BANZA IS WHERE I SENT THE MOOSE FOR GUITAR LESSONS!!
ONE SNIFF OF THE "MEXICALI ROSE" AND THE VICTIM FORGETS EVERYTHING--WHAT A BOON TO POTTSYLVANIA!! THE PEASANTS WON'T REMEMBER ANYTHING AND WE WON'T HAVE TO KEEP RE-WRITING THE HISTORY BOOKS!!
EL FLIGHTO
LINES
NON-SKED AIRLINES
NATASHA! DIDN'T YOU HEAR? THE MOOSE!! I SENT HIM WHERE WE'RE GOING!
HE CAN HAVE AN ACCIDENT ANYWHERE!
YOU'RE RIGHT! IT'S JUST THE STUPID COINCIDENCE THAT BOTHERS ME!!
LET'S FACE IT, DARLING, WITHOUT THOSE COINCIDENCES WE WOULDN'T HAVE A STORY!

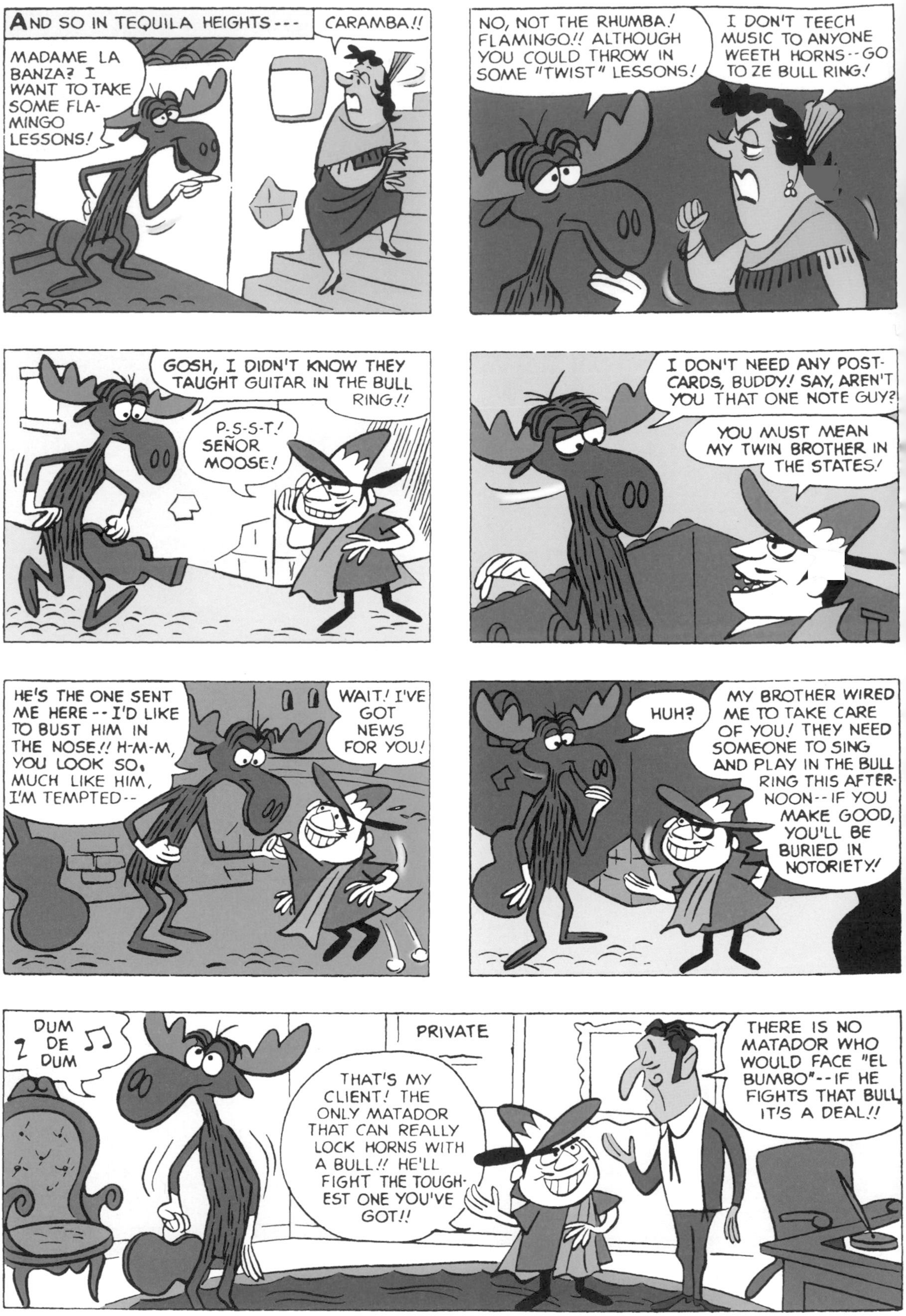
AND SO IN TEQUILA HEIGHTS---
MADAME LA BANZA? I WANT TO TAKE SOME FLAMINGO LESSONS!
CARAMBA!!
NO, NOT THE RHUMBA! FLAMINGO!! ALTHOUGH YOU COULD THROW IN SOME "TWIST" LESSONS!
I DON'T TEECH MUSIC TO ANYONE WEETH HORNS--GO TO ZE BULL RING!
GOSH, I DIDN'T KNOW THEY TAUGHT GUITAR IN THE BULL RING!!
P-S-S-T! SEÑOR MOOSE!
I DON'T NEED ANY POST-CARDS, BUDDY! SAY, AREN'T YOU THAT ONE NOTE GUY?
YOU MUST MEAN MY TWIN BROTHER IN THE STATES!
HE'S THE ONE SENT ME HERE--I'D LIKE TO BUST HIM IN THE NOSE!! H-M-M, YOU LOOK SO. MUCH LIKE HIM, I'M TEMPTED--
WAIT! I'VE GOT NEWS FOR YOU!
HUH?
MY BROTHER WIRED ME TO TAKE CARE OF YOU! THEY NEED SOMEONE TO SING AND PLAY IN THE BULL RING THIS AFTERNOON--IF YOU MAKE GOOD, YOU'LL BE BURIED IN NOTORIETY!
DUM DE DUM
PRIVATE
THAT'S MY CLIENT! THE ONLY MATADOR THAT CAN REALLY LOCK HORNS WITH A BULL!! HE'LL FIGHT THE TOUGHEST ONE YOU'VE GOT!!
THERE IS NO MATADOR WHO WOULD FACE "EL BUMBO"--IF HE FIGHTS THAT BULL, IT'S A DEAL!!

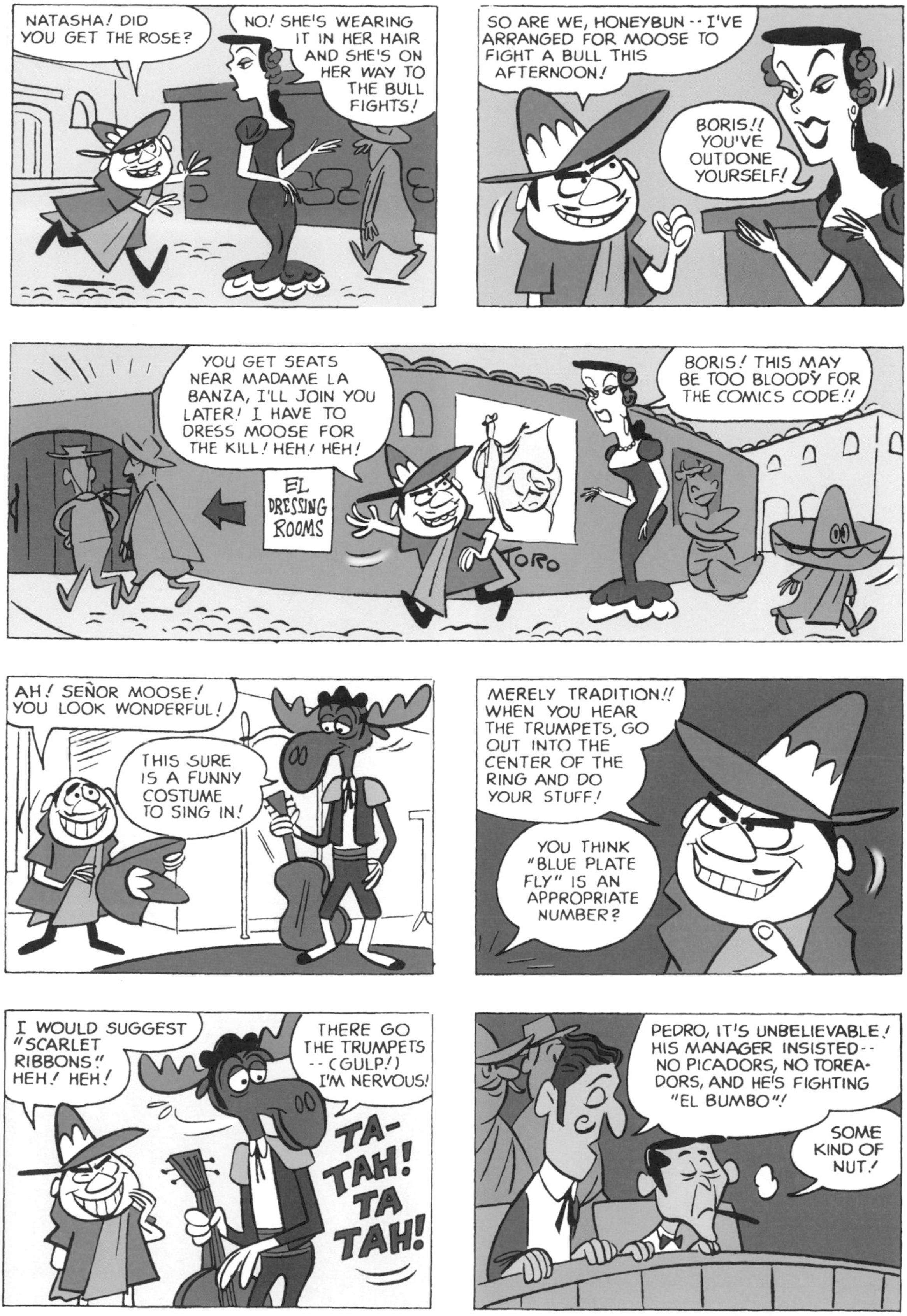
NATASHA! DID YOU GET THE ROSE?
NO! SHE'S WEARING IT IN HER HAIR AND SHE'S ON HER WAY TO THE BULL FIGHTS!
SO ARE WE, HONEYBUN -- I'VE ARRANGED FOR MOOSE TO FIGHT A BULL THIS AFTERNOON!
BORIS!! YOU'VE OUTDONE YOURSELF!
YOU GET SEATS NEAR MADAME LA BANZA, I'LL JOIN YOU LATER! I HAVE TO DRESS MOOSE FOR THE KILL! HEH! HEH!
EL DRESSING ROOMS
TORO
BORIS! THIS MAY BE TOO BLOODY FOR THE COMICS CODE!!
AH! SEÑOR MOOSE! YOU LOOK WONDERFUL!
THIS SURE IS A FUNNY COSTUME TO SING IN!
MERELY TRADITION!! WHEN YOU HEAR THE TRUMPETS, GO OUT INTO THE CENTER OF THE RING AND DO YOUR STUFF!
YOU THINK "BLUE PLATE FLY" IS AN APPROPRIATE NUMBER?
I WOULD SUGGEST "SCARLET RIBBONS!" HEH! HEH!
THERE GO THE TRUMPETS -- (GULP!) I'M NERVOUS!
TA-TAH! TA TAH!
PEDRO, IT'S UNBELIEVABLE! HIS MANAGER INSISTED -- NO PICADORS, NO TOREADORS, AND HE'S FIGHTING "EL BUMBO"!
SOME KIND OF NUT!

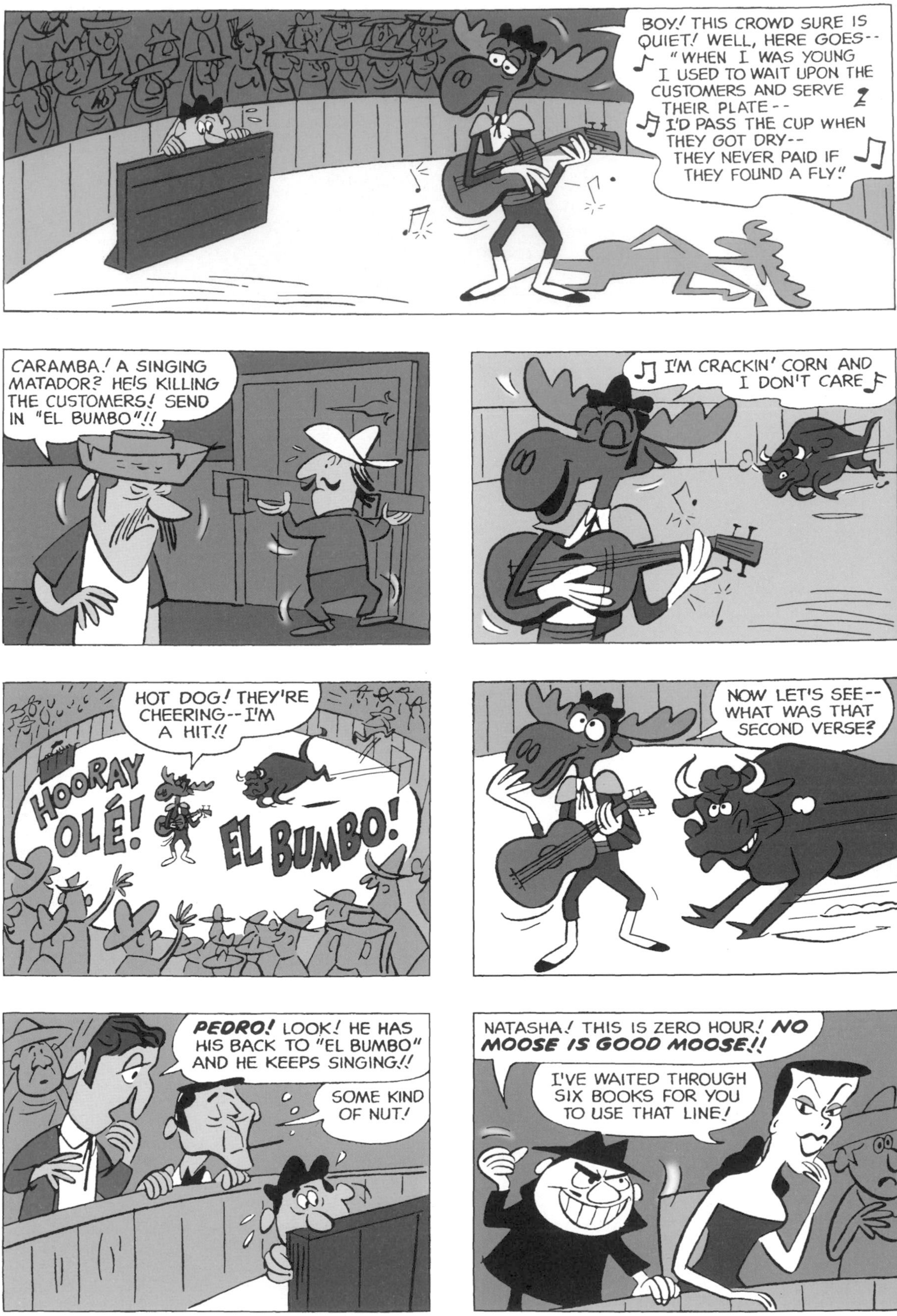
BOY! THIS CROWD SURE IS QUIET! WELL, HERE GOES-- "WHEN I WAS YOUNG I USED TO WAIT UPON THE CUSTOMERS AND SERVE THEIR PLATE-- I'D PASS THE CUP WHEN THEY GOT DRY-- THEY NEVER PAID IF THEY FOUND A FLY!"
CARAMBA! A SINGING MATADOR? HE'S KILLING THE CUSTOMERS! SEND IN "EL BUMBO"!!
I'M CRACKIN' CORN AND I DON'T CARE
HOT DOG! THEY'RE CHEERING--I'M A HIT!!
HOORAY
OLÉ!
EL BUMBO!
NOW LET'S SEE-- WHAT WAS THAT SECOND VERSE?
PEDRO! LOOK! HE HAS HIS BACK TO "EL BUMBO" AND HE KEEPS SINGING!!
SOME KIND OF NUT!
NATASHA! THIS IS ZERO HOUR! ***NO MOOSE IS GOOD MOOSE!!***
I'VE WAITED THROUGH SIX BOOKS FOR YOU TO USE THAT LINE!

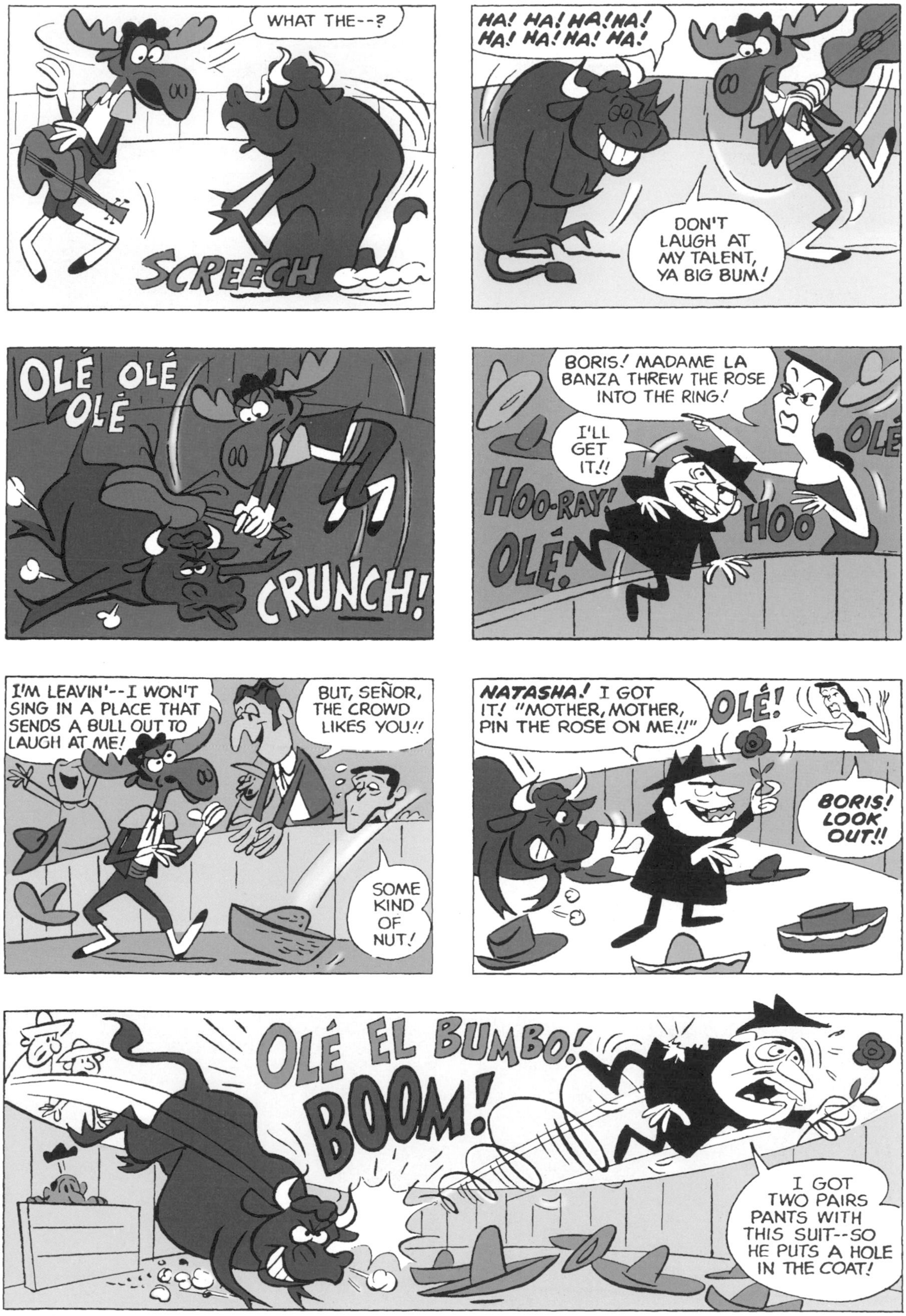
WHAT THE--?
SCREECH
HA! HA! HA! HA! HA! HA! HA! HA!
DON'T LAUGH AT MY TALENT, YA BIG BUM!
OLÉ OLÉ OLÉ
CRUNCH!
BORIS! MADAME LA BANZA THREW THE ROSE INTO THE RING!
I'LL GET IT!!
OLÉ
HOO-RAY!
HOO
OLÉ!
I'M LEAVIN'--I WON'T SING IN A PLACE THAT SENDS A BULL OUT TO LAUGH AT ME!
BUT, SEÑOR, THE CROWD LIKES YOU!!
SOME KIND OF NUT!
NATASHA! I GOT IT! "MOTHER, MOTHER, PIN THE ROSE ON ME!!"
OLÉ!
BORIS! LOOK OUT!!
OLÉ EL BUMBO!
BOOM!
I GOT TWO PAIRS PANTS WITH THIS SUIT--SO HE PUTS A HOLE IN THE COAT!

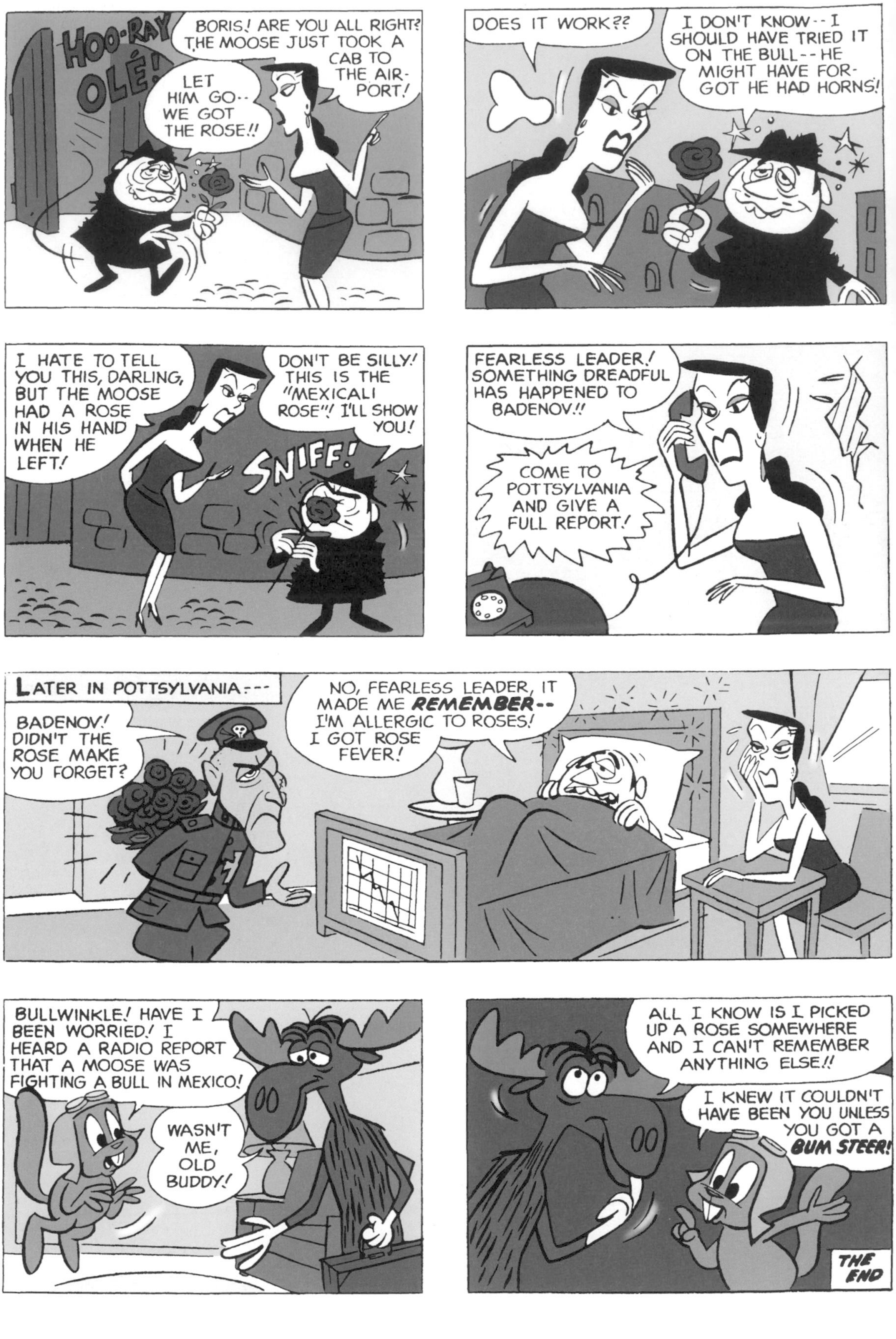
HOO-RAY OLÉ!
BORIS! ARE YOU ALL RIGHT? THE MOOSE JUST TOOK A CAB TO THE AIRPORT!
LET HIM GO-- WE GOT THE ROSE!!
DOES IT WORK??
I DON'T KNOW--I SHOULD HAVE TRIED IT ON THE BULL--HE MIGHT HAVE FORGOT HE HAD HORNS!
I HATE TO TELL YOU THIS, DARLING, BUT THE MOOSE HAD A ROSE IN HIS HAND WHEN HE LEFT!
DON'T BE SILLY! THIS IS THE "MEXICALI ROSE"! I'LL SHOW YOU!
SNIFF!
FEARLESS LEADER! SOMETHING DREADFUL HAS HAPPENED TO BADENOV!!
COME TO POTTSYLVANIA AND GIVE A FULL REPORT!
LATER IN POTTSYLVANIA---
BADENOV! DIDN'T THE ROSE MAKE YOU FORGET?
NO, FEARLESS LEADER, IT MADE ME REMEMBER-- I'M ALLERGIC TO ROSES! I GOT ROSE FEVER!
BULLWINKLE! HAVE I BEEN WORRIED! I HEARD A RADIO REPORT THAT A MOOSE WAS FIGHTING A BULL IN MEXICO!
WASN'T ME, OLD BUDDY!
ALL I KNOW IS I PICKED UP A ROSE SOMEWHERE AND I CAN'T REMEMBER ANYTHING ELSE!!
I KNEW IT COULDN'T HAVE BEEN YOU UNLESS YOU GOT A BUM STEER!
THE END

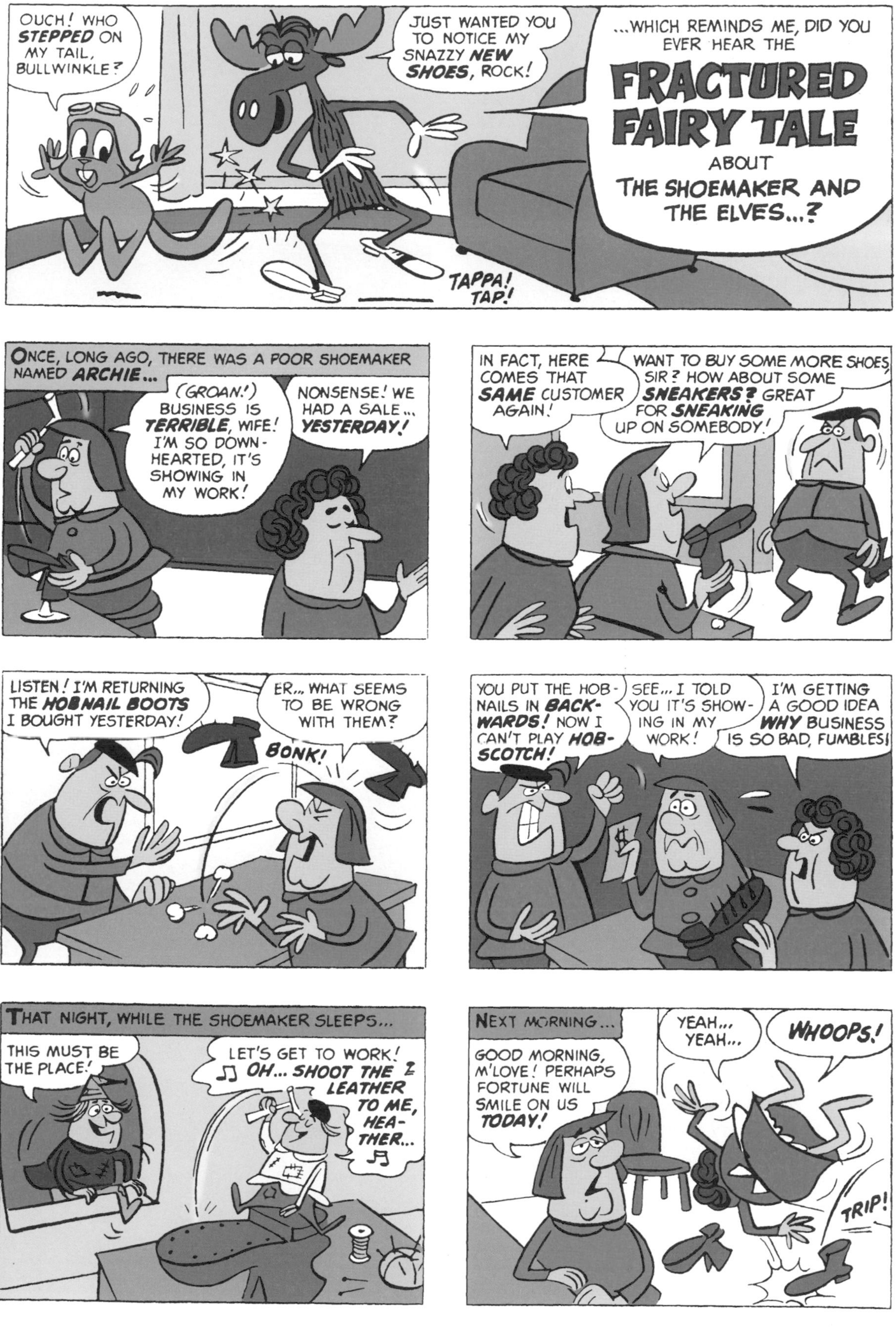
OUCH! WHO STEPPED ON MY TAIL, BULLWINKLE?
JUST WANTED YOU TO NOTICE MY SNAZZY NEW SHOES, ROCK!
...WHICH REMINDS ME, DID YOU EVER HEAR THE FRACTURED FAIRY TALE ABOUT THE SHOEMAKER AND THE ELVES...?
TAPPA! TAP!
ONCE, LONG AGO, THERE WAS A POOR SHOEMAKER NAMED ARCHIE...
(GROAN!) BUSINESS IS TERRIBLE, WIFE! I'M SO DOWN-HEARTED, IT'S SHOWING IN MY WORK!
NONSENSE! WE HAD A SALE... YESTERDAY!
IN FACT, HERE COMES THAT SAME CUSTOMER AGAIN!
WANT TO BUY SOME MORE SHOES, SIR? HOW ABOUT SOME SNEAKERS? GREAT FOR SNEAKING UP ON SOMEBODY!
LISTEN! I'M RETURNING THE HOBNAIL BOOTS I BOUGHT YESTERDAY!
ER... WHAT SEEMS TO BE WRONG WITH THEM?
BONK!
YOU PUT THE HOB-NAILS IN BACK-WARDS! NOW I CAN'T PLAY HOB-SCOTCH!
SEE... I TOLD YOU IT'S SHOW-ING IN MY WORK!
I'M GETTING A GOOD IDEA WHY BUSINESS IS SO BAD, FUMBLES!
THAT NIGHT, WHILE THE SHOEMAKER SLEEPS...
THIS MUST BE THE PLACE!
LET'S GET TO WORK! OH... SHOOT THE LEATHER TO ME, HEA-THER...
NEXT MORNING...
GOOD MORNING, M'LOVE! PERHAPS FORTUNE WILL SMILE ON US TODAY!
YEAH... YEAH...
WHOOPS!
TRIP!

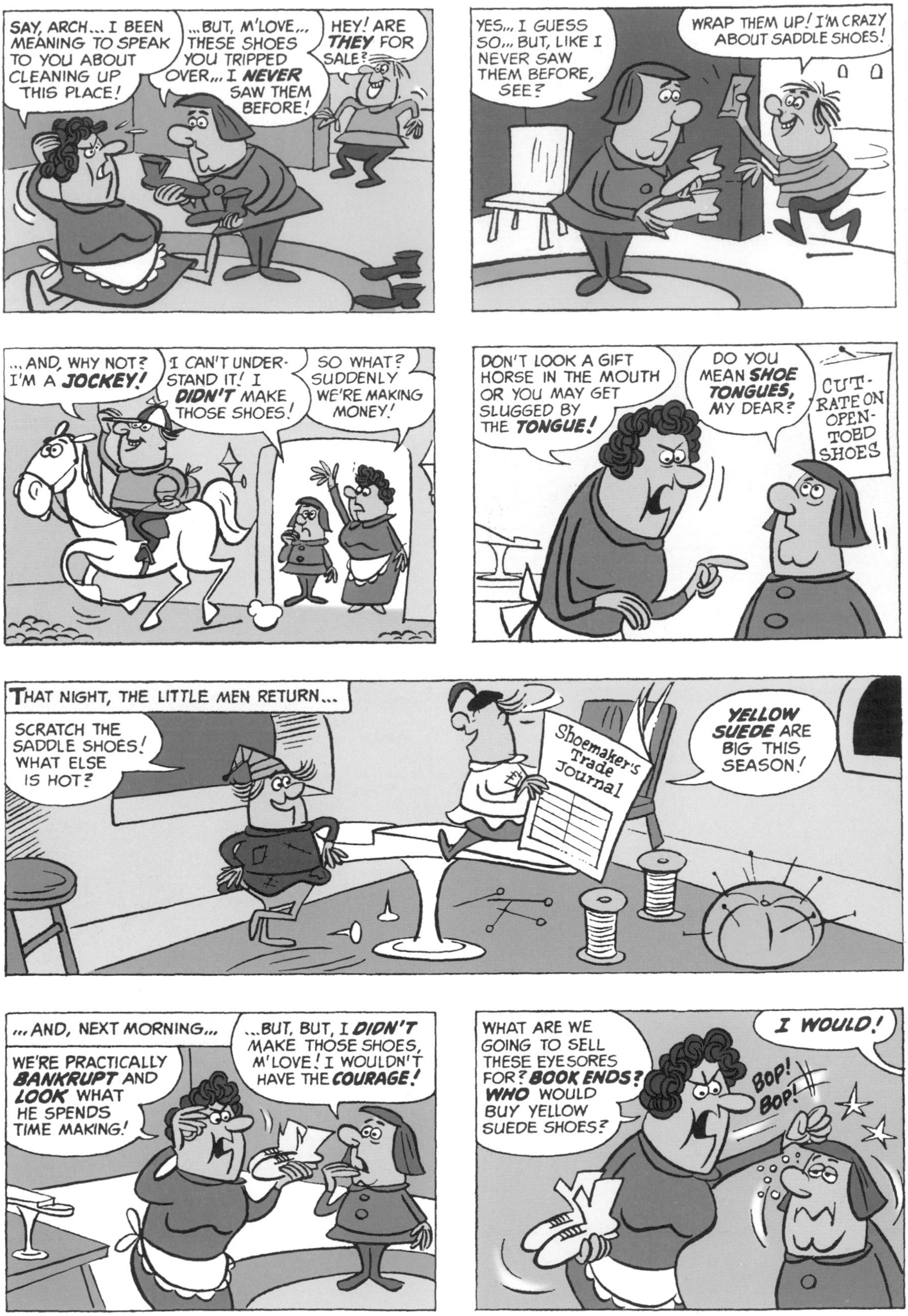
SAY, ARCH... I BEEN MEANING TO SPEAK TO YOU ABOUT CLEANING UP THIS PLACE!
...BUT, M'LOVE... THESE SHOES YOU TRIPPED OVER... I NEVER SAW THEM BEFORE!
HEY! ARE THEY FOR SALE?
YES... I GUESS SO... BUT, LIKE I NEVER SAW THEM BEFORE, SEE?
WRAP THEM UP! I'M CRAZY ABOUT SADDLE SHOES!
...AND, WHY NOT? I'M A JOCKEY!
I CAN'T UNDERSTAND IT! I DIDN'T MAKE THOSE SHOES!
SO WHAT? SUDDENLY WE'RE MAKING MONEY!
DON'T LOOK A GIFT HORSE IN THE MOUTH OR YOU MAY GET SLUGGED BY THE TONGUE!
DO YOU MEAN SHOE TONGUES, MY DEAR?
CUT-RATE ON OPEN-TOED SHOES
THAT NIGHT, THE LITTLE MEN RETURN...
SCRATCH THE SADDLE SHOES! WHAT ELSE IS HOT?
Shoemaker's Trade Journal
YELLOW SUEDE ARE BIG THIS SEASON!
...AND, NEXT MORNING...
WE'RE PRACTICALLY BANKRUPT AND LOOK WHAT HE SPENDS TIME MAKING!
...BUT, BUT, I DIDN'T MAKE THOSE SHOES, M'LOVE! I WOULDN'T HAVE THE COURAGE!
WHAT ARE WE GOING TO SELL THESE EYESORES FOR? BOOK ENDS? WHO WOULD BUY YELLOW SUEDE SHOES?
I WOULD!
BOP! BOP!

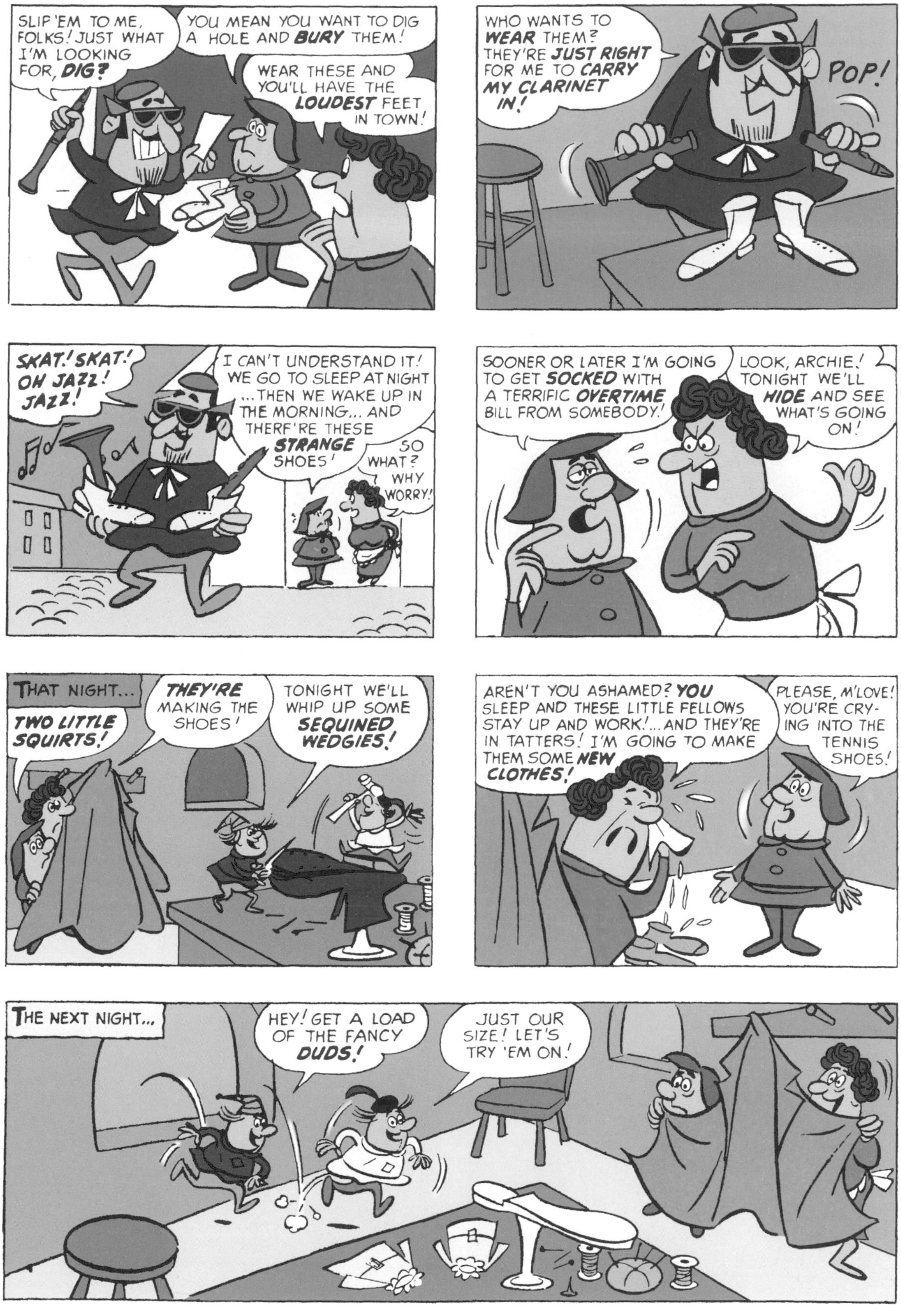
SLIP 'EM TO ME, FOLKS! JUST WHAT I'M LOOKING FOR, DIG?
YOU MEAN YOU WANT TO DIG A HOLE AND BURY THEM!
WEAR THESE AND YOU'LL HAVE THE LOUDEST FEET IN TOWN!
WHO WANTS TO WEAR THEM? THEY'RE JUST RIGHT FOR ME TO CARRY MY CLARINET IN!
POP!
SKAT! SKAT! OH JAZZ! JAZZ!
I CAN'T UNDERSTAND IT! WE GO TO SLEEP AT NIGHT ...THEN WE WAKE UP IN THE MORNING... AND THERE'RE THESE STRANGE SHOES!
SO WHAT? WHY WORRY!
SOONER OR LATER I'M GOING TO GET SOCKED WITH A TERRIFIC OVERTIME BILL FROM SOMEBODY!
LOOK, ARCHIE! TONIGHT WE'LL HIDE AND SEE WHAT'S GOING ON!
THAT NIGHT...
TWO LITTLE SQUIRTS!
THEY'RE MAKING THE SHOES!
TONIGHT WE'LL WHIP UP SOME SEQUINED WEDGIES!
AREN'T YOU ASHAMED? YOU SLEEP AND THESE LITTLE FELLOWS STAY UP AND WORK!... AND THEY'RE IN TATTERS! I'M GOING TO MAKE THEM SOME NEW CLOTHES!
PLEASE, M'LOVE! YOU'RE CRYING INTO THE TENNIS SHOES!
THE NEXT NIGHT...
HEY! GET A LOAD OF THE FANCY DUDS!
JUST OUR SIZE! LET'S TRY 'EM ON!

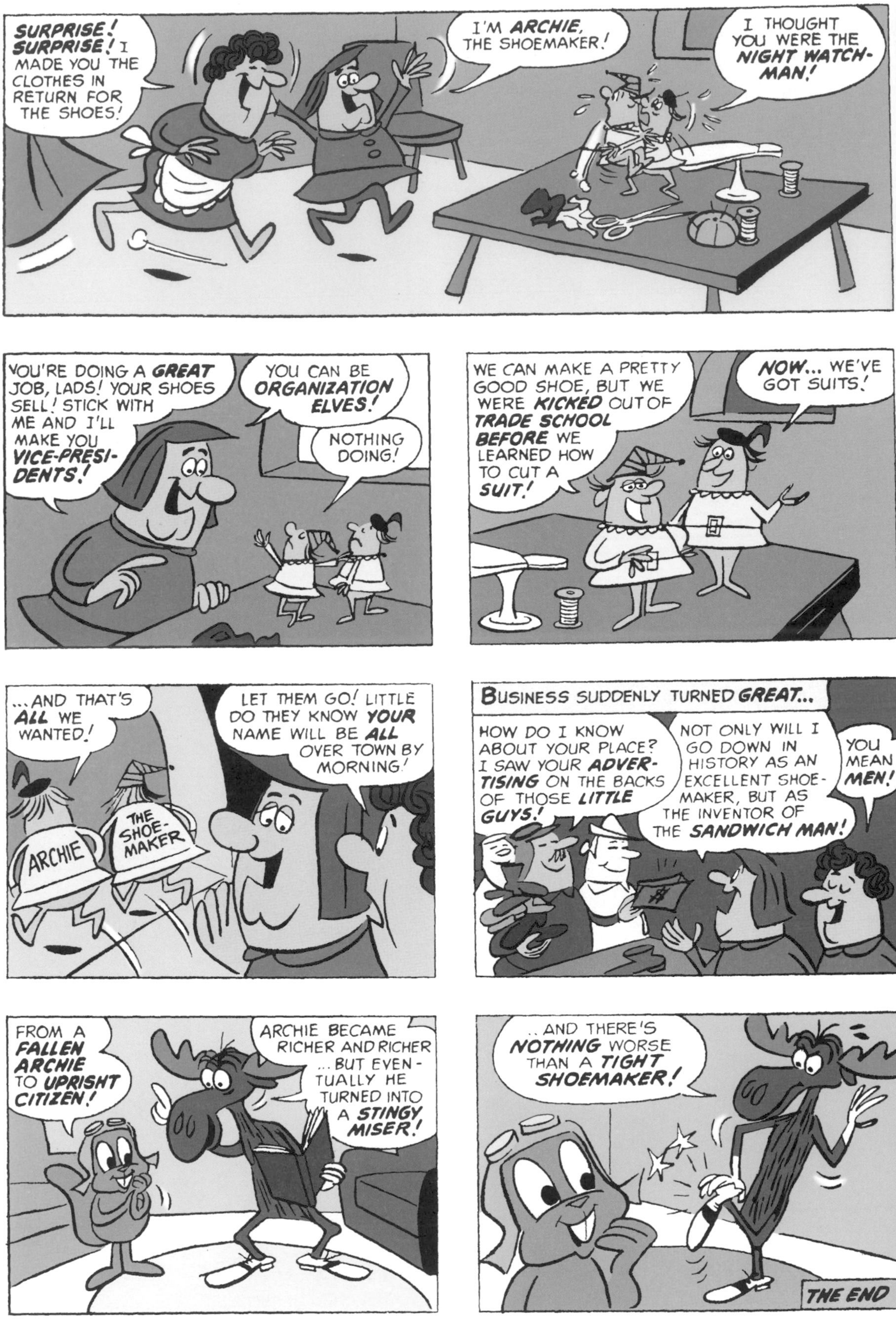
SURPRISE! SURPRISE! I MADE YOU THE CLOTHES IN RETURN FOR THE SHOES!
I'M ARCHIE, THE SHOEMAKER!
I THOUGHT YOU WERE THE NIGHT WATCH-MAN!
YOU'RE DOING A GREAT JOB, LADS! YOUR SHOES SELL! STICK WITH ME AND I'LL MAKE YOU VICE-PRESI-DENTS!
YOU CAN BE ORGANIZATION ELVES!
NOTHING DOING!
WE CAN MAKE A PRETTY GOOD SHOE, BUT WE WERE KICKED OUT OF TRADE SCHOOL BEFORE WE LEARNED HOW TO CUT A SUIT!
NOW... WE'VE GOT SUITS!
...AND THAT'S ALL WE WANTED!
LET THEM GO! LITTLE DO THEY KNOW YOUR NAME WILL BE ALL OVER TOWN BY MORNING!
ARCHIE
THE SHOE-MAKER
BUSINESS SUDDENLY TURNED GREAT...
HOW DO I KNOW ABOUT YOUR PLACE? I SAW YOUR ADVER-TISING ON THE BACKS OF THOSE LITTLE GUYS!
NOT ONLY WILL I GO DOWN IN HISTORY AS AN EXCELLENT SHOE-MAKER, BUT AS THE INVENTOR OF THE SANDWICH MAN!
YOU MEAN MEN!
FROM A FALLEN ARCHIE TO UPRIGHT CITIZEN!
ARCHIE BECAME RICHER AND RICHER ...BUT EVEN-TUALLY HE TURNED INTO A STINGY MISER!
..AND THERE'S NOTHING WORSE THAN A TIGHT SHOEMAKER!
THE END

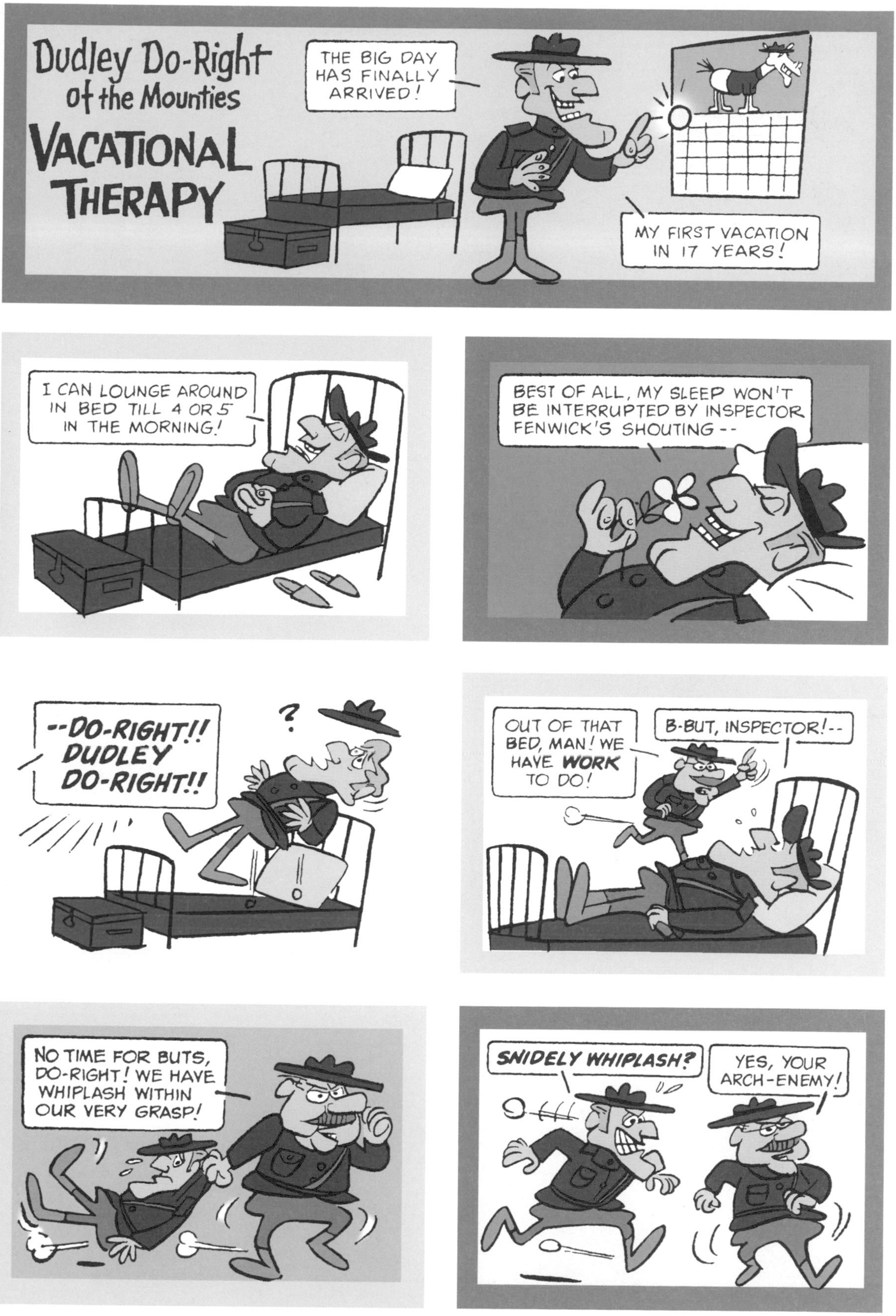
Dudley Do-Right of the Mounties
VACATIONAL THERAPY
THE BIG DAY HAS FINALLY ARRIVED!
MY FIRST VACATION IN 17 YEARS!
I CAN LOUNGE AROUND IN BED TILL 4 OR 5 IN THE MORNING!
BEST OF ALL, MY SLEEP WON'T BE INTERRUPTED BY INSPECTOR FENWICK'S SHOUTING --
--DO-RIGHT!! DUDLEY DO-RIGHT!!
?
OUT OF THAT BED, MAN! WE HAVE WORK TO DO!
B-BUT, INSPECTOR!--
NO TIME FOR BUTS, DO-RIGHT! WE HAVE WHIPLASH WITHIN OUR VERY GRASP!
SNIDELY WHIPLASH?
YES, YOUR ARCH-ENEMY!

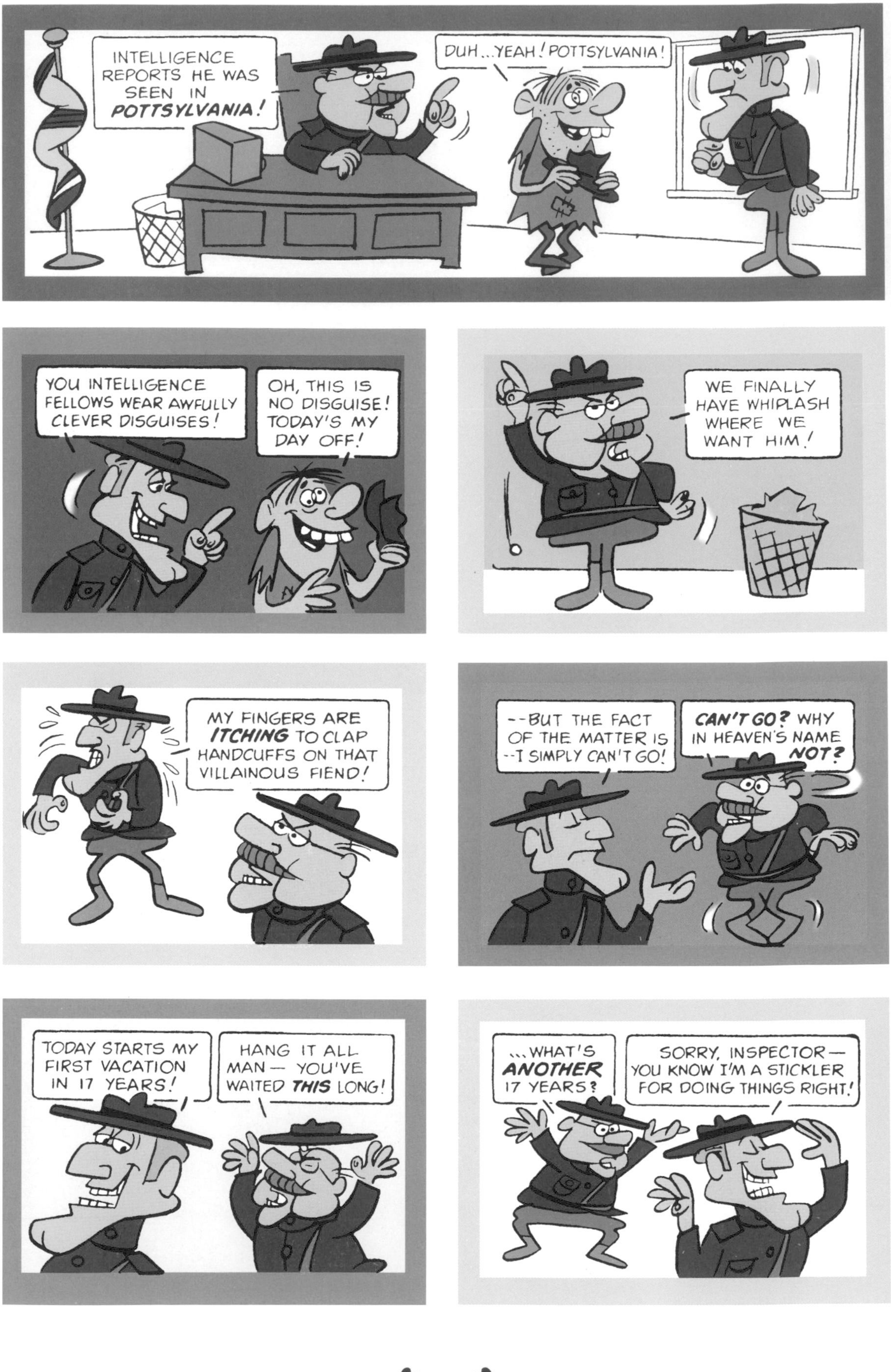
INTELLIGENCE REPORTS HE WAS SEEN IN **POTTSYLVANIA!**
DUH...YEAH! POTTSYLVANIA!
YOU INTELLIGENCE FELLOWS WEAR AWFULLY CLEVER DISGUISES!
OH, THIS IS NO DISGUISE! TODAY'S MY DAY OFF!
WE FINALLY HAVE WHIPLASH WHERE WE WANT HIM!
MY FINGERS ARE **ITCHING** TO CLAP HANDCUFFS ON THAT VILLAINOUS FIEND!
--BUT THE FACT OF THE MATTER IS --I SIMPLY CAN'T GO!
CAN'T GO? WHY IN HEAVEN'S NAME **NOT?**
TODAY STARTS MY FIRST VACATION IN 17 YEARS!
HANG IT ALL MAN— YOU'VE WAITED **THIS** LONG!
...WHAT'S **ANOTHER** 17 YEARS?
SORRY, INSPECTOR— YOU KNOW I'M A STICKLER FOR DOING THINGS RIGHT!

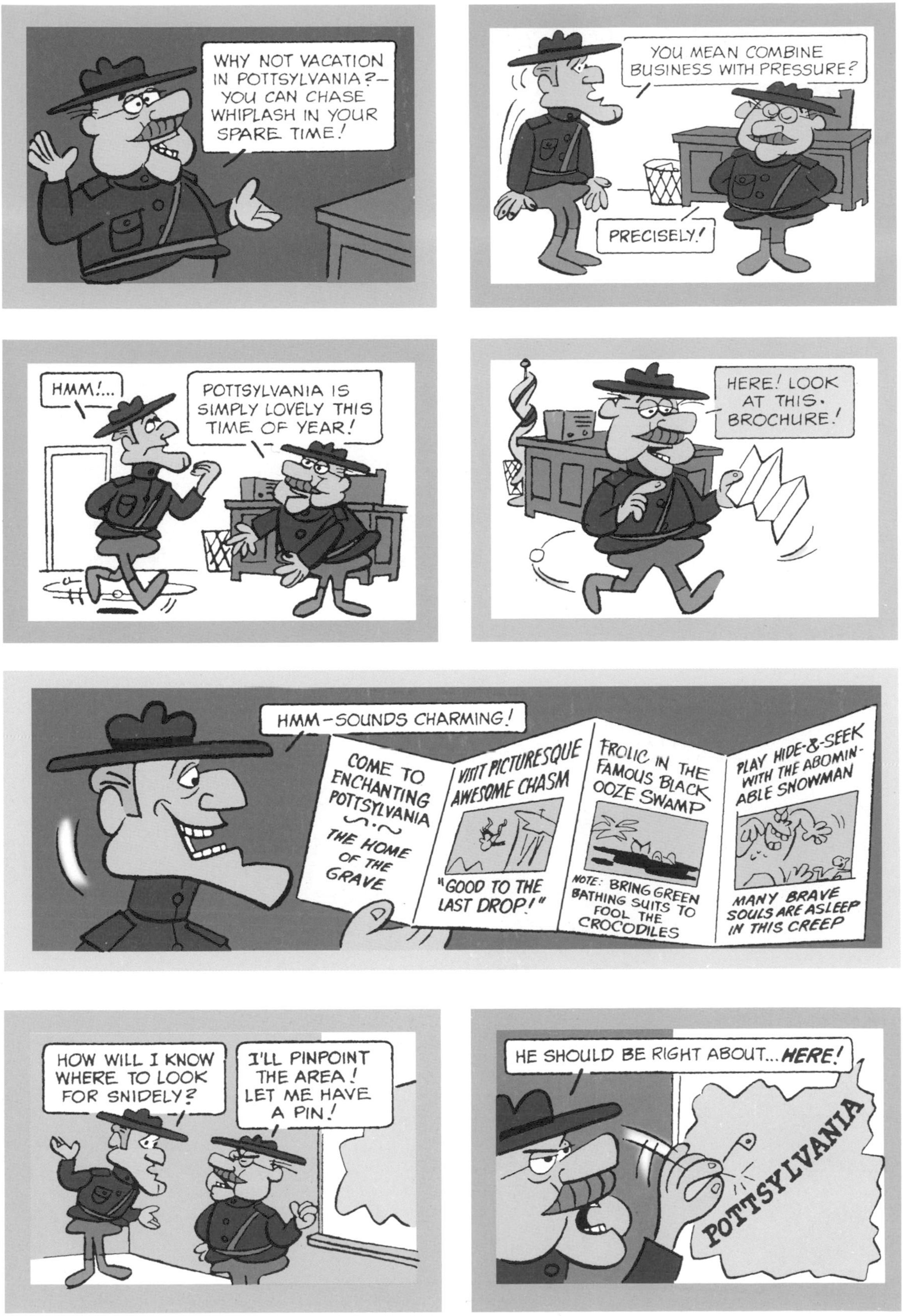
WHY NOT VACATION IN POTTSYLVANIA?— YOU CAN CHASE WHIPLASH IN YOUR SPARE TIME!
YOU MEAN COMBINE BUSINESS WITH PRESSURE?
PRECISELY!
HMM!...
POTTSYLVANIA IS SIMPLY LOVELY THIS TIME OF YEAR!
HERE! LOOK AT THIS. BROCHURE!
HMM—SOUNDS CHARMING!
COME TO ENCHANTING POTTSYLVANIA
THE HOME OF THE GRAVE
VISIT PICTURESQUE AWESOME CHASM
"GOOD TO THE LAST DROP!"
FROLIC IN THE FAMOUS BLACK OOZE SWAMP
NOTE: BRING GREEN BATHING SUITS TO FOOL THE CROCODILES
PLAY HIDE-&-SEEK WITH THE ABOMIN-ABLE SNOWMAN
MANY BRAVE SOULS ARE ASLEEP IN THIS CREEP
HOW WILL I KNOW WHERE TO LOOK FOR SNIDELY?
I'LL PINPOINT THE AREA! LET ME HAVE A PIN!
HE SHOULD BE RIGHT ABOUT... HERE!
POTTSYLVANIA

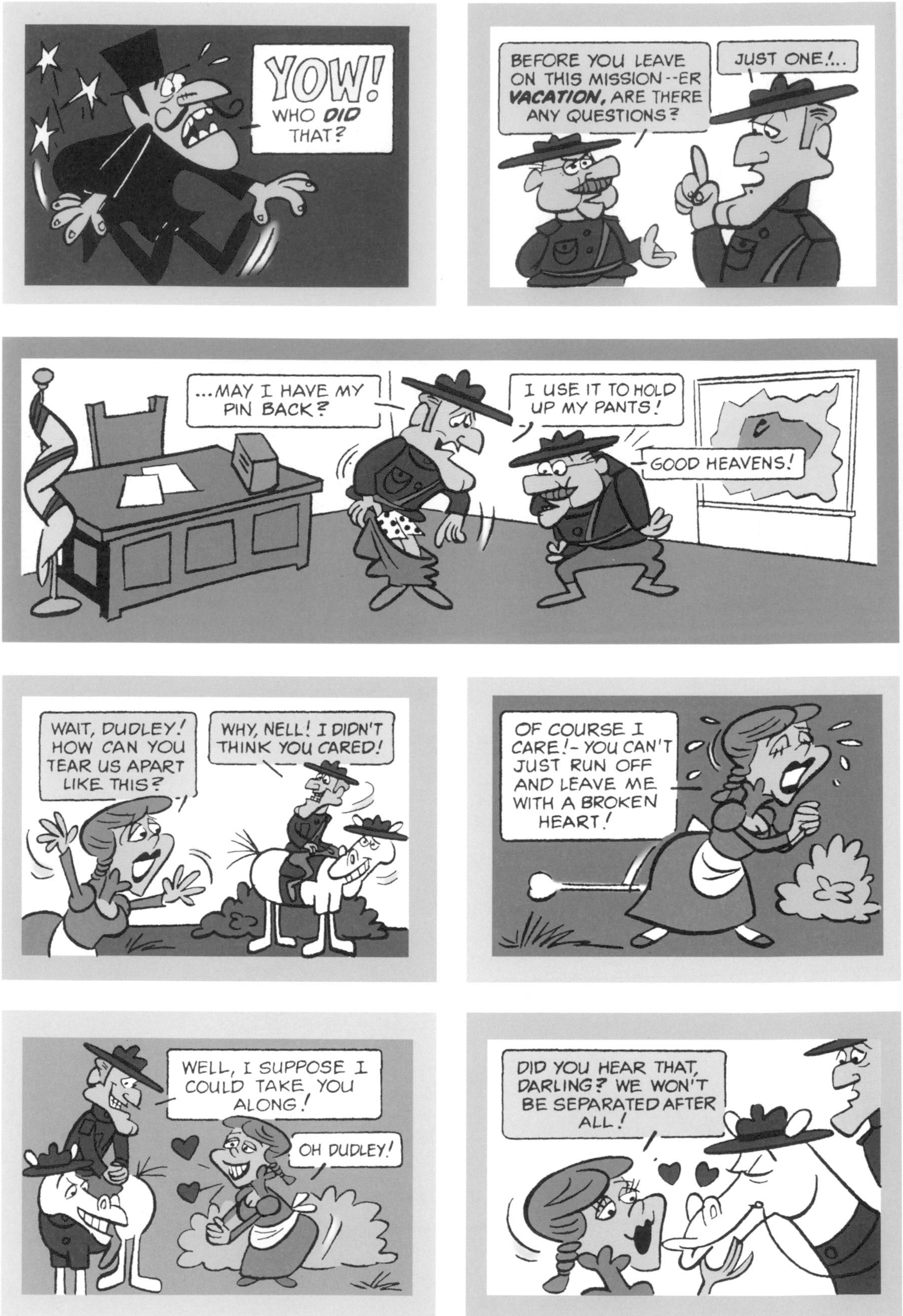
YOW!
WHO DID THAT?
BEFORE YOU LEAVE ON THIS MISSION--ER VACATION, ARE THERE ANY QUESTIONS?
JUST ONE!...
...MAY I HAVE MY PIN BACK?
I USE IT TO HOLD UP MY PANTS!
GOOD HEAVENS!
WAIT, DUDLEY! HOW CAN YOU TEAR US APART LIKE THIS?
WHY, NELL! I DIDN'T THINK YOU CARED!
OF COURSE I CARE!- YOU CAN'T JUST RUN OFF AND LEAVE ME WITH A BROKEN HEART!
WELL, I SUPPOSE I COULD TAKE YOU ALONG!
OH DUDLEY!
DID YOU HEAR THAT, DARLING? WE WON'T BE SEPARATED AFTER ALL!

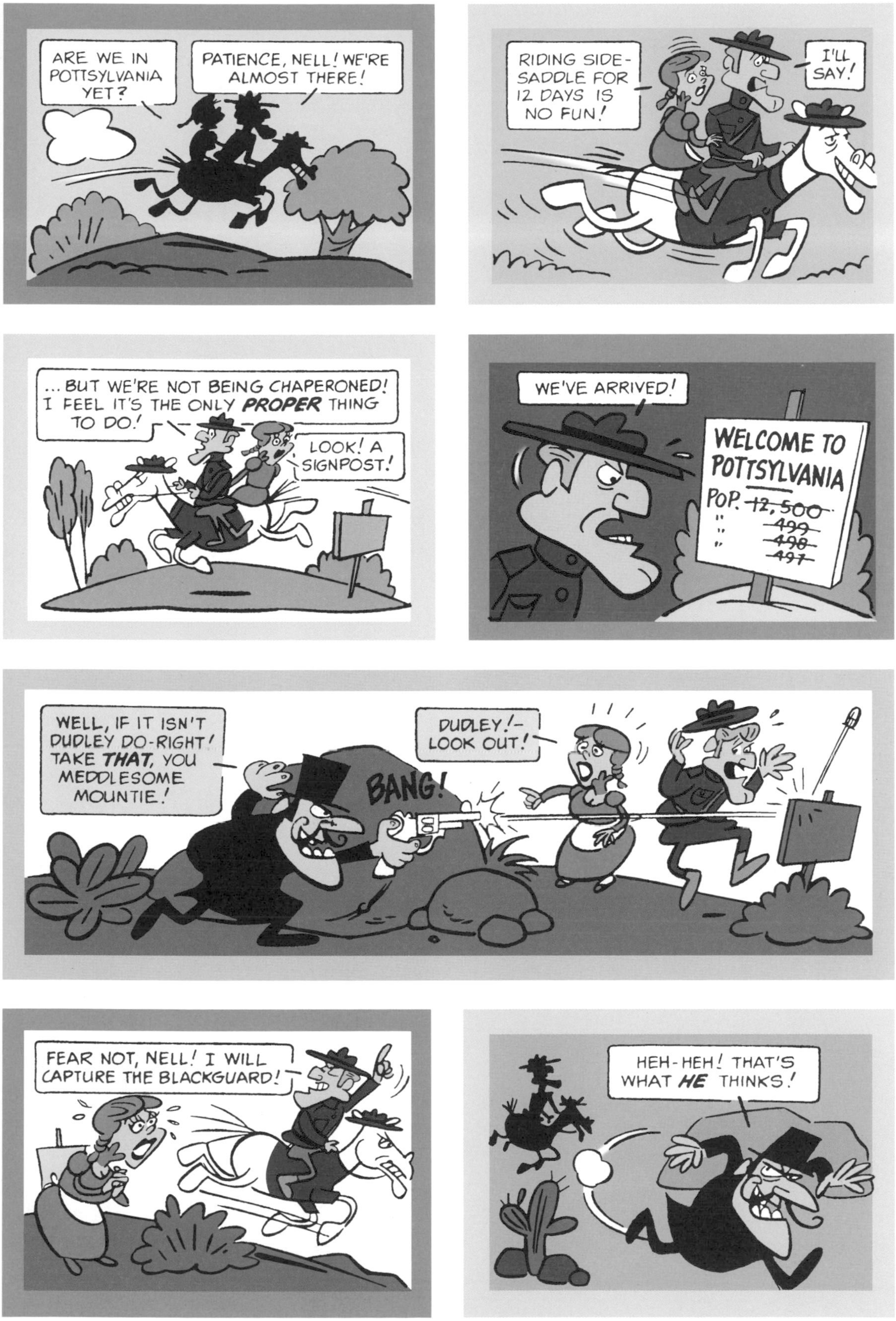
ARE WE IN POTTSYLVANIA YET?
PATIENCE, NELL! WE'RE ALMOST THERE!
RIDING SIDE-SADDLE FOR 12 DAYS IS NO FUN!
I'LL SAY!
...BUT WE'RE NOT BEING CHAPERONED! I FEEL IT'S THE ONLY PROPER THING TO DO!
LOOK! A SIGNPOST!
WE'VE ARRIVED!
WELCOME TO POTTSYLVANIA
POP. 12,500
" 499
" 498
" 497
WELL, IF IT ISN'T DUDLEY DO-RIGHT! TAKE THAT, YOU MEDDLESOME MOUNTIE!
BANG!
DUDLEY!– LOOK OUT!
FEAR NOT, NELL! I WILL CAPTURE THE BLACKGUARD!
HEH-HEH! THAT'S WHAT HE THINKS!

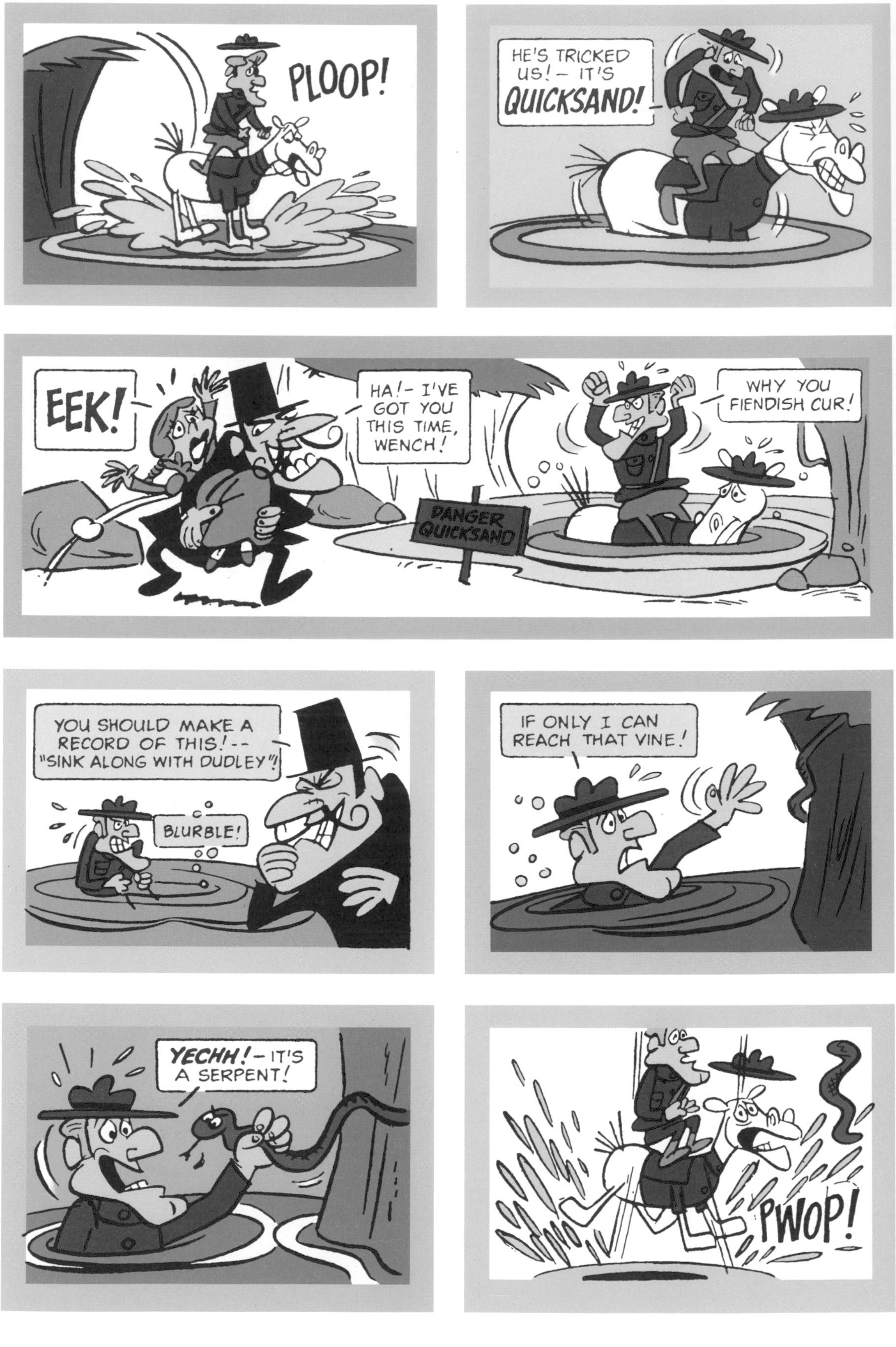
PLOOP!
HE'S TRICKED US! – IT'S QUICKSAND!
EEK!
HA! – I'VE GOT YOU THIS TIME, WENCH!
DANGER QUICKSAND
WHY YOU FIENDISH CUR!
YOU SHOULD MAKE A RECORD OF THIS! -- "SINK ALONG WITH DUDLEY"!
BLURBLE!
IF ONLY I CAN REACH THAT VINE!
YECHH! – IT'S A SERPENT!
PWOP!

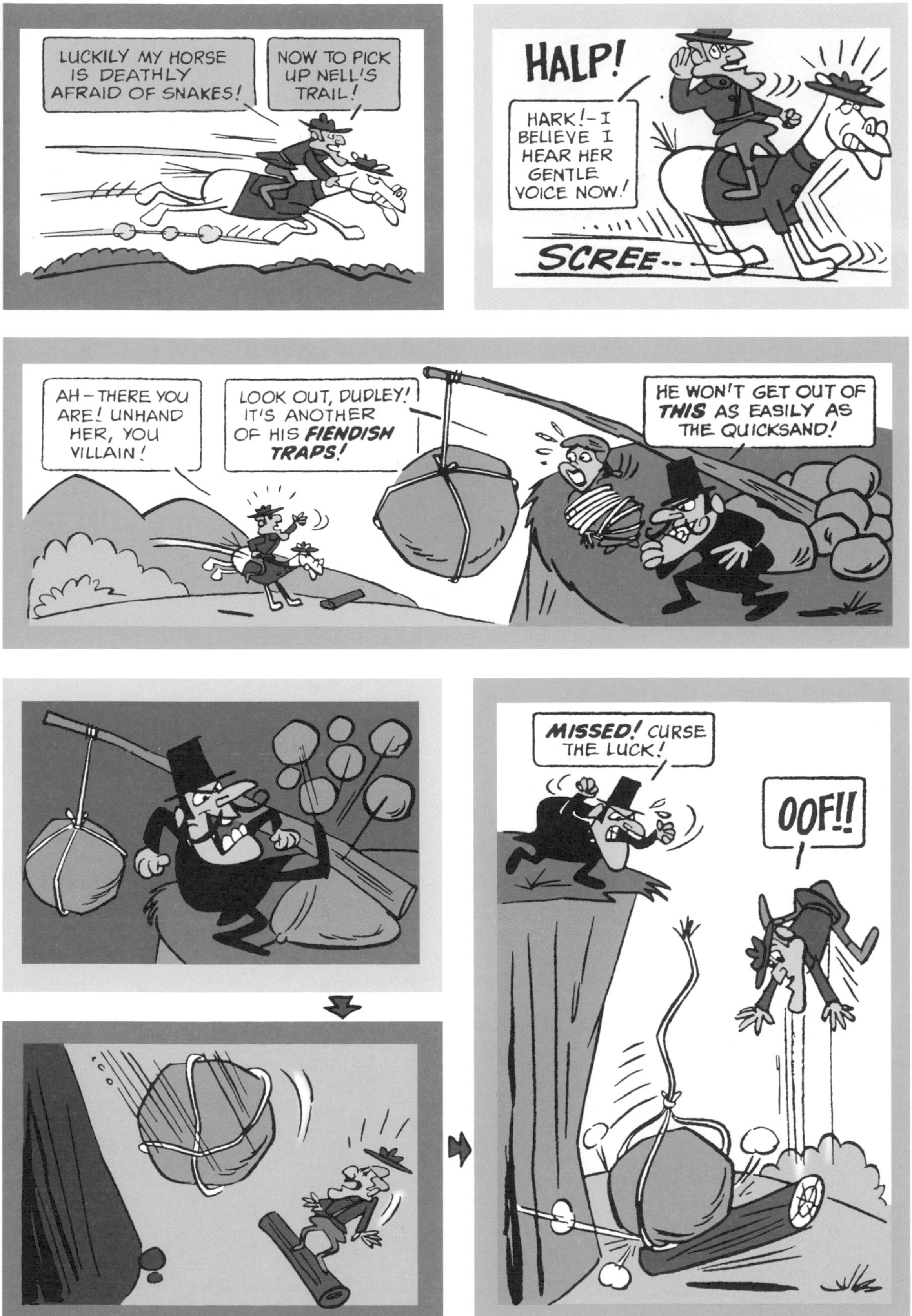
LUCKILY MY HORSE IS DEATHLY AFRAID OF SNAKES!
NOW TO PICK UP NELL'S TRAIL!
HALP!
HARK!–I BELIEVE I HEAR HER GENTLE VOICE NOW!
SCREE--
AH–THERE YOU ARE! UNHAND HER, YOU VILLAIN!
LOOK OUT, DUDLEY! IT'S ANOTHER OF HIS FIENDISH TRAPS!
HE WON'T GET OUT OF THIS AS EASILY AS THE QUICKSAND!
MISSED! CURSE THE LUCK!
OOF!!

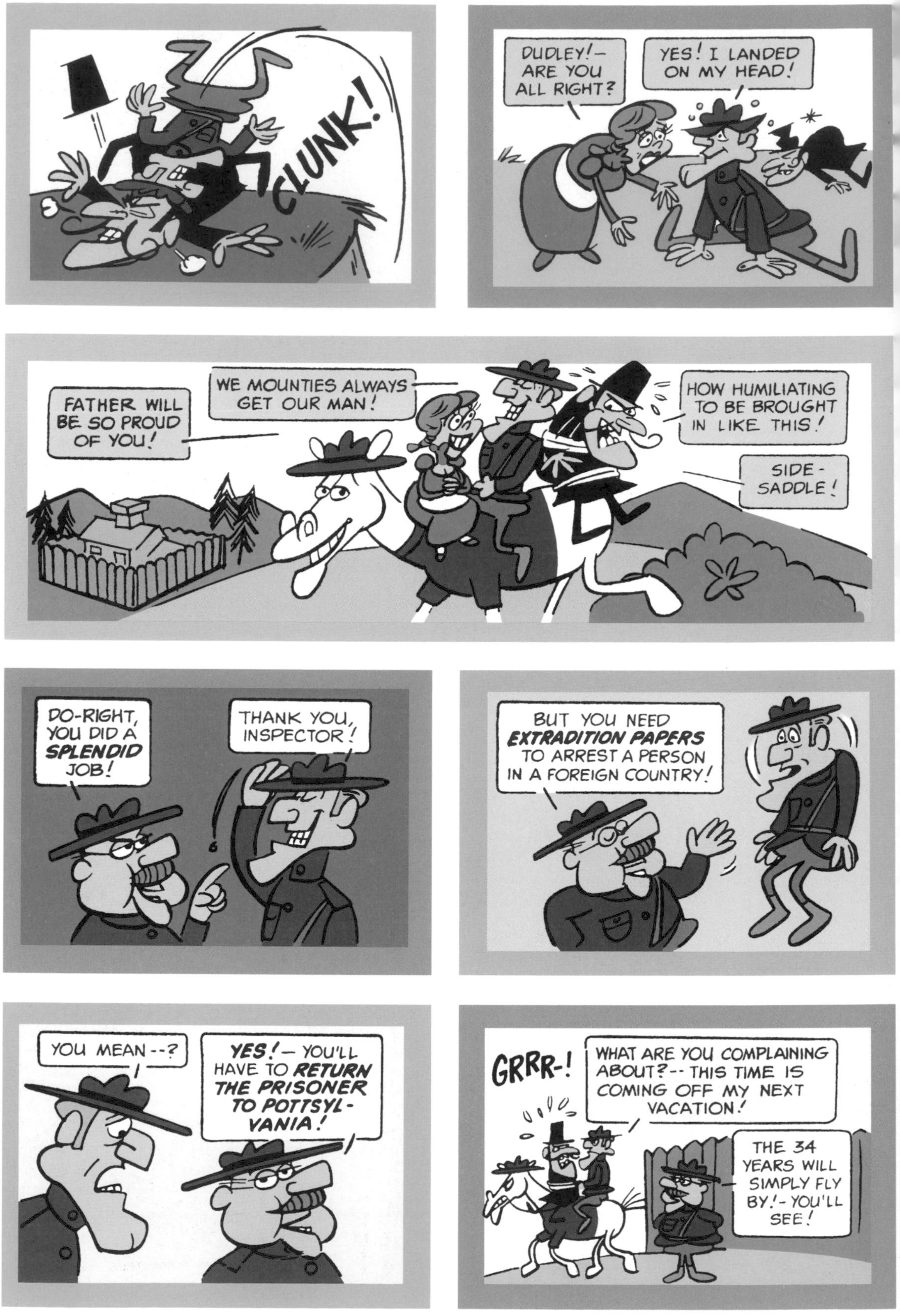
CLUNK!
DUDLEY!— ARE YOU ALL RIGHT?
YES! I LANDED ON MY HEAD!
FATHER WILL BE SO PROUD OF YOU!
WE MOUNTIES ALWAYS GET OUR MAN!
HOW HUMILIATING TO BE BROUGHT IN LIKE THIS!
SIDE-SADDLE!
DO-RIGHT, YOU DID A SPLENDID JOB!
THANK YOU, INSPECTOR!
BUT YOU NEED EXTRADITION PAPERS TO ARREST A PERSON IN A FOREIGN COUNTRY!
YOU MEAN --?
YES!— YOU'LL HAVE TO RETURN THE PRISONER TO POTTSYL-VANIA!
GRRR-!
WHAT ARE YOU COMPLAINING ABOUT?-- THIS TIME IS COMING OFF MY NEXT VACATION!
THE 34 YEARS WILL SIMPLY FLY BY!- YOU'LL SEE!

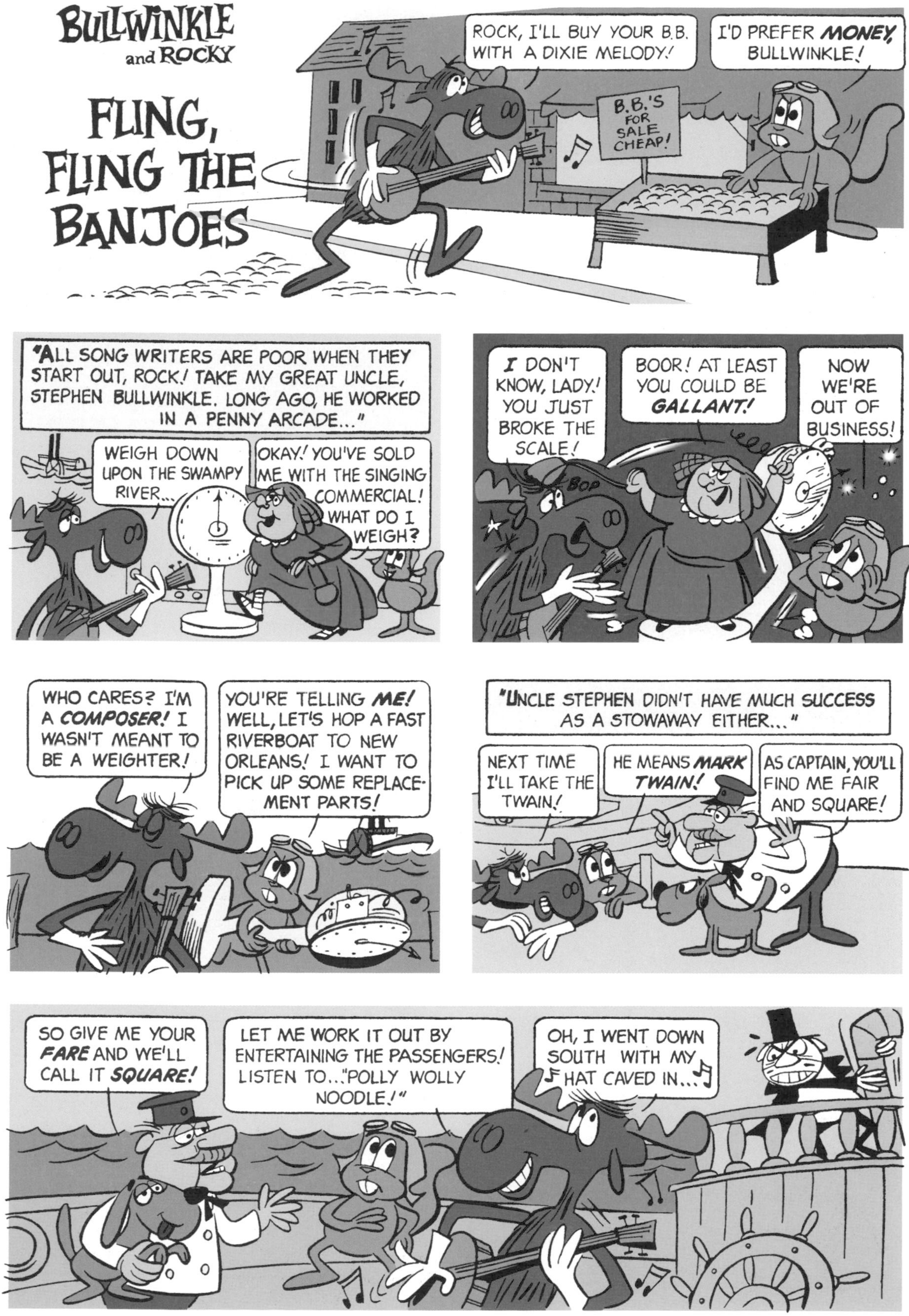
BULLWINKLE and ROCKY
FLING, FLING THE BANJOES
ROCK, I'LL BUY YOUR B.B. WITH A DIXIE MELODY!
I'D PREFER MONEY, BULLWINKLE!
B.B.'S FOR SALE CHEAP!
"ALL SONG WRITERS ARE POOR WHEN THEY START OUT, ROCK! TAKE MY GREAT UNCLE, STEPHEN BULLWINKLE. LONG AGO, HE WORKED IN A PENNY ARCADE..."
WEIGH DOWN UPON THE SWAMPY RIVER...
OKAY! YOU'VE SOLD ME WITH THE SINGING COMMERCIAL! WHAT DO I WEIGH?
I DON'T KNOW, LADY! YOU JUST BROKE THE SCALE!
BOOR! AT LEAST YOU COULD BE GALLANT!
NOW WE'RE OUT OF BUSINESS!
BOP
WHO CARES? I'M A COMPOSER! I WASN'T MEANT TO BE A WEIGHTER!
YOU'RE TELLING ME! WELL, LET'S HOP A FAST RIVERBOAT TO NEW ORLEANS! I WANT TO PICK UP SOME REPLACEMENT PARTS!
"UNCLE STEPHEN DIDN'T HAVE MUCH SUCCESS AS A STOWAWAY EITHER..."
NEXT TIME I'LL TAKE THE TWAIN!
HE MEANS MARK TWAIN!
AS CAPTAIN, YOU'LL FIND ME FAIR AND SQUARE!
SO GIVE ME YOUR FARE AND WE'LL CALL IT SQUARE!
LET ME WORK IT OUT BY ENTERTAINING THE PASSENGERS! LISTEN TO..."POLLY WOLLY NOODLE!"
OH, I WENT DOWN SOUTH WITH MY HAT CAVED IN...

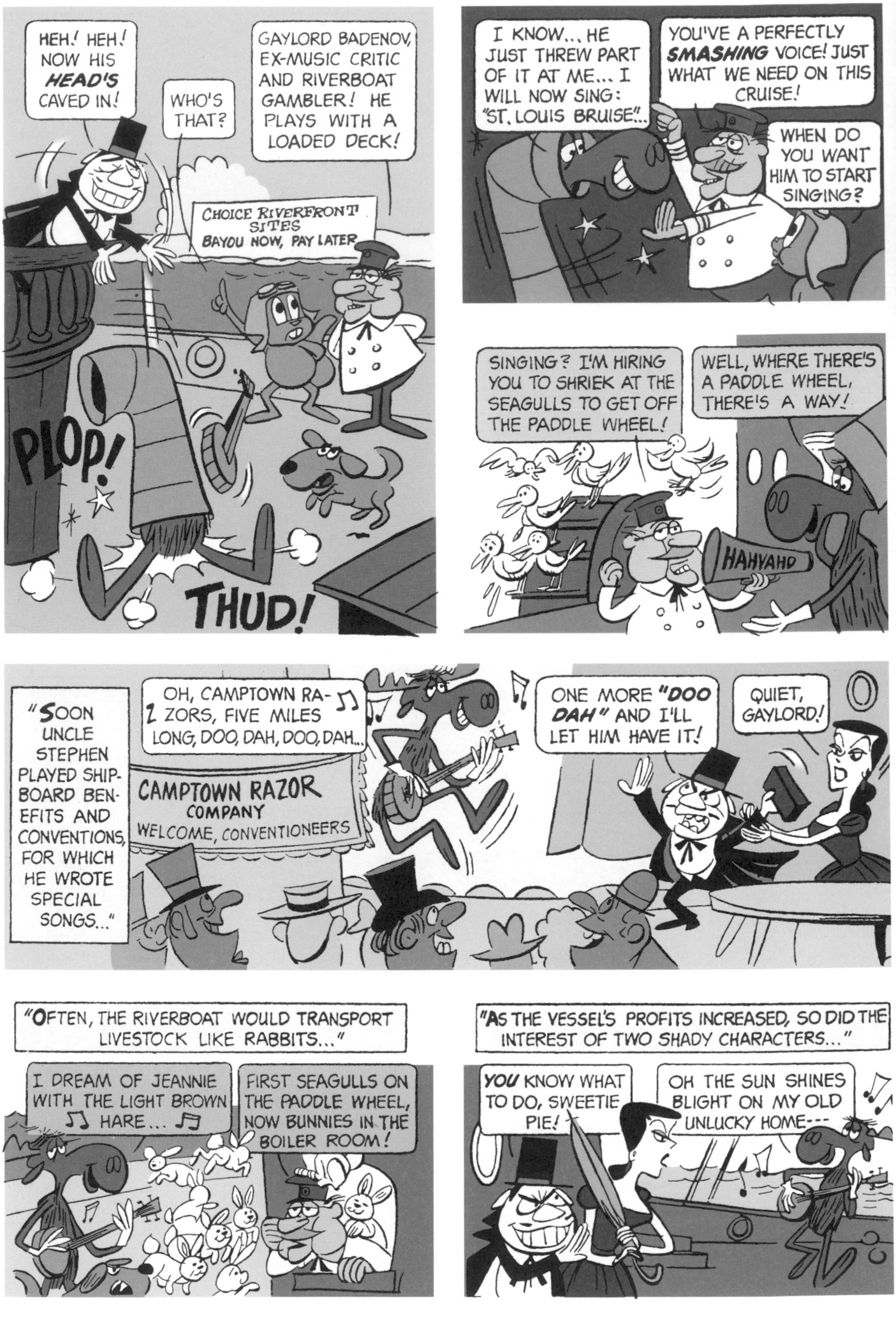
HEH! HEH! NOW HIS HEAD'S CAVED IN!
WHO'S THAT?
GAYLORD BADENOV, EX-MUSIC CRITIC AND RIVERBOAT GAMBLER! HE PLAYS WITH A LOADED DECK!
CHOICE RIVERFRONT SITES BAYOU NOW, PAY LATER
PLOP!
THUD!
I KNOW... HE JUST THREW PART OF IT AT ME... I WILL NOW SING: "ST. LOUIS BRUISE"...
YOU'VE A PERFECTLY SMASHING VOICE! JUST WHAT WE NEED ON THIS CRUISE!
WHEN DO YOU WANT HIM TO START SINGING?
SINGING? I'M HIRING YOU TO SHRIEK AT THE SEAGULLS TO GET OFF THE PADDLE WHEEL!
WELL, WHERE THERE'S A PADDLE WHEEL, THERE'S A WAY!
HAHYAHD
"SOON UNCLE STEPHEN PLAYED SHIP-BOARD BEN-EFITS AND CONVENTIONS, FOR WHICH HE WROTE SPECIAL SONGS..."
OH, CAMPTOWN RA-ZORS, FIVE MILES LONG, DOO, DAH, DOO, DAH...
CAMPTOWN RAZOR COMPANY WELCOME, CONVENTIONEERS
ONE MORE "DOO DAH" AND I'LL LET HIM HAVE IT!
QUIET, GAYLORD!
"OFTEN, THE RIVERBOAT WOULD TRANSPORT LIVESTOCK LIKE RABBITS..."
I DREAM OF JEANNIE WITH THE LIGHT BROWN HARE...
FIRST SEAGULLS ON THE PADDLE WHEEL, NOW BUNNIES IN THE BOILER ROOM!
"AS THE VESSEL'S PROFITS INCREASED, SO DID THE INTEREST OF TWO SHADY CHARACTERS..."
YOU KNOW WHAT TO DO, SWEETIE PIE!
OH THE SUN SHINES BLIGHT ON MY OLD UNLUCKY HOME---

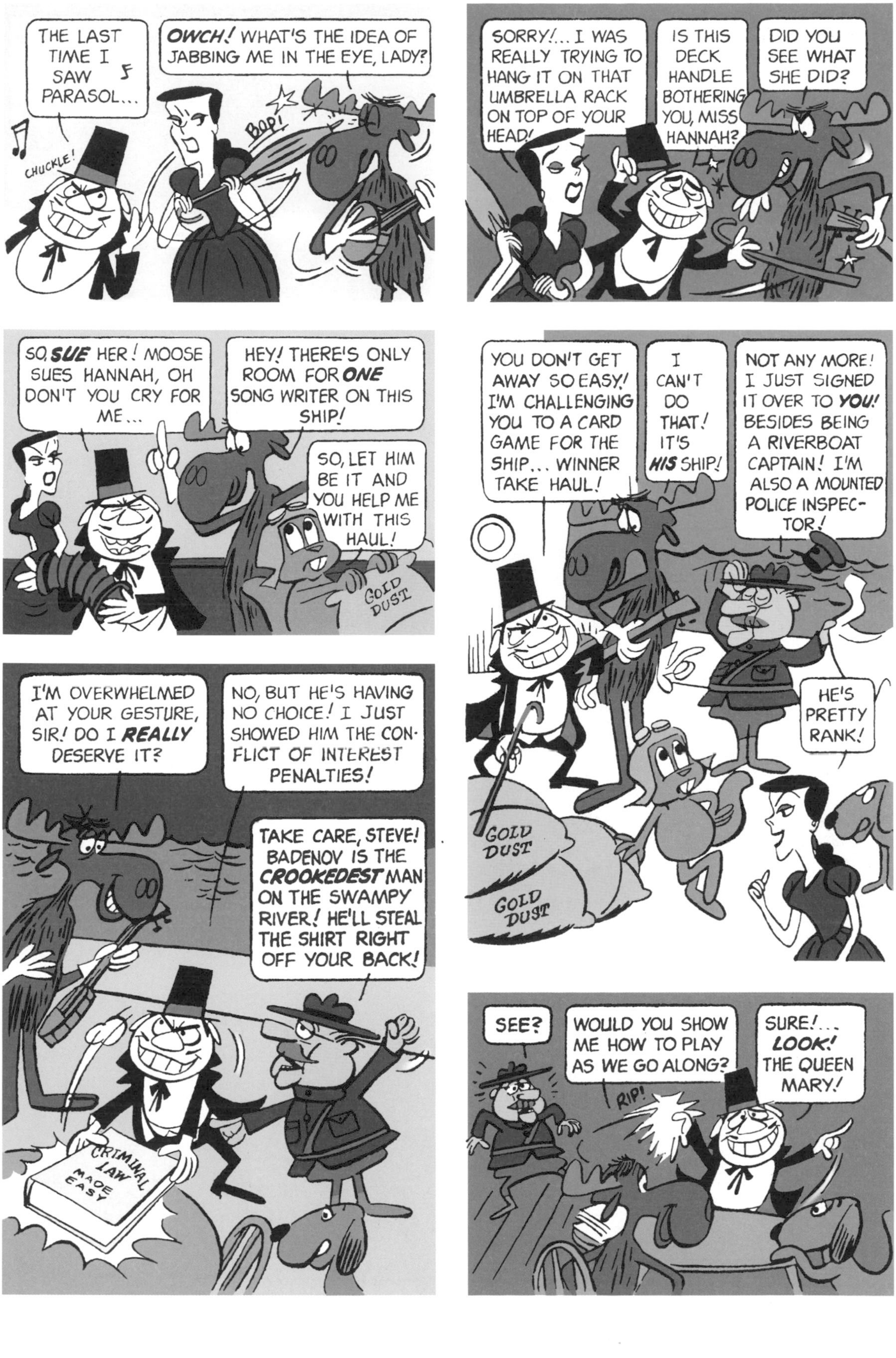
THE LAST TIME I SAW PARASOL...
CHUCKLE!
OWCH! WHAT'S THE IDEA OF JABBING ME IN THE EYE, LADY?
BOP!
SORRY!... I WAS REALLY TRYING TO HANG IT ON THAT UMBRELLA RACK ON TOP OF YOUR HEAD!
IS THIS DECK HANDLE BOTHERING YOU, MISS HANNAH?
DID YOU SEE WHAT SHE DID?
SO, SUE HER! MOOSE SUES HANNAH, OH DON'T YOU CRY FOR ME...
HEY! THERE'S ONLY ROOM FOR ONE SONG WRITER ON THIS SHIP!
SO, LET HIM BE IT AND YOU HELP ME WITH THIS HAUL!
GOLD DUST
YOU DON'T GET AWAY SO EASY! I'M CHALLENGING YOU TO A CARD GAME FOR THE SHIP... WINNER TAKE HAUL!
I CAN'T DO THAT! IT'S HIS SHIP!
NOT ANY MORE! I JUST SIGNED IT OVER TO YOU! BESIDES BEING A RIVERBOAT CAPTAIN! I'M ALSO A MOUNTED POLICE INSPECTOR!
HE'S PRETTY RANK!
GOLD DUST
GOLD DUST
I'M OVERWHELMED AT YOUR GESTURE, SIR! DO I REALLY DESERVE IT?
NO, BUT HE'S HAVING NO CHOICE! I JUST SHOWED HIM THE CONFLICT OF INTEREST PENALTIES!
TAKE CARE, STEVE! BADENOV IS THE CROOKEDEST MAN ON THE SWAMPY RIVER! HE'LL STEAL THE SHIRT RIGHT OFF YOUR BACK!
CRIMINAL LAW MADE EASY
SEE?
WOULD YOU SHOW ME HOW TO PLAY AS WE GO ALONG?
RIP!
SURE!... LOOK! THE QUEEN MARY!

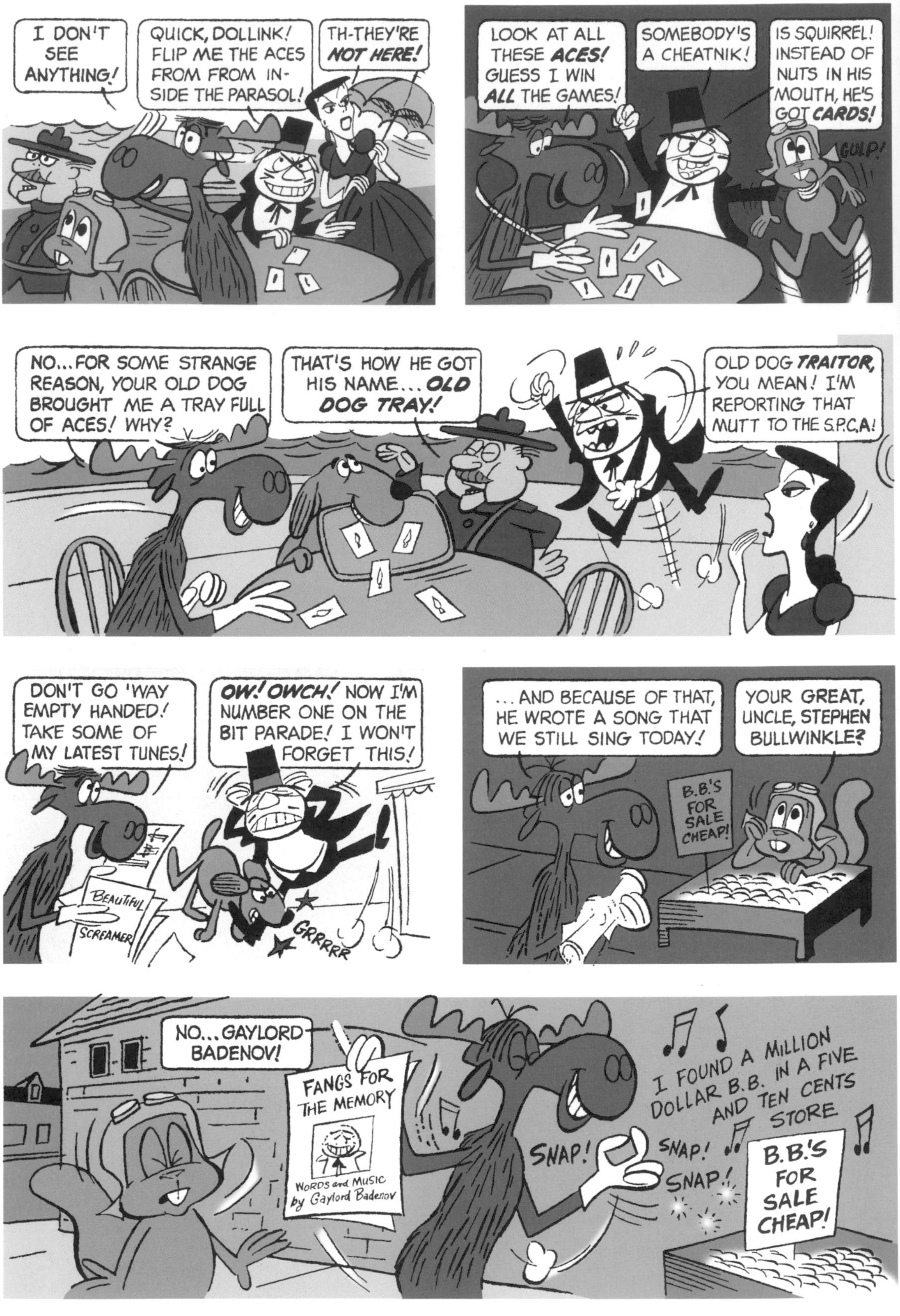
I DON'T SEE ANYTHING!
QUICK, DOLLINK! FLIP ME THE ACES FROM FROM INSIDE THE PARASOL!
TH-THEY'RE NOT HERE!
LOOK AT ALL THESE ACES! GUESS I WIN ALL THE GAMES!
SOMEBODY'S A CHEATNIK!
IS SQUIRREL! INSTEAD OF NUTS IN HIS MOUTH, HE'S GOT CARDS!
GULP!
NO...FOR SOME STRANGE REASON, YOUR OLD DOG BROUGHT ME A TRAY FULL OF ACES! WHY?
THAT'S HOW HE GOT HIS NAME... OLD DOG TRAY!
OLD DOG TRAITOR, YOU MEAN! I'M REPORTING THAT MUTT TO THE S.P.C.A!
DON'T GO 'WAY EMPTY HANDED! TAKE SOME OF MY LATEST TUNES!
OW! OWCH! NOW I'M NUMBER ONE ON THE BIT PARADE! I WON'T FORGET THIS!
BEAUTIFUL
SCREAMER
GRRRRR
...AND BECAUSE OF THAT, HE WROTE A SONG THAT WE STILL SING TODAY!
YOUR GREAT, UNCLE, STEPHEN BULLWINKLE?
B.B.'S FOR SALE CHEAP!
NO...GAYLORD BADENOV!
FANGS FOR THE MEMORY
WORDS and MUSIC by Gaylord Badenov
I FOUND A MILLION DOLLAR B.B. IN A FIVE AND TEN CENTS STORE
SNAP!
SNAP!
SNAP!
B.B.'S FOR SALE CHEAP!

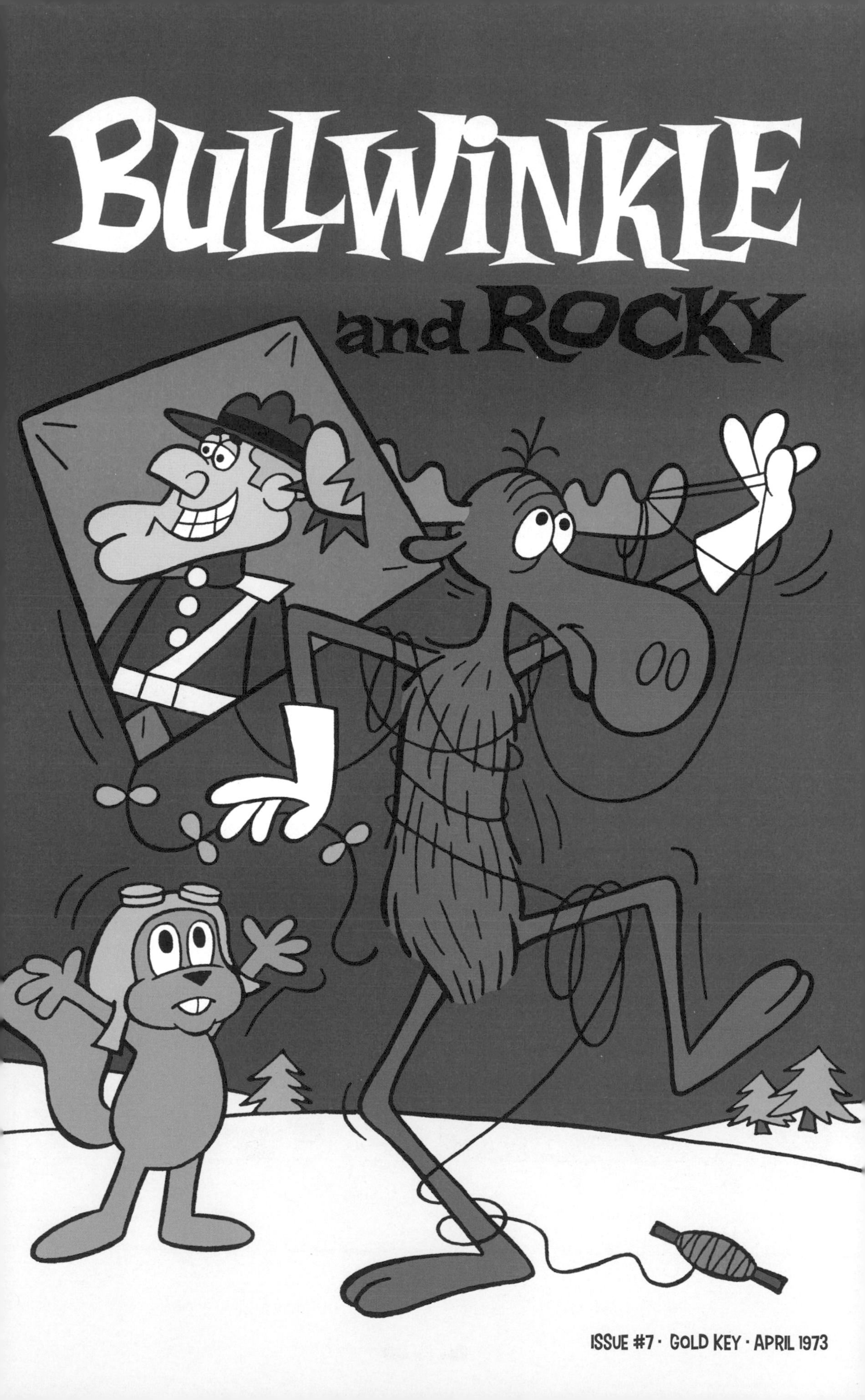
BULLWINKLE
and ROCKY
ISSUE #7 · GOLD KEY · APRIL 1973

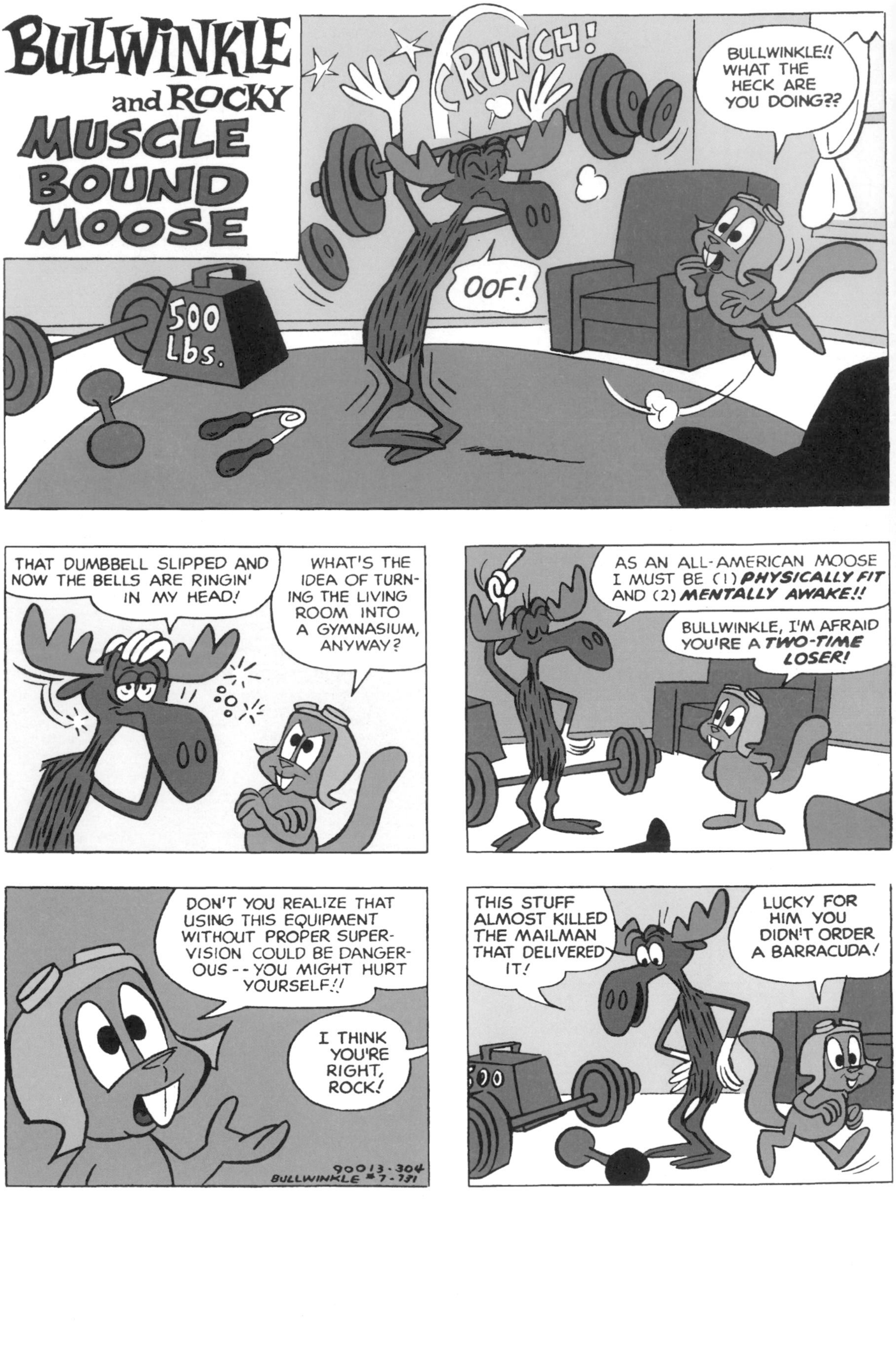
BULLWINKLE and ROCKY
MUSCLE BOUND MOOSE
CRUNCH!
BULLWINKLE!! WHAT THE HECK ARE YOU DOING??
OOF!
500 Lbs.
THAT DUMBBELL SLIPPED AND NOW THE BELLS ARE RINGIN' IN MY HEAD!
WHAT'S THE IDEA OF TURNING THE LIVING ROOM INTO A GYMNASIUM, ANYWAY?
AS AN ALL-AMERICAN MOOSE I MUST BE (1) PHYSICALLY FIT AND (2) MENTALLY AWAKE!!
BULLWINKLE, I'M AFRAID YOU'RE A TWO-TIME LOSER!
DON'T YOU REALIZE THAT USING THIS EQUIPMENT WITHOUT PROPER SUPERVISION COULD BE DANGEROUS--YOU MIGHT HURT YOURSELF!!
I THINK YOU'RE RIGHT, ROCK!
90013-304 BULLWINKLE #7-731
THIS STUFF ALMOST KILLED THE MAILMAN THAT DELIVERED IT!
LUCKY FOR HIM YOU DIDN'T ORDER A BARRACUDA!

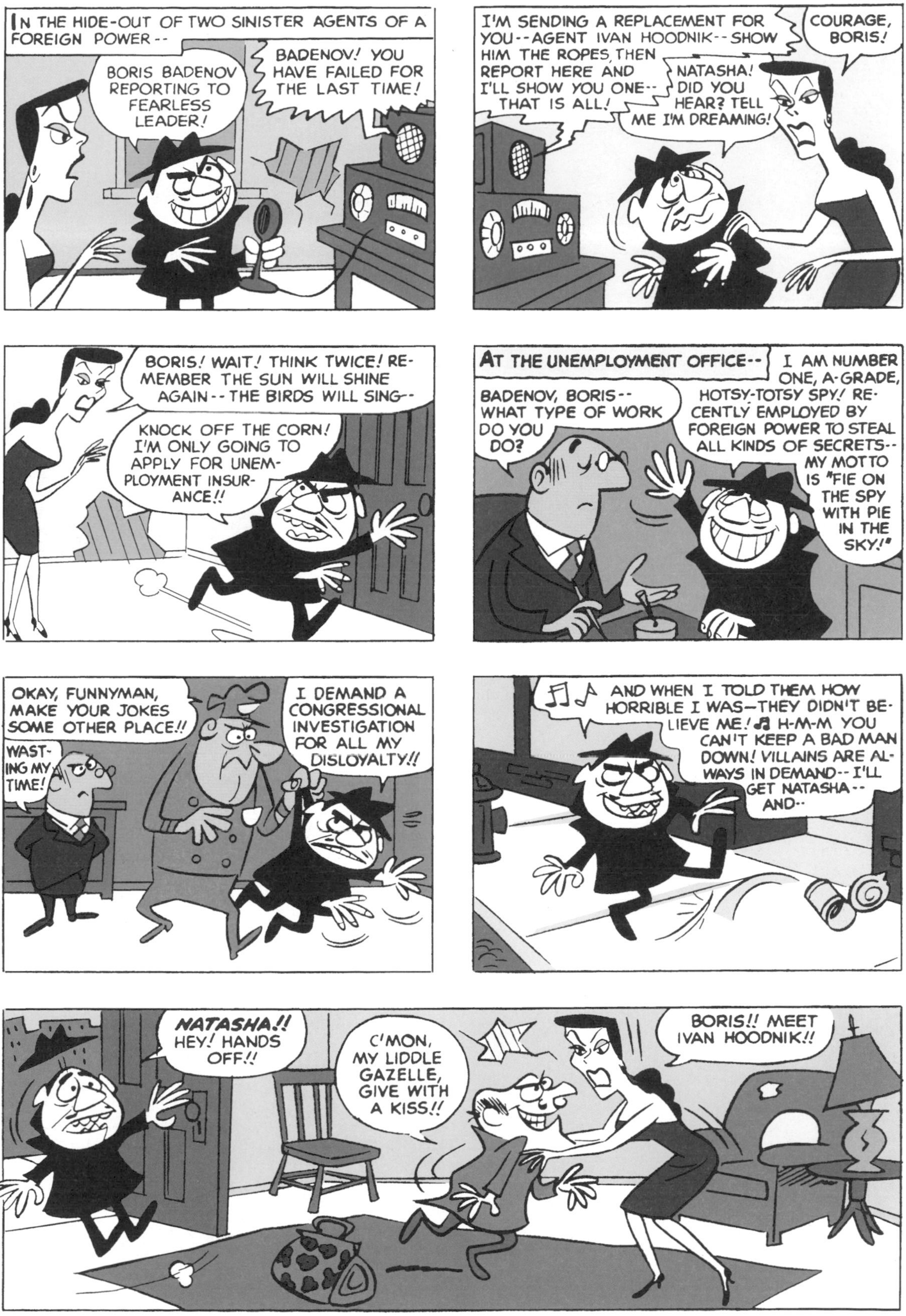
IN THE HIDE-OUT OF TWO SINISTER AGENTS OF A FOREIGN POWER--
BORIS BADENOV REPORTING TO FEARLESS LEADER!
BADENOV! YOU HAVE FAILED FOR THE LAST TIME!
I'M SENDING A REPLACEMENT FOR YOU--AGENT IVAN HOODNIK--SHOW HIM THE ROPES, THEN REPORT HERE AND I'LL SHOW YOU ONE--THAT IS ALL!
NATASHA! DID YOU HEAR? TELL ME I'M DREAMING!
COURAGE, BORIS!
BORIS! WAIT! THINK TWICE! REMEMBER THE SUN WILL SHINE AGAIN--THE BIRDS WILL SING--
KNOCK OFF THE CORN! I'M ONLY GOING TO APPLY FOR UNEMPLOYMENT INSURANCE!!
AT THE UNEMPLOYMENT OFFICE--
BADENOV, BORIS--WHAT TYPE OF WORK DO YOU DO?
I AM NUMBER ONE, A-GRADE, HOTSY-TOTSY SPY! RECENTLY EMPLOYED BY FOREIGN POWER TO STEAL ALL KINDS OF SECRETS--MY MOTTO IS "FIE ON THE SPY WITH PIE IN THE SKY!"
OKAY, FUNNYMAN, MAKE YOUR JOKES SOME OTHER PLACE!!
WASTING MY TIME!
I DEMAND A CONGRESSIONAL INVESTIGATION FOR ALL MY DISLOYALTY!!
AND WHEN I TOLD THEM HOW HORRIBLE I WAS—THEY DIDN'T BELIEVE ME! H-M-M YOU CAN'T KEEP A BAD MAN DOWN! VILLAINS ARE ALWAYS IN DEMAND--I'LL GET NATASHA--AND--
NATASHA!! HEY! HANDS OFF!!
C'MON, MY LIDDLE GAZELLE, GIVE WITH A KISS!!
BORIS!! MEET IVAN HOODNIK!!

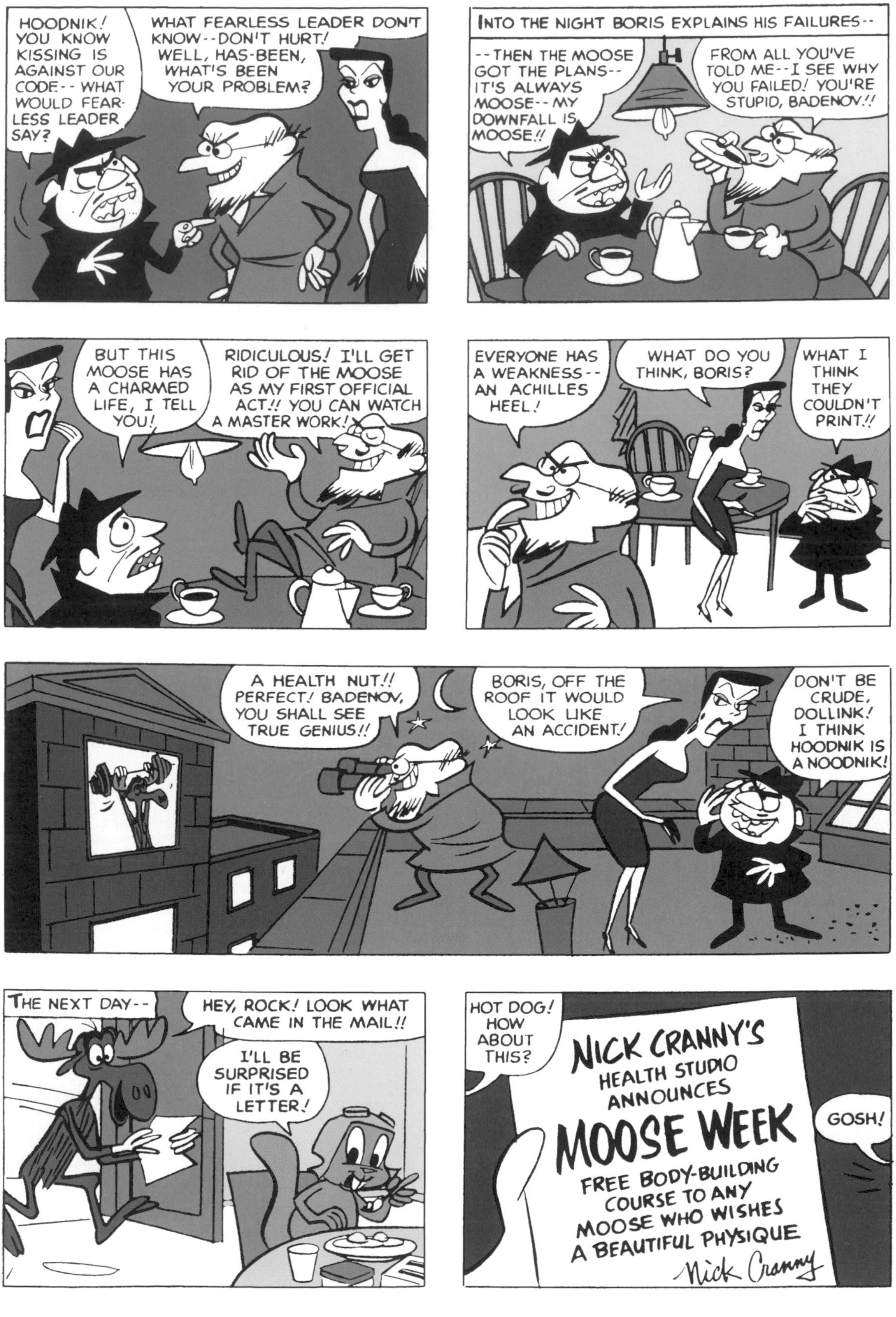
HOODNIK! YOU KNOW KISSING IS AGAINST OUR CODE--WHAT WOULD FEARLESS LEADER SAY?
WHAT FEARLESS LEADER DON'T KNOW--DON'T HURT! WELL, HAS-BEEN, WHAT'S BEEN YOUR PROBLEM?
INTO THE NIGHT BORIS EXPLAINS HIS FAILURES--
--THEN THE MOOSE GOT THE PLANS--IT'S ALWAYS MOOSE--MY DOWNFALL IS MOOSE!!
FROM ALL YOU'VE TOLD ME--I SEE WHY YOU FAILED! YOU'RE STUPID, BADENOV!!
BUT THIS MOOSE HAS A CHARMED LIFE, I TELL YOU!
RIDICULOUS! I'LL GET RID OF THE MOOSE AS MY FIRST OFFICIAL ACT!! YOU CAN WATCH A MASTER WORK!
EVERYONE HAS A WEAKNESS--AN ACHILLES HEEL!
WHAT DO YOU THINK, BORIS?
WHAT I THINK THEY COULDN'T PRINT!!
A HEALTH NUT!! PERFECT! BADENOV, YOU SHALL SEE TRUE GENIUS!!
BORIS, OFF THE ROOF IT WOULD LOOK LIKE AN ACCIDENT!
DON'T BE CRUDE, DOLLINK! I THINK HOODNIK IS A NOODNIK!
THE NEXT DAY--
HEY, ROCK! LOOK WHAT CAME IN THE MAIL!!
I'LL BE SURPRISED IF IT'S A LETTER!
HOT DOG! HOW ABOUT THIS?
NICK CRANNY'S HEALTH STUDIO ANNOUNCES MOOSE WEEK
FREE BODY-BUILDING COURSE TO ANY MOOSE WHO WISHES A BEAUTIFUL PHYSIQUE
Nick Cranny
GOSH!

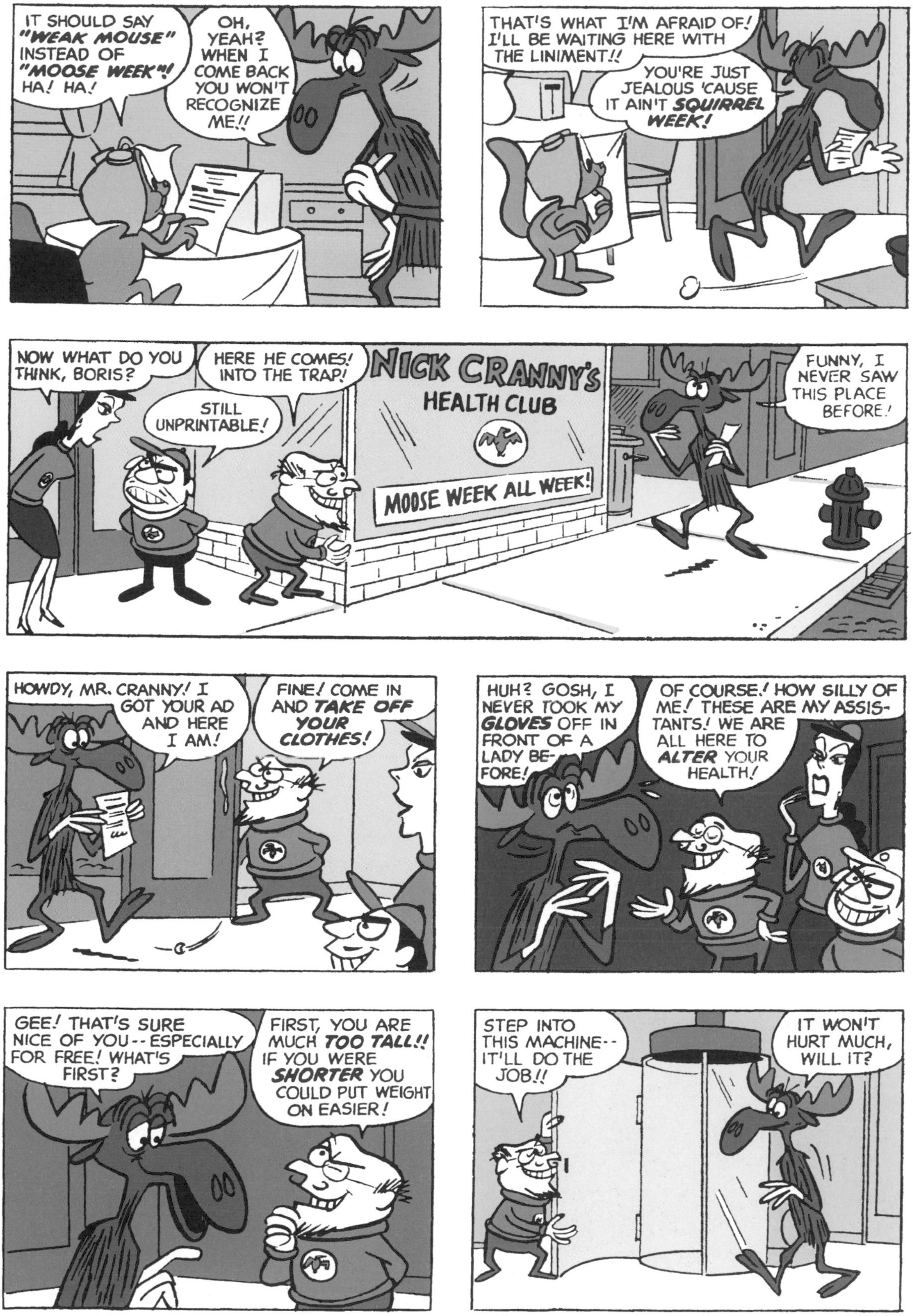
IT SHOULD SAY "WEAK MOUSE" INSTEAD OF "MOOSE WEEK"! HA! HA!
OH, YEAH? WHEN I COME BACK YOU WON'T RECOGNIZE ME!!
THAT'S WHAT I'M AFRAID OF! I'LL BE WAITING HERE WITH THE LINIMENT!!
YOU'RE JUST JEALOUS 'CAUSE IT AIN'T SQUIRREL WEEK!
NOW WHAT DO YOU THINK, BORIS?
STILL UNPRINTABLE!
HERE HE COMES! INTO THE TRAP!
NICK CRANNY'S
HEALTH CLUB
MOOSE WEEK ALL WEEK!
FUNNY, I NEVER SAW THIS PLACE BEFORE!
HOWDY, MR. CRANNY! I GOT YOUR AD AND HERE I AM!
FINE! COME IN AND TAKE OFF YOUR CLOTHES!
HUH? GOSH, I NEVER TOOK MY GLOVES OFF IN FRONT OF A LADY BEFORE!
OF COURSE! HOW SILLY OF ME! THESE ARE MY ASSISTANTS! WE ARE ALL HERE TO ALTER YOUR HEALTH!
GEE! THAT'S SURE NICE OF YOU--ESPECIALLY FOR FREE! WHAT'S FIRST?
FIRST, YOU ARE MUCH TOO TALL!! IF YOU WERE SHORTER YOU COULD PUT WEIGHT ON EASIER!
STEP INTO THIS MACHINE--IT'LL DO THE JOB!!
IT WON'T HURT MUCH, WILL IT?

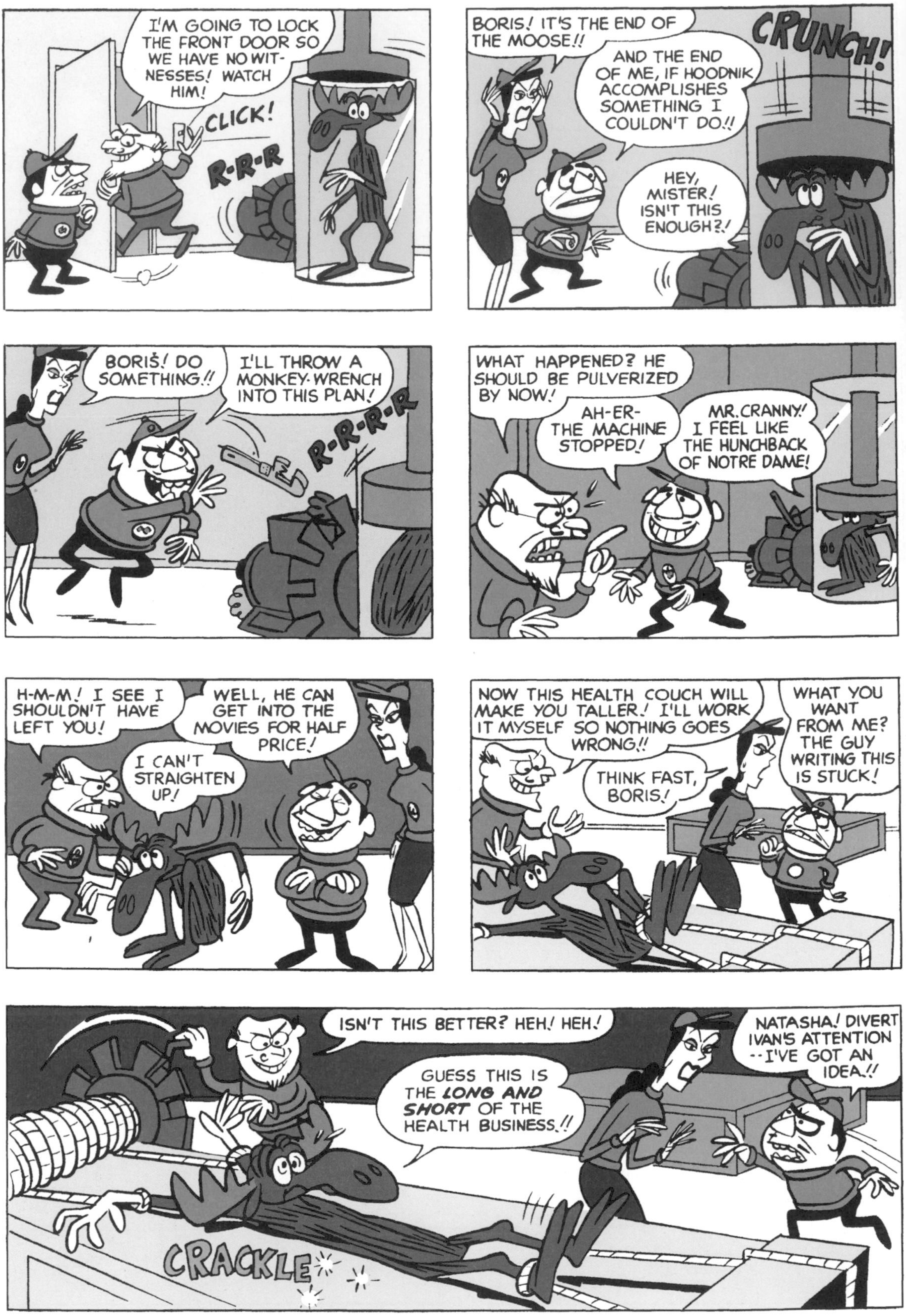
I'M GOING TO LOCK THE FRONT DOOR SO WE HAVE NO WITNESSES! WATCH HIM!
CLICK!
R-R-R
BORIS! IT'S THE END OF THE MOOSE!!
AND THE END OF ME, IF HOODNIK ACCOMPLISHES SOMETHING I COULDN'T DO!!
CRUNCH!
HEY, MISTER! ISN'T THIS ENOUGH?!
BORIS! DO SOMETHING!!
I'LL THROW A MONKEY-WRENCH INTO THIS PLAN!
R-R-R-R
WHAT HAPPENED? HE SHOULD BE PULVERIZED BY NOW!
AH-ER- THE MACHINE STOPPED!
MR. CRANNY! I FEEL LIKE THE HUNCHBACK OF NOTRE DAME!
H-M-M! I SEE I SHOULDN'T HAVE LEFT YOU!
WELL, HE CAN GET INTO THE MOVIES FOR HALF PRICE!
I CAN'T STRAIGHTEN UP!
NOW THIS HEALTH COUCH WILL MAKE YOU TALLER! I'LL WORK IT MYSELF SO NOTHING GOES WRONG!!
THINK FAST, BORIS!
WHAT YOU WANT FROM ME? THE GUY WRITING THIS IS STUCK!
ISN'T THIS BETTER? HEH! HEH!
GUESS THIS IS THE LONG AND SHORT OF THE HEALTH BUSINESS!!
NATASHA! DIVERT IVAN'S ATTENTION --I'VE GOT AN IDEA!!
CRACKLE

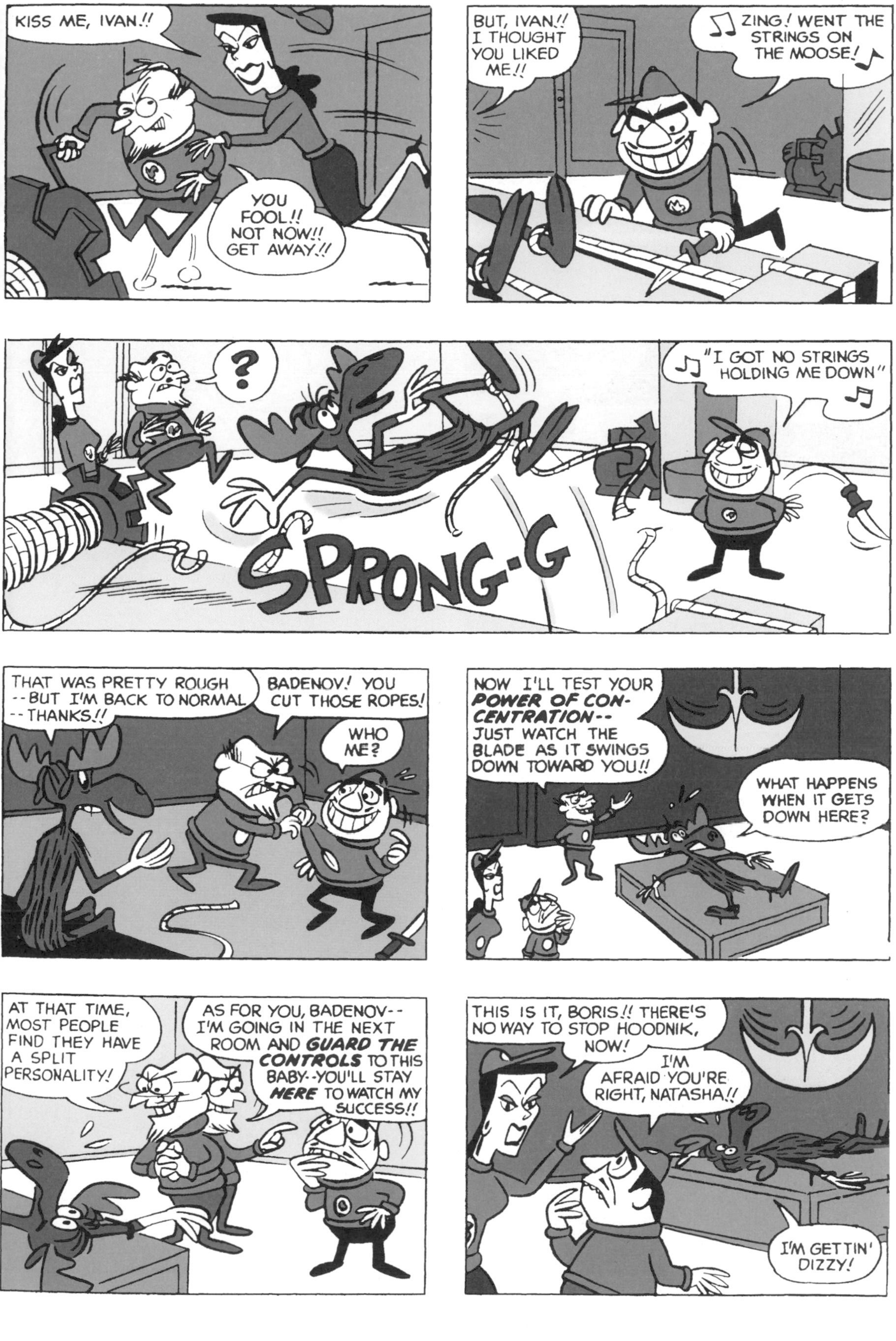
KISS ME, IVAN!!
YOU FOOL!! NOT NOW!! GET AWAY!!
BUT, IVAN!! I THOUGHT YOU LIKED ME!!
ZING! WENT THE STRINGS ON THE MOOSE!
?
"I GOT NO STRINGS HOLDING ME DOWN"
SPRONG-G
THAT WAS PRETTY ROUGH --BUT I'M BACK TO NORMAL --THANKS!!
BADENOV! YOU CUT THOSE ROPES!
WHO ME?
NOW I'LL TEST YOUR POWER OF CONCENTRATION-- JUST WATCH THE BLADE AS IT SWINGS DOWN TOWARD YOU!!
WHAT HAPPENS WHEN IT GETS DOWN HERE?
AT THAT TIME, MOST PEOPLE FIND THEY HAVE A SPLIT PERSONALITY!
AS FOR YOU, BADENOV-- I'M GOING IN THE NEXT ROOM AND GUARD THE CONTROLS TO THIS BABY--YOU'LL STAY HERE TO WATCH MY SUCCESS!!
THIS IS IT, BORIS!! THERE'S NO WAY TO STOP HOODNIK, NOW!
I'M AFRAID YOU'RE RIGHT, NATASHA!!
I'M GETTIN' DIZZY!

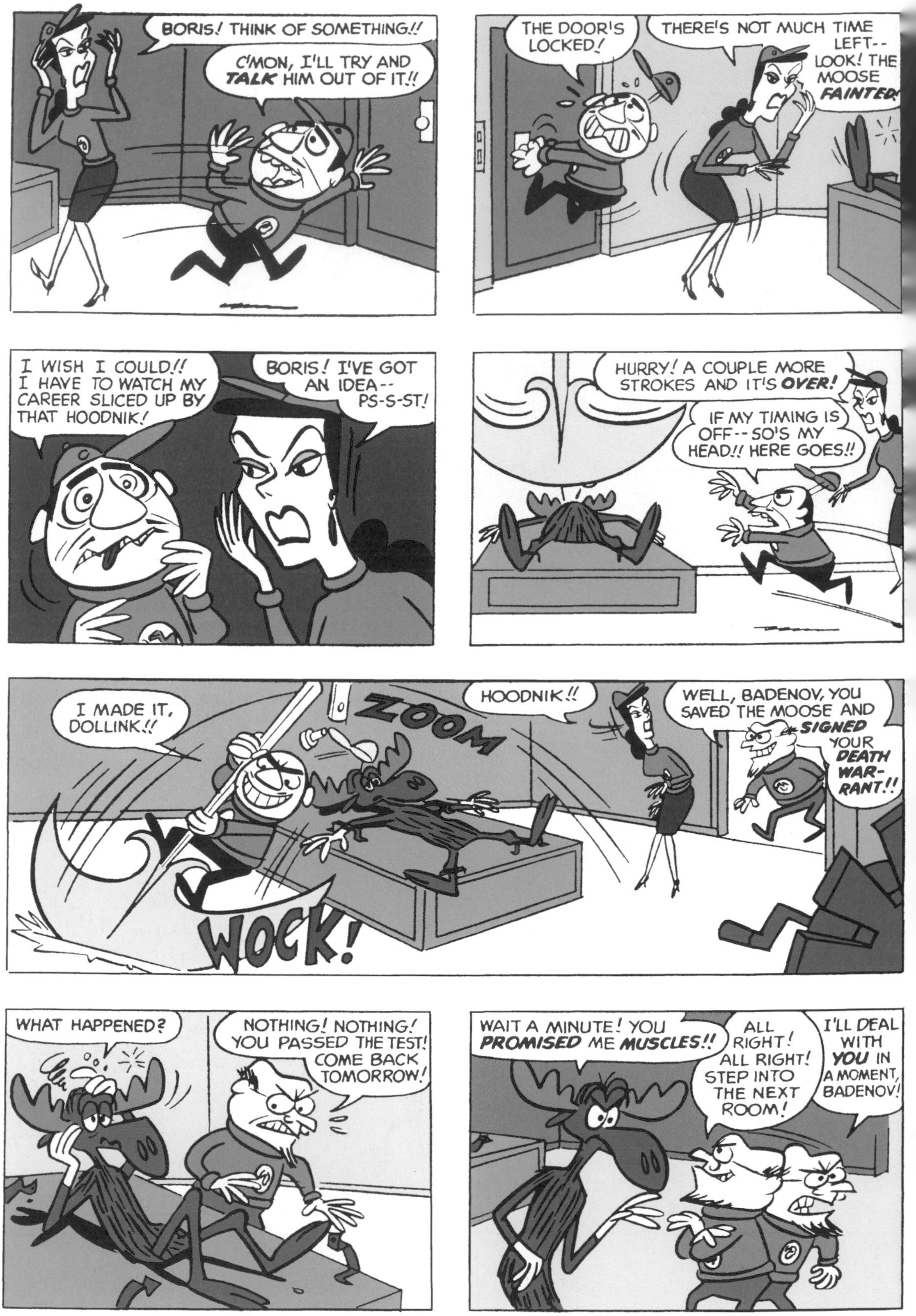
BORIS! THINK OF SOMETHING!!
C'MON, I'LL TRY AND TALK HIM OUT OF IT!!
THE DOOR'S LOCKED!
THERE'S NOT MUCH TIME LEFT-- LOOK! THE MOOSE FAINTED!
I WISH I COULD!! I HAVE TO WATCH MY CAREER SLICED UP BY THAT HOODNIK!
BORIS! I'VE GOT AN IDEA-- PS-S-ST!
HURRY! A COUPLE MORE STROKES AND IT'S OVER!
IF MY TIMING IS OFF--SO'S MY HEAD!! HERE GOES!!
I MADE IT, DOLLINK!!
ZOOM
HOODNIK!!
WELL, BADENOV, YOU SAVED THE MOOSE AND SIGNED YOUR DEATH WAR-RANT!!
WOCK!
WHAT HAPPENED?
NOTHING! NOTHING! YOU PASSED THE TEST! COME BACK TOMORROW!
WAIT A MINUTE! YOU PROMISED ME MUSCLES!!
ALL RIGHT! ALL RIGHT! STEP INTO THE NEXT ROOM!
I'LL DEAL WITH YOU IN A MOMENT, BADENOV!

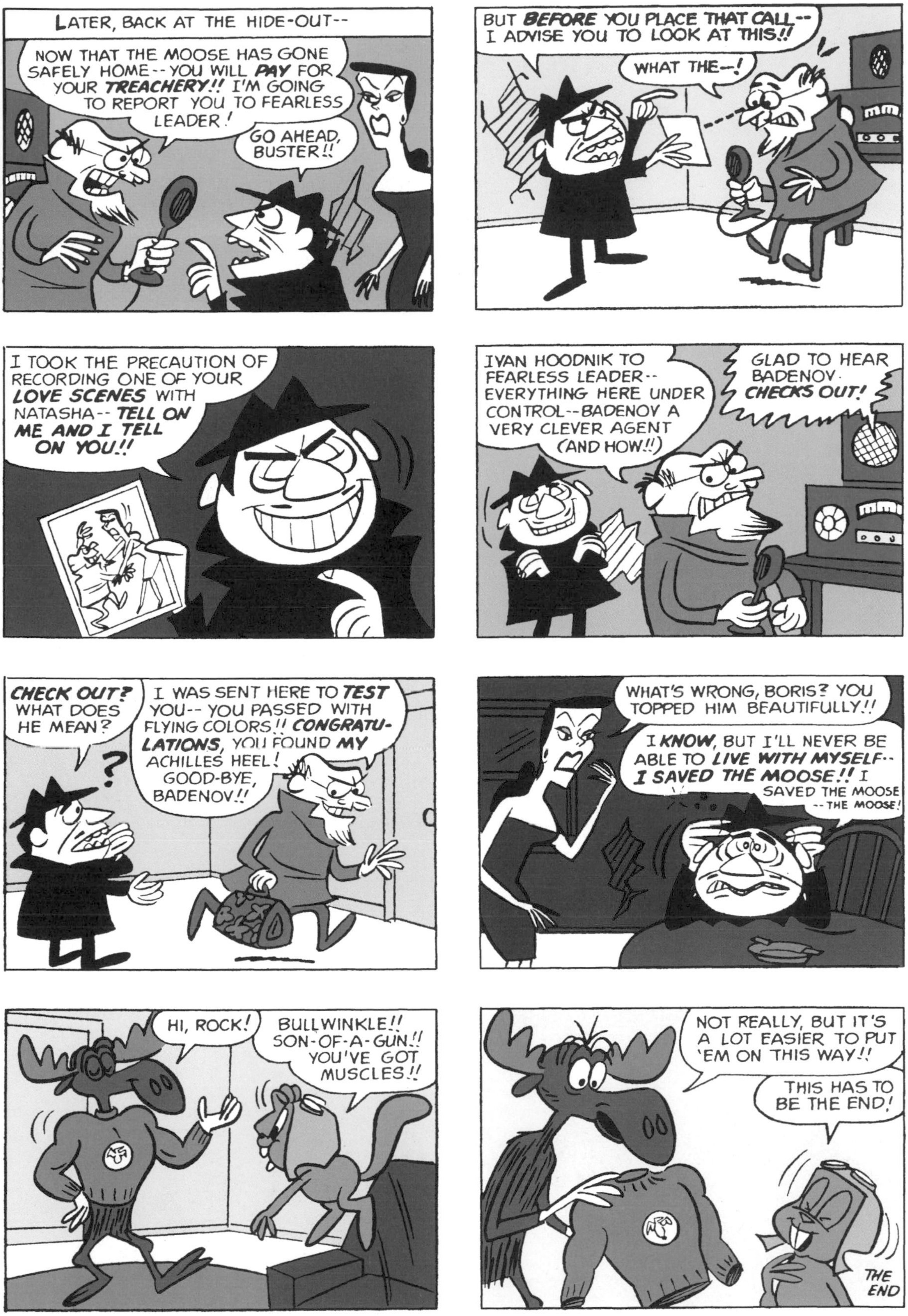
LATER, BACK AT THE HIDE-OUT--
NOW THAT THE MOOSE HAS GONE SAFELY HOME--YOU WILL PAY FOR YOUR TREACHERY!! I'M GOING TO REPORT YOU TO FEARLESS LEADER!
GO AHEAD, BUSTER!!
BUT BEFORE YOU PLACE THAT CALL-- I ADVISE YOU TO LOOK AT THIS!!
WHAT THE--!
I TOOK THE PRECAUTION OF RECORDING ONE OF YOUR LOVE SCENES WITH NATASHA-- TELL ON ME AND I TELL ON YOU!!
IVAN HOODNIK TO FEARLESS LEADER-- EVERYTHING HERE UNDER CONTROL--BADENOV A VERY CLEVER AGENT (AND HOW!!)
GLAD TO HEAR BADENOV. CHECKS OUT!
CHECK OUT? WHAT DOES HE MEAN?
I WAS SENT HERE TO TEST YOU-- YOU PASSED WITH FLYING COLORS!! CONGRATULATIONS, YOU FOUND MY ACHILLES HEEL! GOOD-BYE, BADENOV!!
WHAT'S WRONG, BORIS? YOU TOPPED HIM BEAUTIFULLY!!
I KNOW, BUT I'LL NEVER BE ABLE TO LIVE WITH MYSELF-- I SAVED THE MOOSE!! I SAVED THE MOOSE --THE MOOSE!
HI, ROCK!
BULLWINKLE!! SON-OF-A-GUN!! YOU'VE GOT MUSCLES!!
NOT REALLY, BUT IT'S A LOT EASIER TO PUT 'EM ON THIS WAY!!
THIS HAS TO BE THE END!
THE END

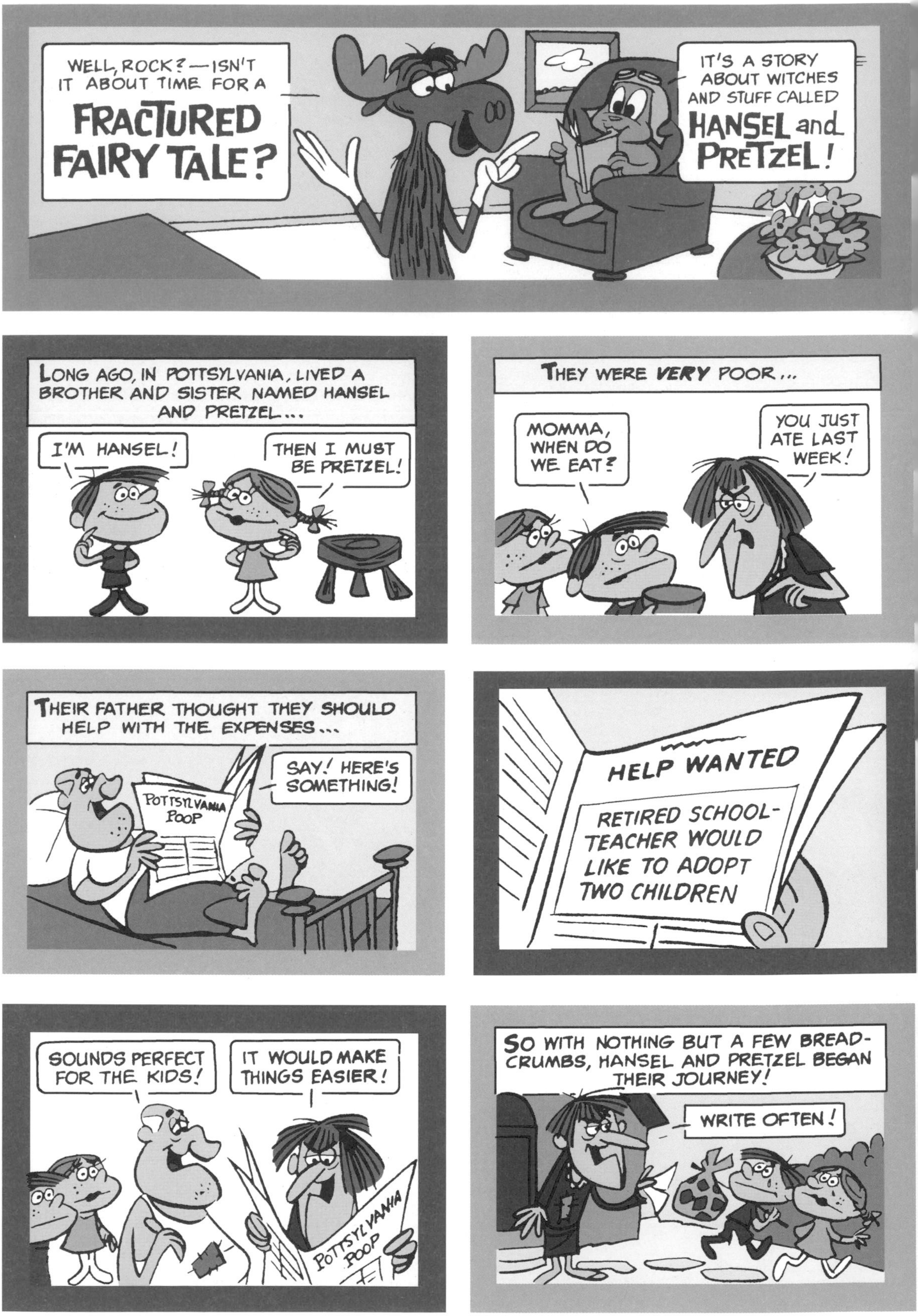
WELL, ROCK?—ISN'T IT ABOUT TIME FOR A FRACTURED FAIRY TALE?
IT'S A STORY ABOUT WITCHES AND STUFF CALLED HANSEL and PRETZEL!
LONG AGO, IN POTTSYLVANIA, LIVED A BROTHER AND SISTER NAMED HANSEL AND PRETZEL...
I'M HANSEL!
THEN I MUST BE PRETZEL!
THEY WERE VERY POOR...
MOMMA, WHEN DO WE EAT?
YOU JUST ATE LAST WEEK!
THEIR FATHER THOUGHT THEY SHOULD HELP WITH THE EXPENSES...
POTTSYLVANIA POOP
SAY! HERE'S SOMETHING!
HELP WANTED
RETIRED SCHOOL-TEACHER WOULD LIKE TO ADOPT TWO CHILDREN
SOUNDS PERFECT FOR THE KIDS!
IT WOULD MAKE THINGS EASIER!
POTTSYLVANIA POOP
SO WITH NOTHING BUT A FEW BREAD-CRUMBS, HANSEL AND PRETZEL BEGAN THEIR JOURNEY!
WRITE OFTEN!

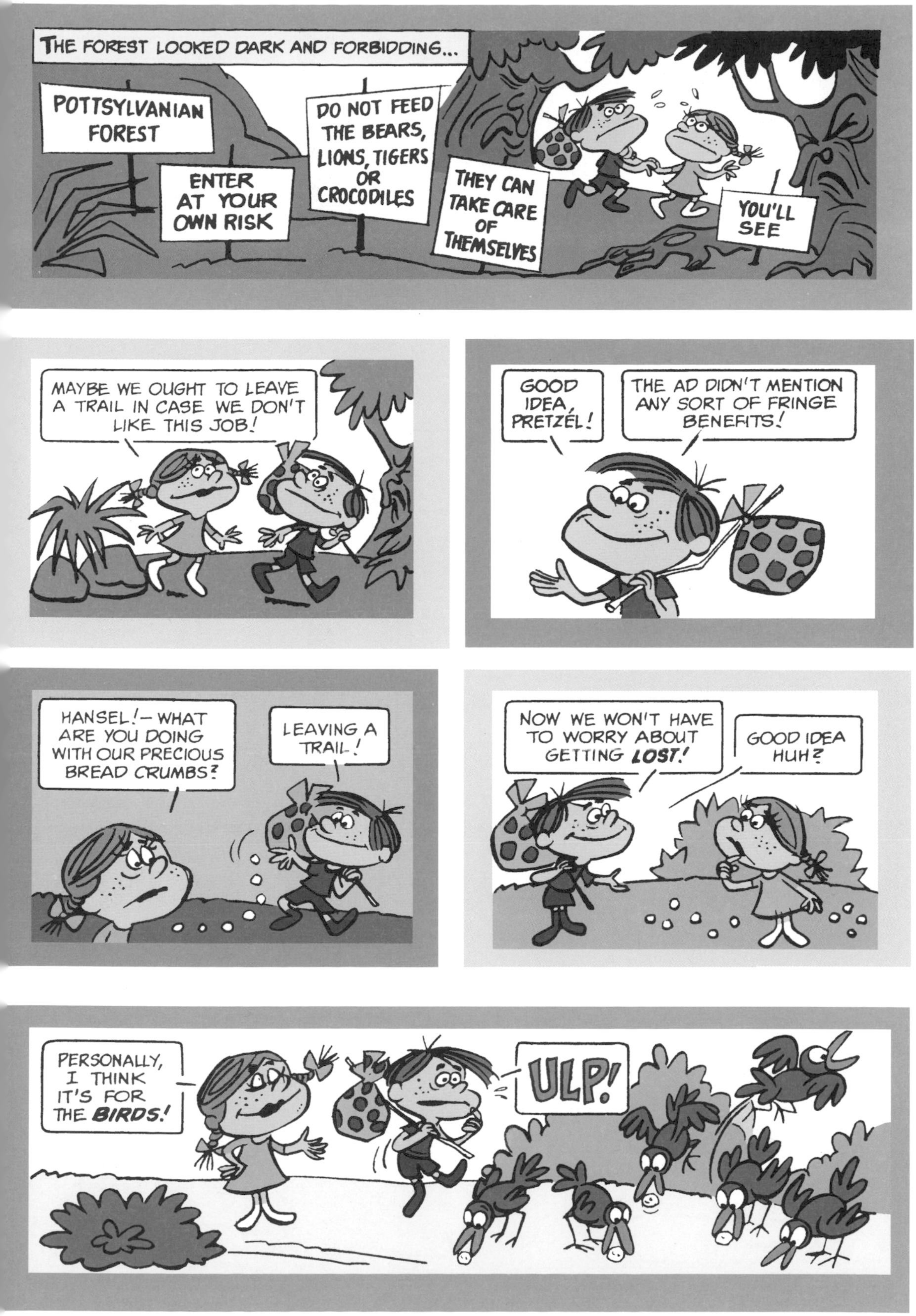
THE FOREST LOOKED DARK AND FORBIDDING...
POTTSYLVANIAN FOREST
ENTER AT YOUR OWN RISK
DO NOT FEED THE BEARS, LIONS, TIGERS OR CROCODILES
THEY CAN TAKE CARE OF THEMSELVES
YOU'LL SEE
MAYBE WE OUGHT TO LEAVE A TRAIL IN CASE WE DON'T LIKE THIS JOB!
GOOD IDEA, PRETZEL!
THE AD DIDN'T MENTION ANY SORT OF FRINGE BENEFITS!
HANSEL!—WHAT ARE YOU DOING WITH OUR PRECIOUS BREAD CRUMBS?
LEAVING A TRAIL!
NOW WE WON'T HAVE TO WORRY ABOUT GETTING LOST!
GOOD IDEA HUH?
PERSONALLY, I THINK IT'S FOR THE BIRDS!
ULP!

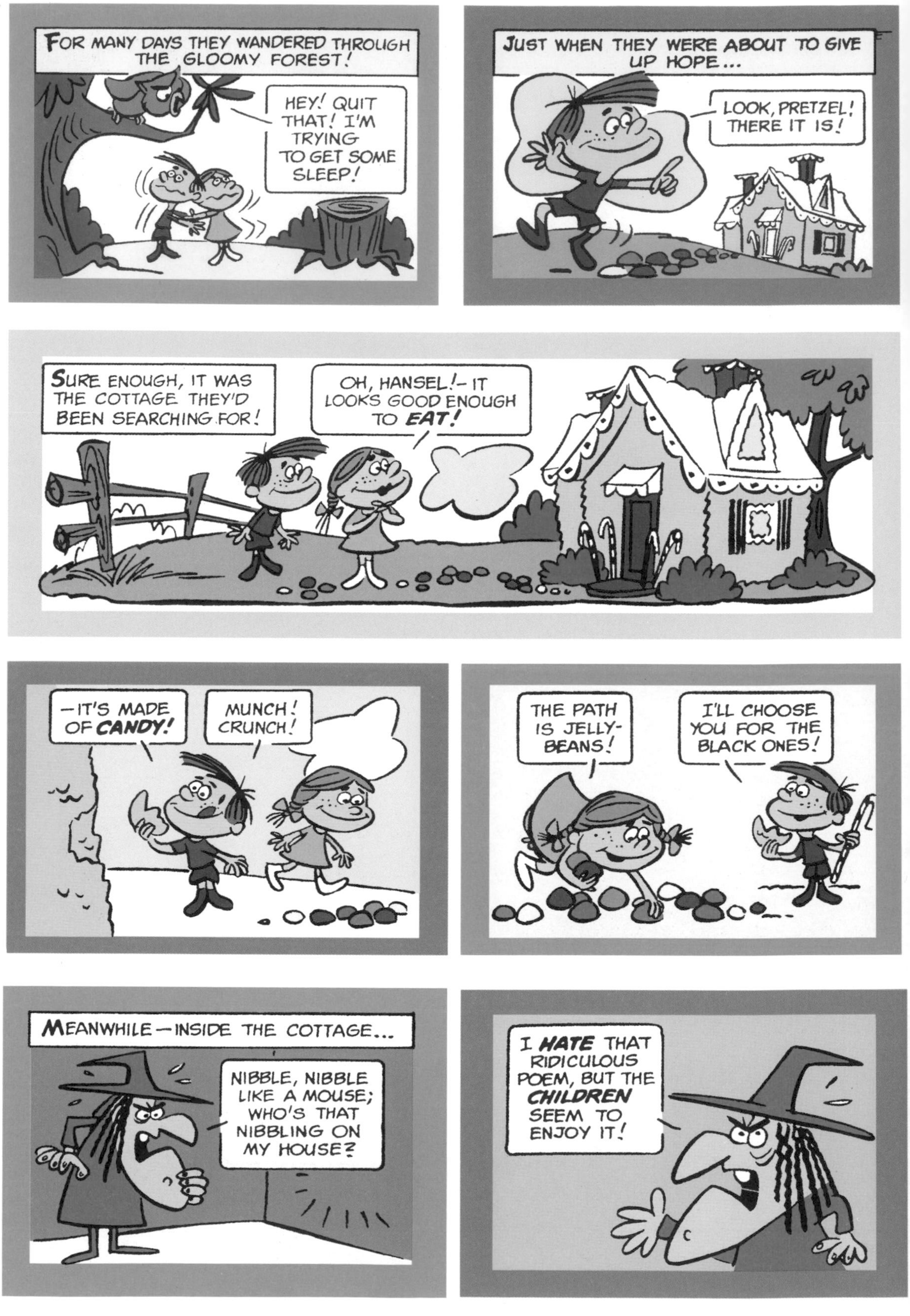
FOR MANY DAYS THEY WANDERED THROUGH THE GLOOMY FOREST!
HEY! QUIT THAT! I'M TRYING TO GET SOME SLEEP!
JUST WHEN THEY WERE ABOUT TO GIVE UP HOPE...
LOOK, PRETZEL! THERE IT IS!
SURE ENOUGH, IT WAS THE COTTAGE THEY'D BEEN SEARCHING FOR!
OH, HANSEL!— IT LOOKS GOOD ENOUGH TO EAT!
—IT'S MADE OF CANDY!
MUNCH! CRUNCH!
THE PATH IS JELLY-BEANS!
I'LL CHOOSE YOU FOR THE BLACK ONES!
MEANWHILE—INSIDE THE COTTAGE...
NIBBLE, NIBBLE LIKE A MOUSE; WHO'S THAT NIBBLING ON MY HOUSE?
I HATE THAT RIDICULOUS POEM, BUT THE CHILDREN SEEM TO ENJOY IT!

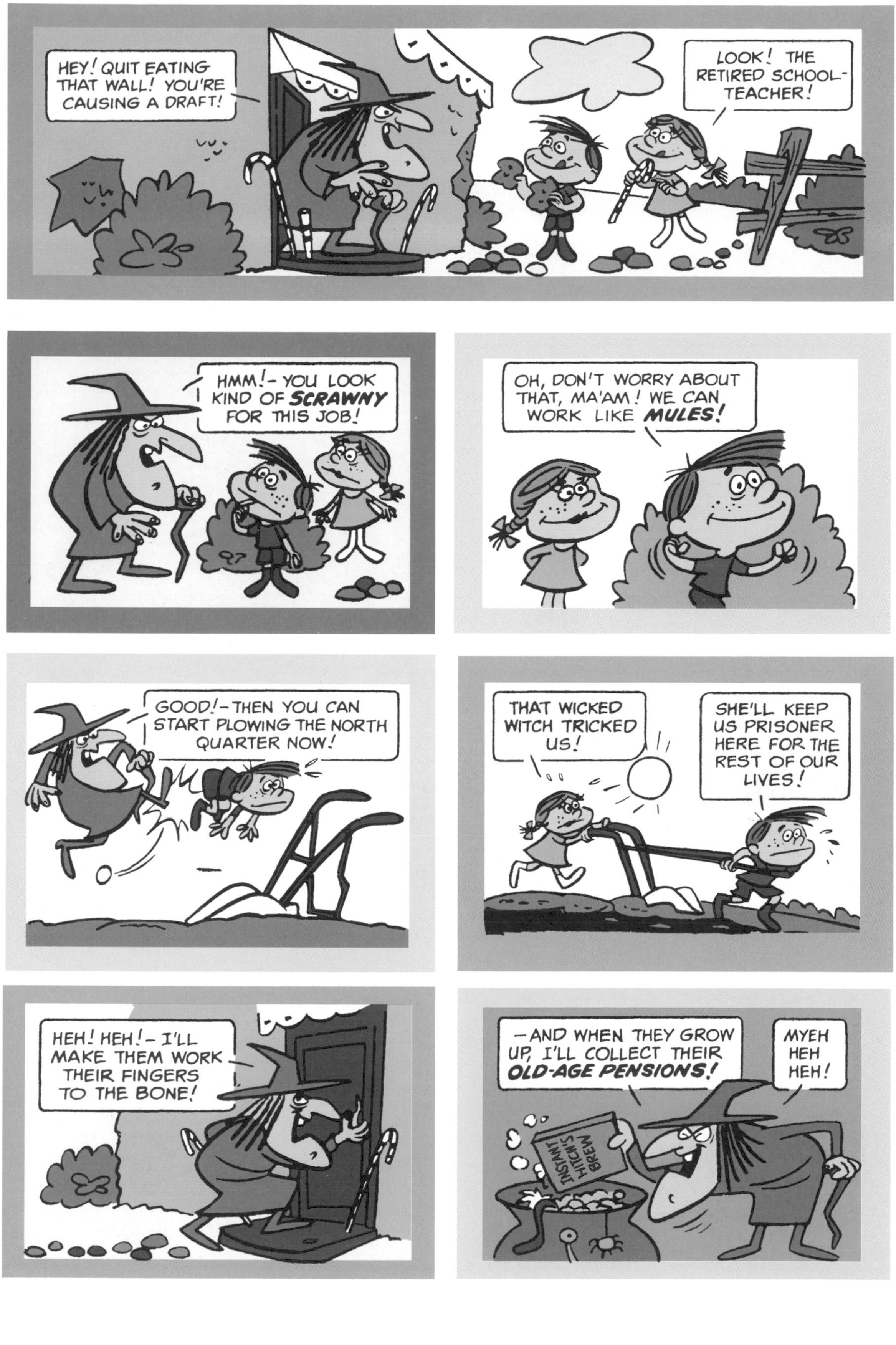
HEY! QUIT EATING THAT WALL! YOU'RE CAUSING A DRAFT!
LOOK! THE RETIRED SCHOOL-TEACHER!
HMM!– YOU LOOK KIND OF SCRAWNY FOR THIS JOB!
OH, DON'T WORRY ABOUT THAT, MA'AM! WE CAN WORK LIKE MULES!
GOOD!– THEN YOU CAN START PLOWING THE NORTH QUARTER NOW!
THAT WICKED WITCH TRICKED US!
SHE'LL KEEP US PRISONER HERE FOR THE REST OF OUR LIVES!
HEH! HEH!– I'LL MAKE THEM WORK THEIR FINGERS TO THE BONE!
–AND WHEN THEY GROW UP, I'LL COLLECT THEIR OLD-AGE PENSIONS!
MYEH HEH HEH!
INSTANT WITCH'S BREW

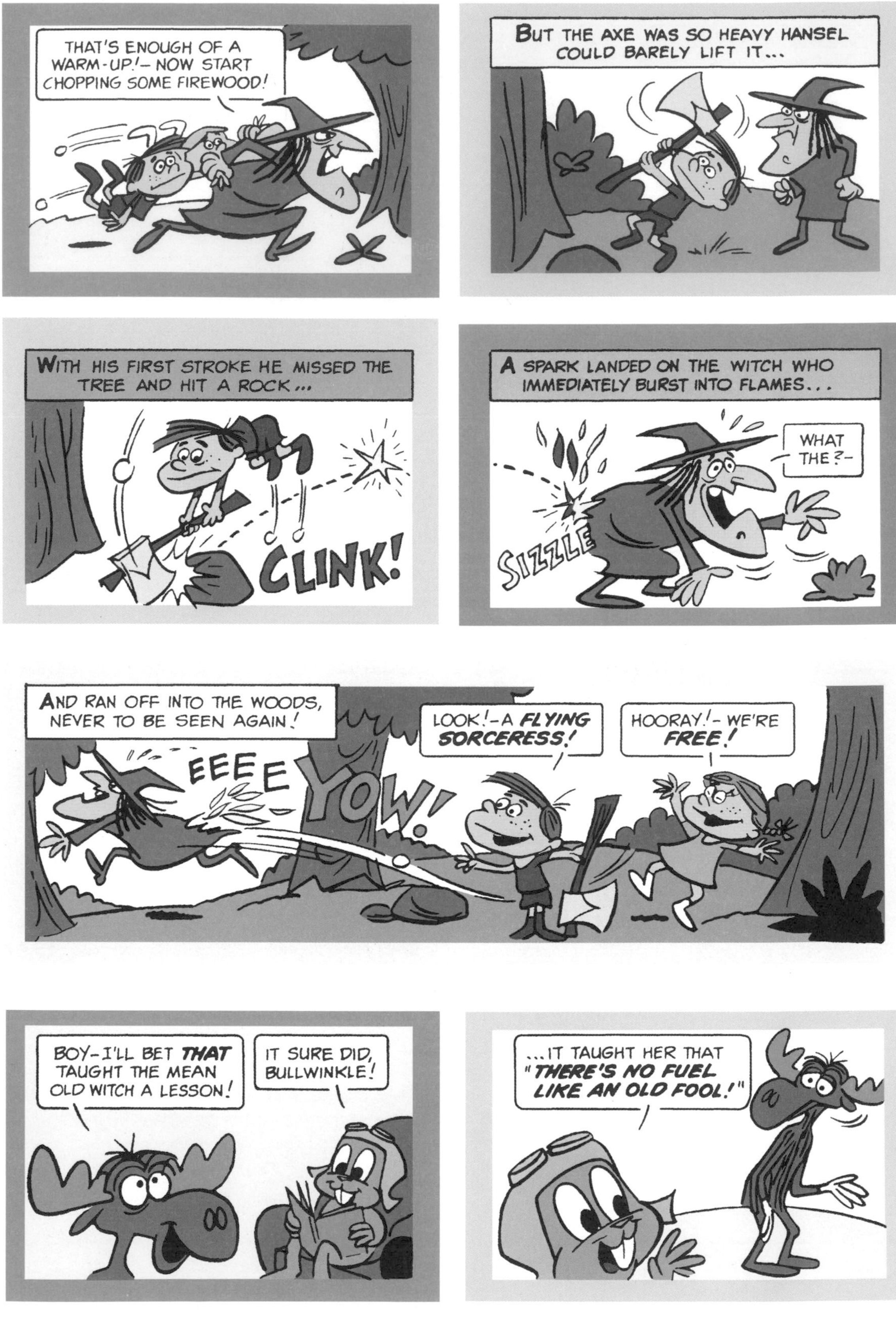
THAT'S ENOUGH OF A WARM-UP!– NOW START CHOPPING SOME FIREWOOD!
BUT THE AXE WAS SO HEAVY HANSEL COULD BARELY LIFT IT...
WITH HIS FIRST STROKE HE MISSED THE TREE AND HIT A ROCK...
CLINK!
A SPARK LANDED ON THE WITCH WHO IMMEDIATELY BURST INTO FLAMES...
WHAT THE?–
SIZZLE
AND RAN OFF INTO THE WOODS, NEVER TO BE SEEN AGAIN!
EEEEEYOW!
LOOK!–A **FLYING SORCERESS!**
HOORAY!– WE'RE **FREE!**
BOY–I'LL BET **THAT** TAUGHT THE MEAN OLD WITCH A LESSON!
IT SURE DID, BULLWINKLE!
...IT TAUGHT HER THAT "**THERE'S NO FUEL LIKE AN OLD FOOL!**"

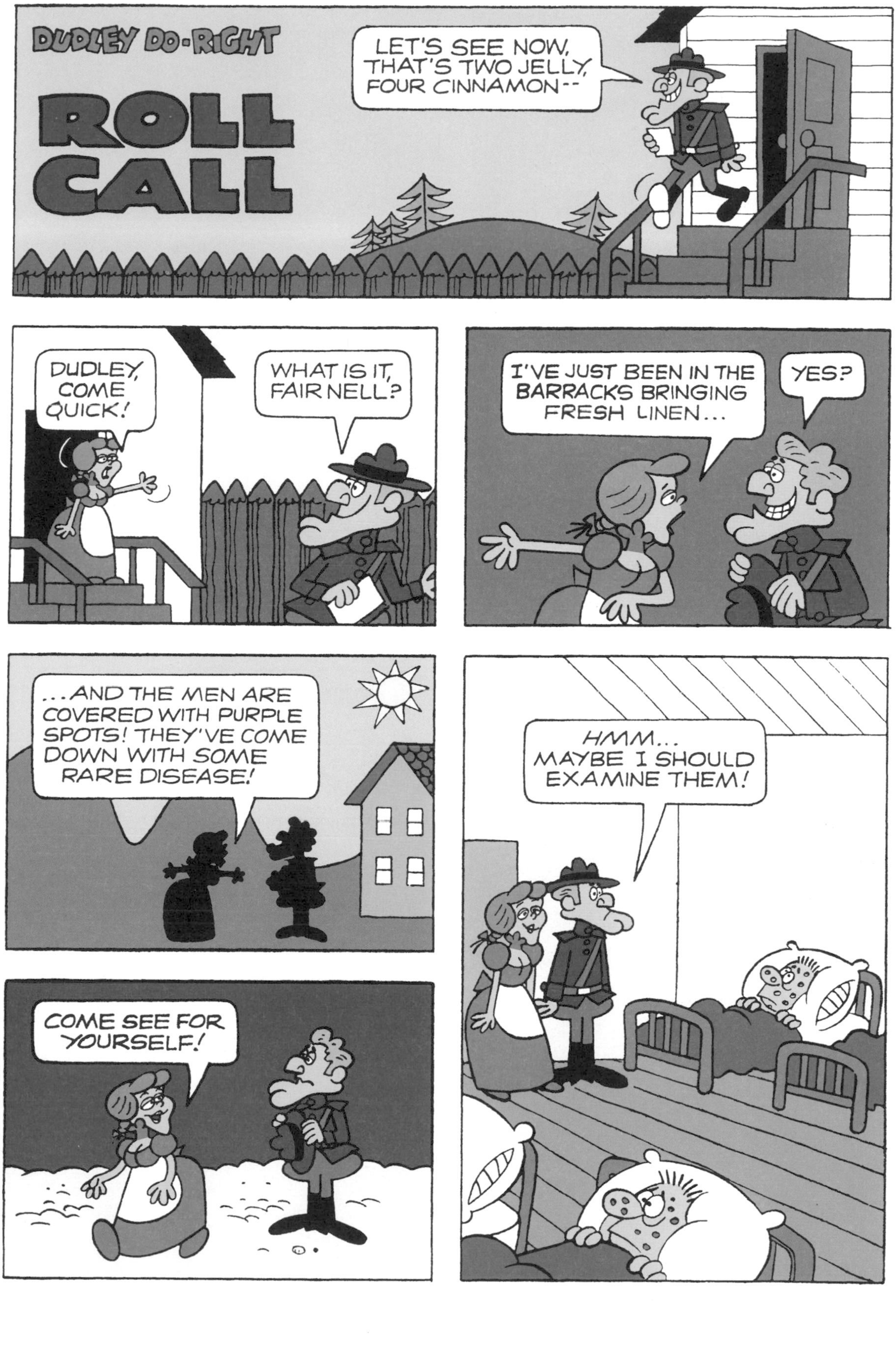
DUDLEY DO-RIGHT
ROLL CALL
LET'S SEE NOW, THAT'S TWO JELLY, FOUR CINNAMON--
DUDLEY, COME QUICK!
WHAT IS IT, FAIR NELL?
I'VE JUST BEEN IN THE BARRACKS BRINGING FRESH LINEN...
YES?
...AND THE MEN ARE COVERED WITH PURPLE SPOTS! THEY'VE COME DOWN WITH SOME RARE DISEASE!
COME SEE FOR YOURSELF!
HMM... MAYBE I SHOULD EXAMINE THEM!

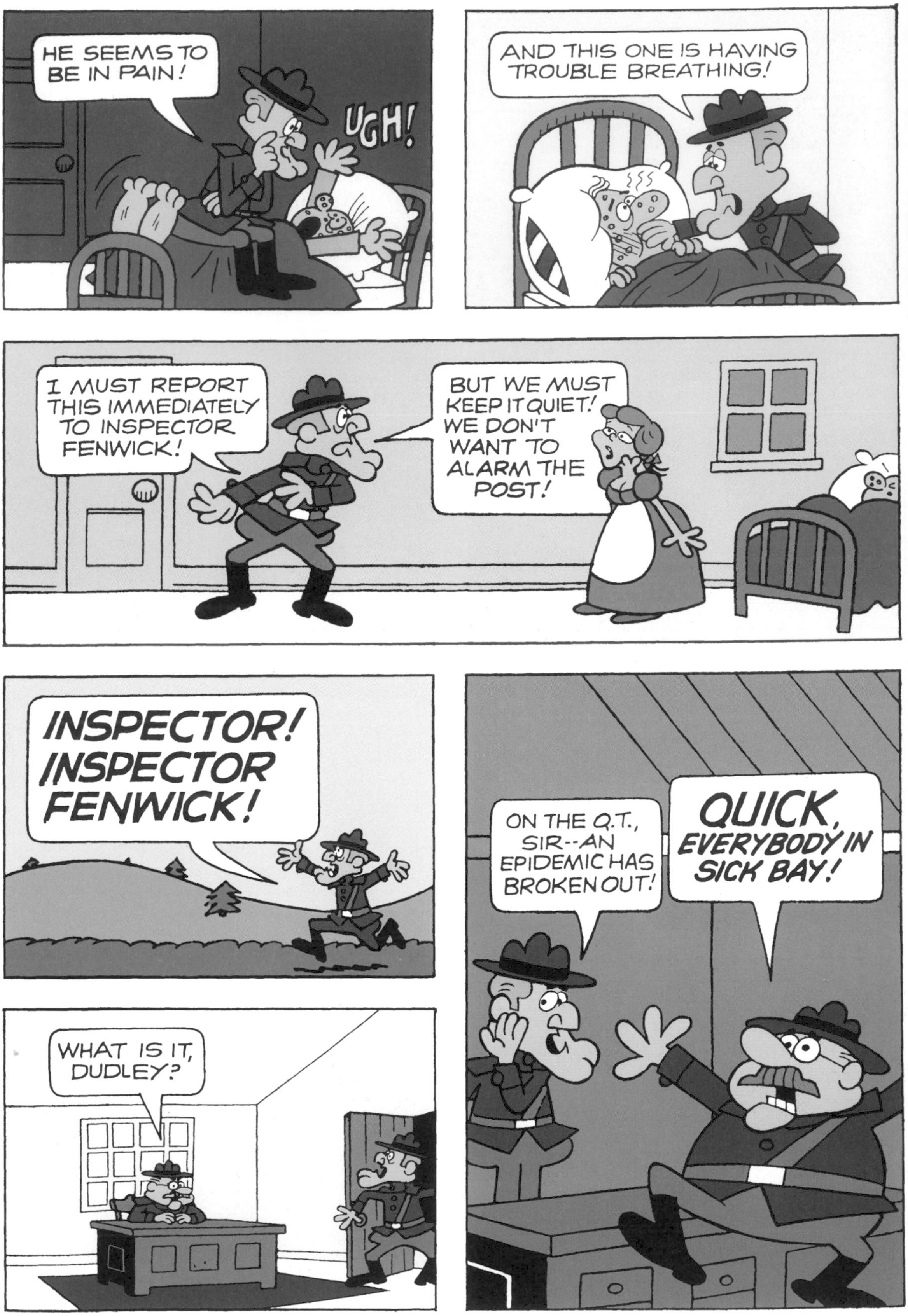
HE SEEMS TO BE IN PAIN!
UGH!
AND THIS ONE IS HAVING TROUBLE BREATHING!
I MUST REPORT THIS IMMEDIATELY TO INSPECTOR FENWICK!
BUT WE MUST KEEP IT QUIET! WE DON'T WANT TO ALARM THE POST!
INSPECTOR! INSPECTOR FENWICK!
WHAT IS IT, DUDLEY?
ON THE Q.T., SIR--AN EPIDEMIC HAS BROKEN OUT!
QUICK, EVERYBODY IN SICK BAY!

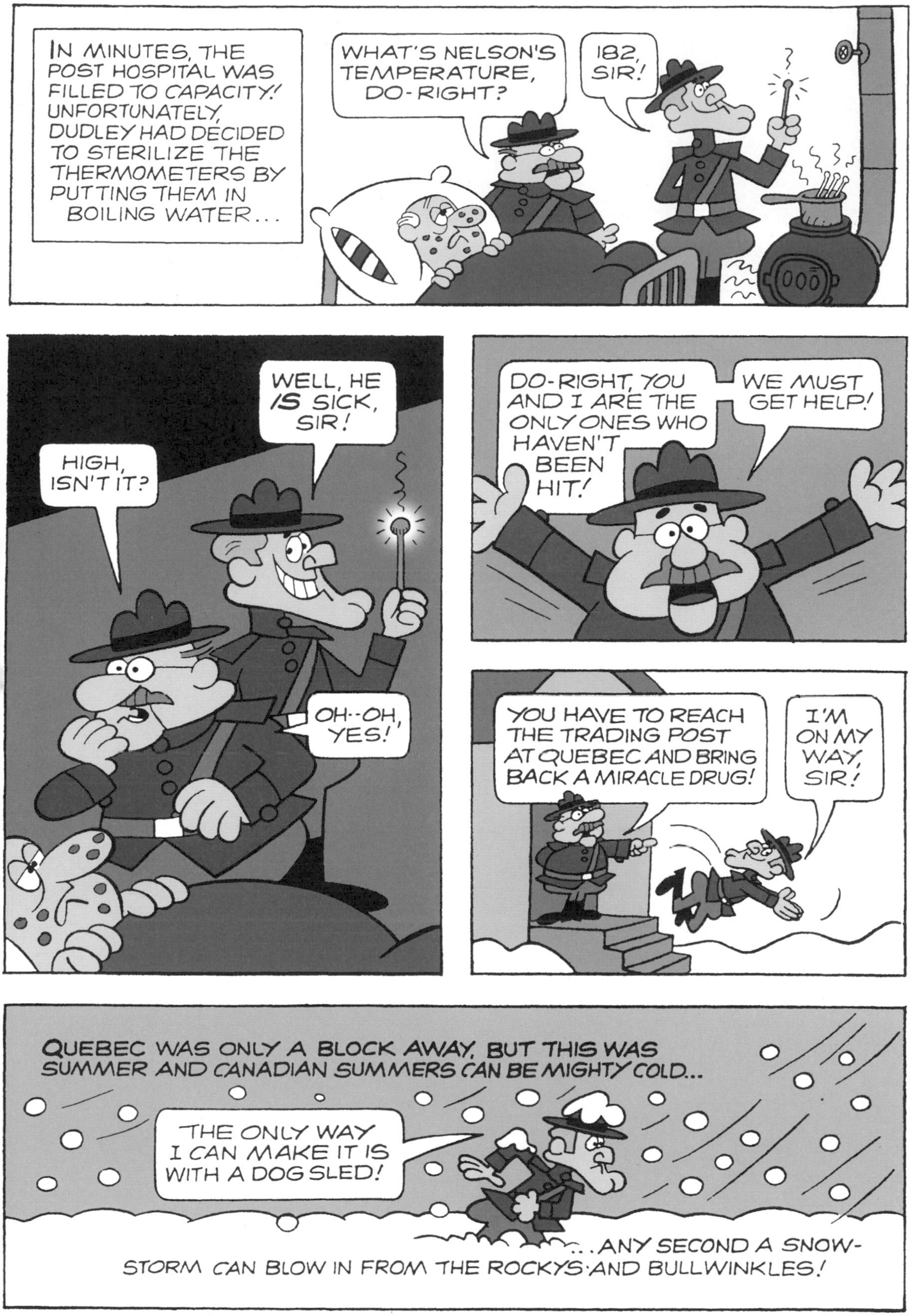

IN MINUTES, THE POST HOSPITAL WAS FILLED TO CAPACITY! UNFORTUNATELY, DUDLEY HAD DECIDED TO STERILIZE THE THERMOMETERS BY PUTTING THEM IN BOILING WATER...
WHAT'S NELSON'S TEMPERATURE, DO-RIGHT?
182, SIR!
HIGH, ISN'T IT?
WELL, HE IS SICK, SIR!
OH--OH, YES!
DO-RIGHT, YOU AND I ARE THE ONLY ONES WHO HAVEN'T BEEN HIT!
WE MUST GET HELP!
YOU HAVE TO REACH THE TRADING POST AT QUEBEC AND BRING BACK A MIRACLE DRUG!
I'M ON MY WAY, SIR!
QUEBEC WAS ONLY A BLOCK AWAY, BUT THIS WAS SUMMER AND CANADIAN SUMMERS CAN BE MIGHTY COLD...
THE ONLY WAY I CAN MAKE IT IS WITH A DOG SLED!
...ANY SECOND A SNOW-STORM CAN BLOW IN FROM THE ROCKYS AND BULLWINKLES!

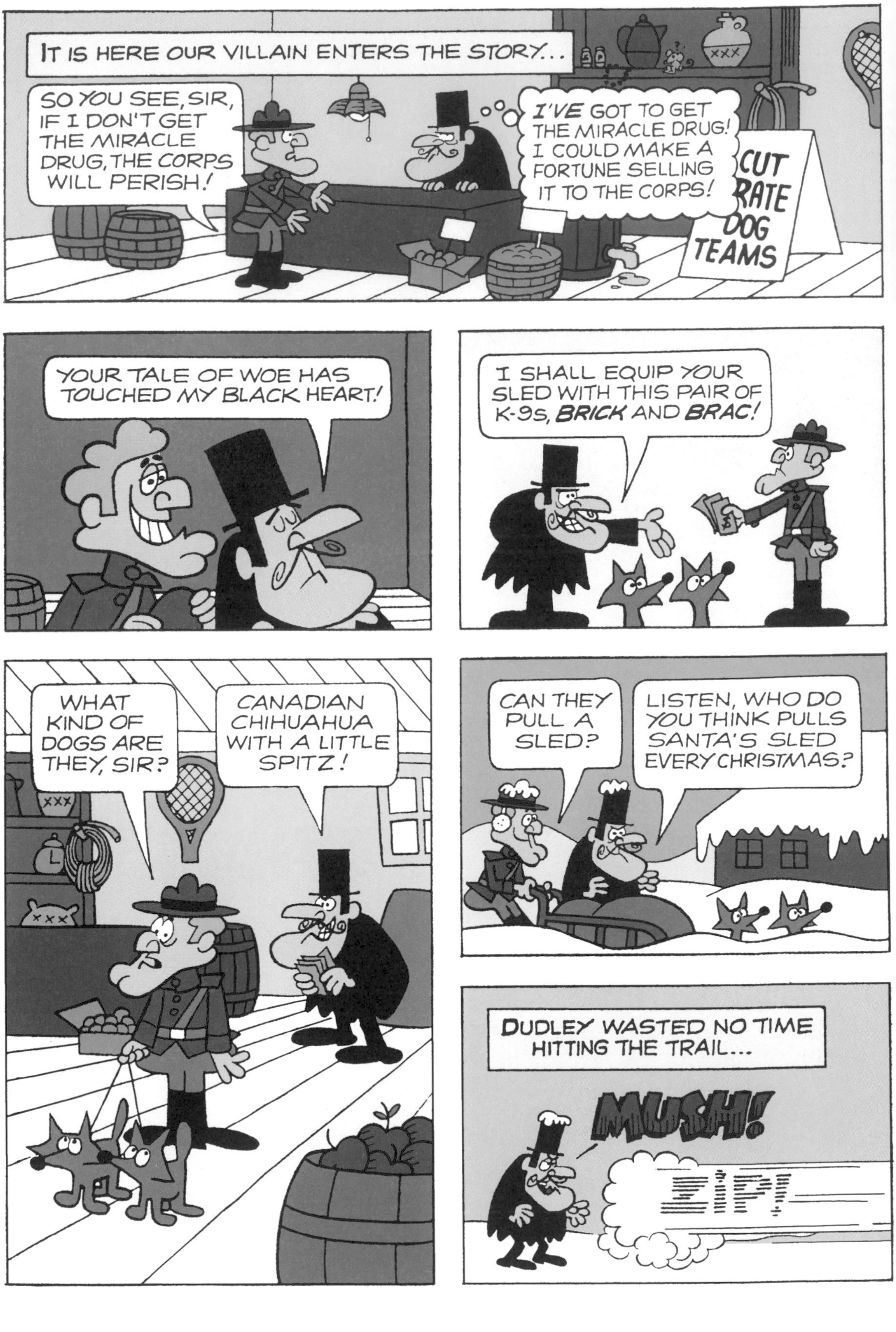
IT IS HERE OUR VILLAIN ENTERS THE STORY...
SO YOU SEE, SIR, IF I DON'T GET THE MIRACLE DRUG, THE CORPS WILL PERISH!
I'VE GOT TO GET THE MIRACLE DRUG! I COULD MAKE A FORTUNE SELLING IT TO THE CORPS!
CUT RATE DOG TEAMS
YOUR TALE OF WOE HAS TOUCHED MY BLACK HEART!
I SHALL EQUIP YOUR SLED WITH THIS PAIR OF K-9S, BRICK AND BRAC!
WHAT KIND OF DOGS ARE THEY, SIR?
CANADIAN CHIHUAHUA WITH A LITTLE SPITZ!
CAN THEY PULL A SLED?
LISTEN, WHO DO YOU THINK PULLS SANTA'S SLED EVERY CHRISTMAS?
DUDLEY WASTED NO TIME HITTING THE TRAIL...
MUSH!
ZIP!

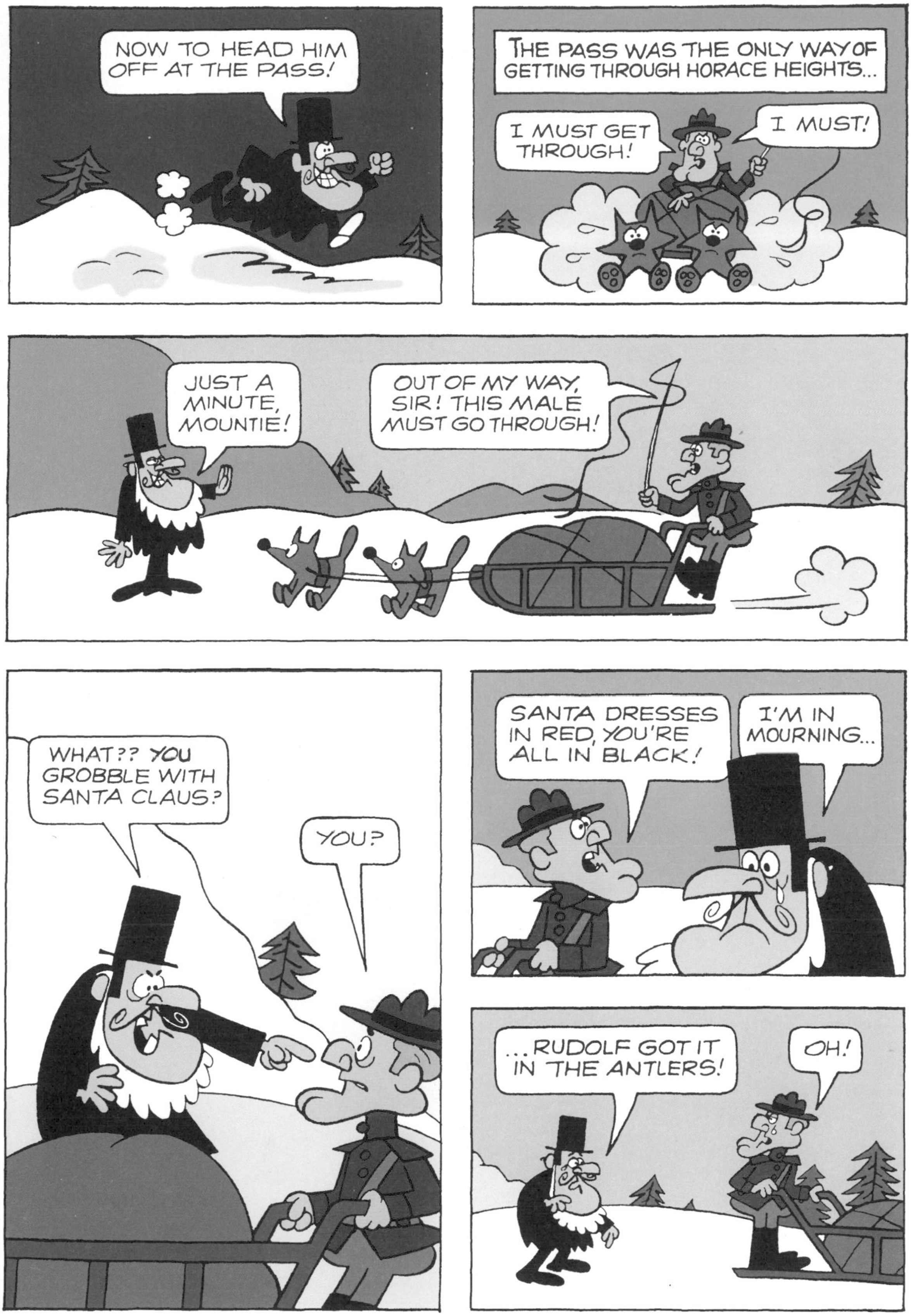
NOW TO HEAD HIM OFF AT THE PASS!
THE PASS WAS THE ONLY WAY OF GETTING THROUGH HORACE HEIGHTS...
I MUST GET THROUGH!
I MUST!
JUST A MINUTE, MOUNTIE!
OUT OF MY WAY, SIR! THIS MALE MUST GO THROUGH!
WHAT?? YOU GROBBLE WITH SANTA CLAUS?
YOU?
SANTA DRESSES IN RED, YOU'RE ALL IN BLACK!
I'M IN MOURNING...
...RUDOLF GOT IT IN THE ANTLERS!
OH!

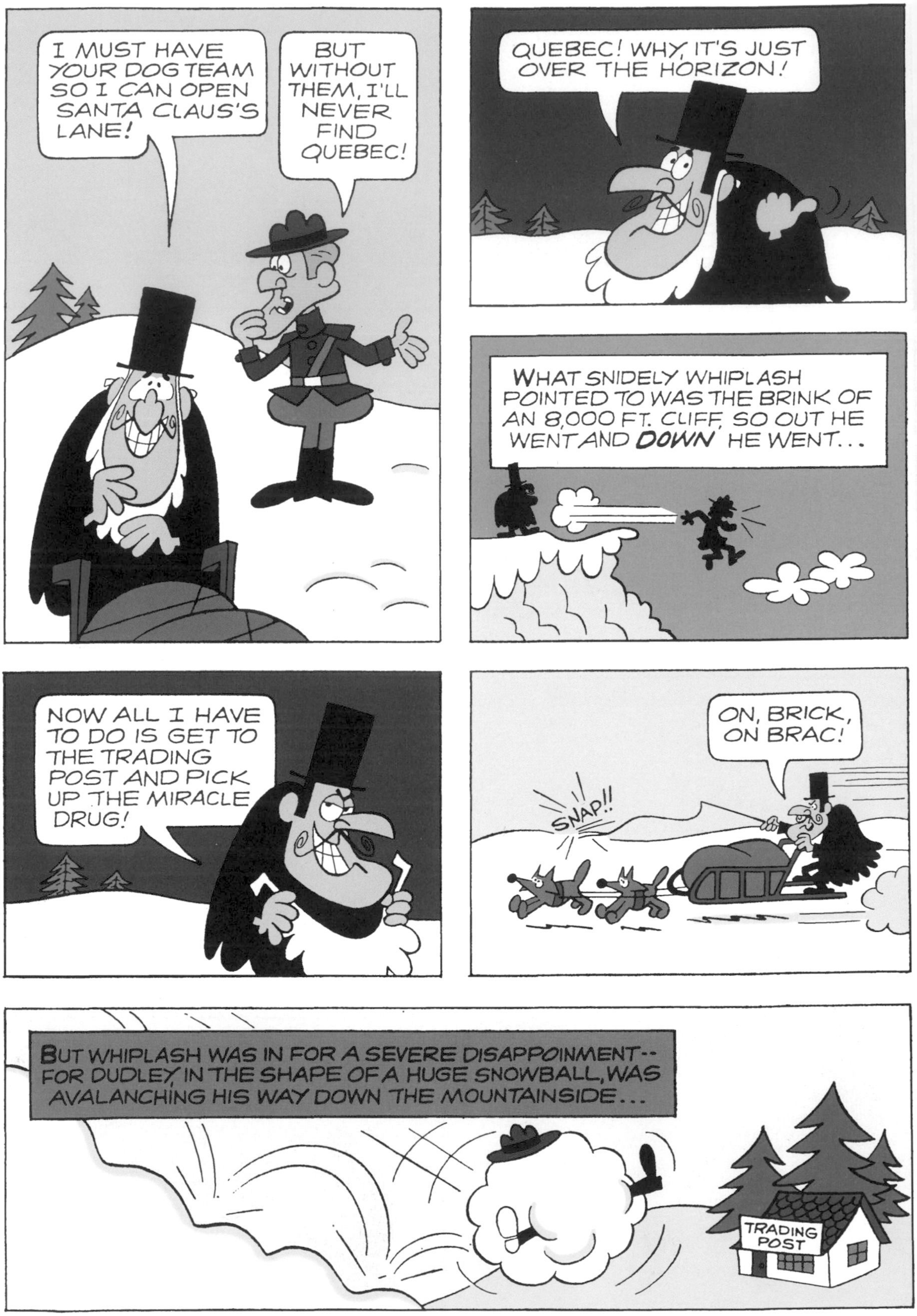
I MUST HAVE YOUR DOG TEAM SO I CAN OPEN SANTA CLAUS'S LANE!
BUT WITHOUT THEM, I'LL NEVER FIND QUEBEC!
QUEBEC! WHY, IT'S JUST OVER THE HORIZON!
WHAT SNIDELY WHIPLASH POINTED TO WAS THE BRINK OF AN 8,000 FT. CLIFF, SO OUT HE WENT AND DOWN HE WENT...
NOW ALL I HAVE TO DO IS GET TO THE TRADING POST AND PICK UP THE MIRACLE DRUG!
ON, BRICK, ON BRAC!
SNAP!!
BUT WHIPLASH WAS IN FOR A SEVERE DISAPPOINTMENT-- FOR DUDLEY, IN THE SHAPE OF A HUGE SNOWBALL, WAS AVALANCHING HIS WAY DOWN THE MOUNTAINSIDE...
TRADING POST

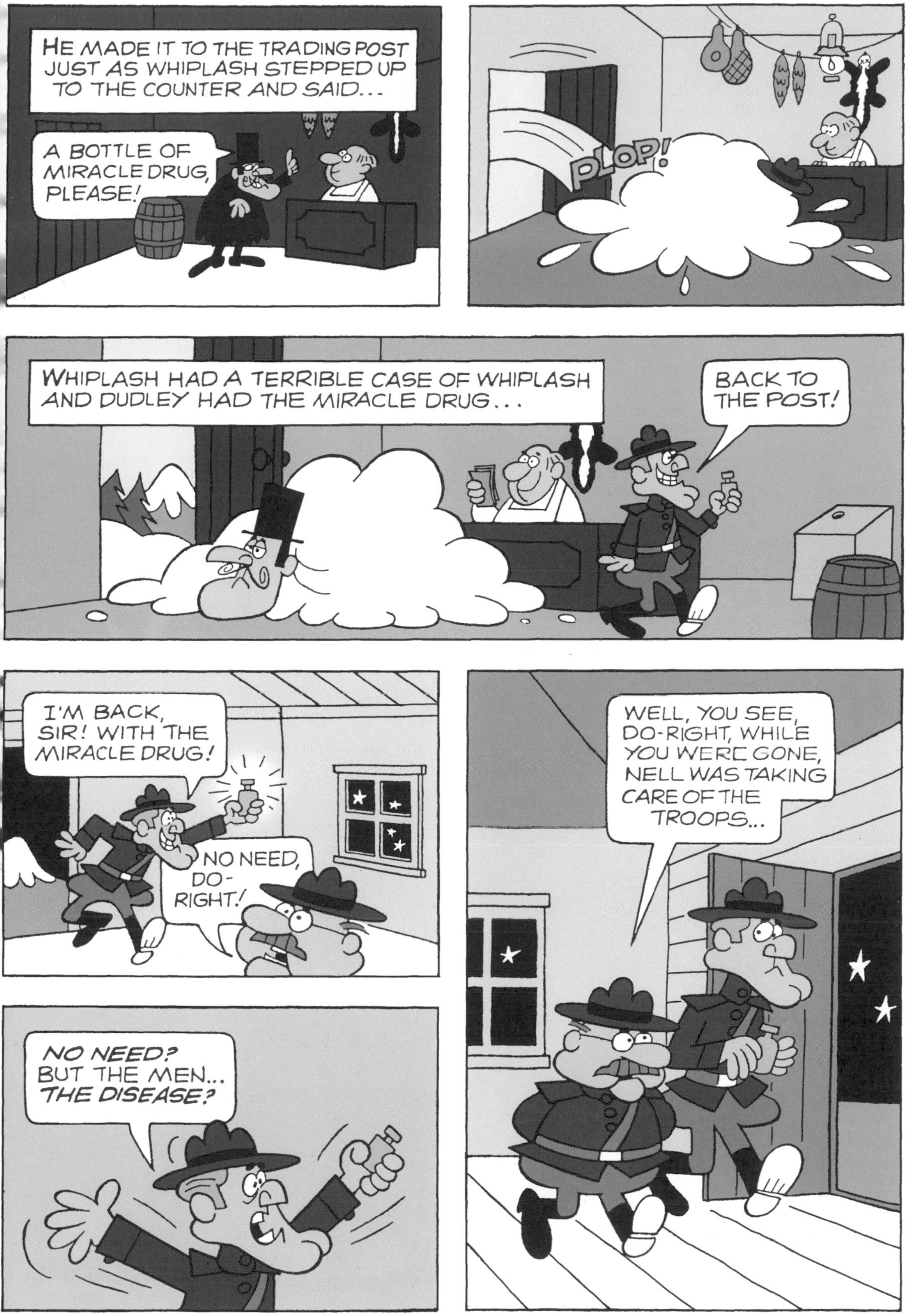
HE MADE IT TO THE TRADING POST JUST AS WHIPLASH STEPPED UP TO THE COUNTER AND SAID...
A BOTTLE OF MIRACLE DRUG, PLEASE!
PLOP!
WHIPLASH HAD A TERRIBLE CASE OF WHIPLASH AND DUDLEY HAD THE MIRACLE DRUG...
BACK TO THE POST!
I'M BACK, SIR! WITH THE MIRACLE DRUG!
NO NEED, DO-RIGHT!
WELL, YOU SEE, DO-RIGHT, WHILE YOU WERE GONE, NELL WAS TAKING CARE OF THE TROOPS...
NO NEED? BUT THE MEN... THE DISEASE?

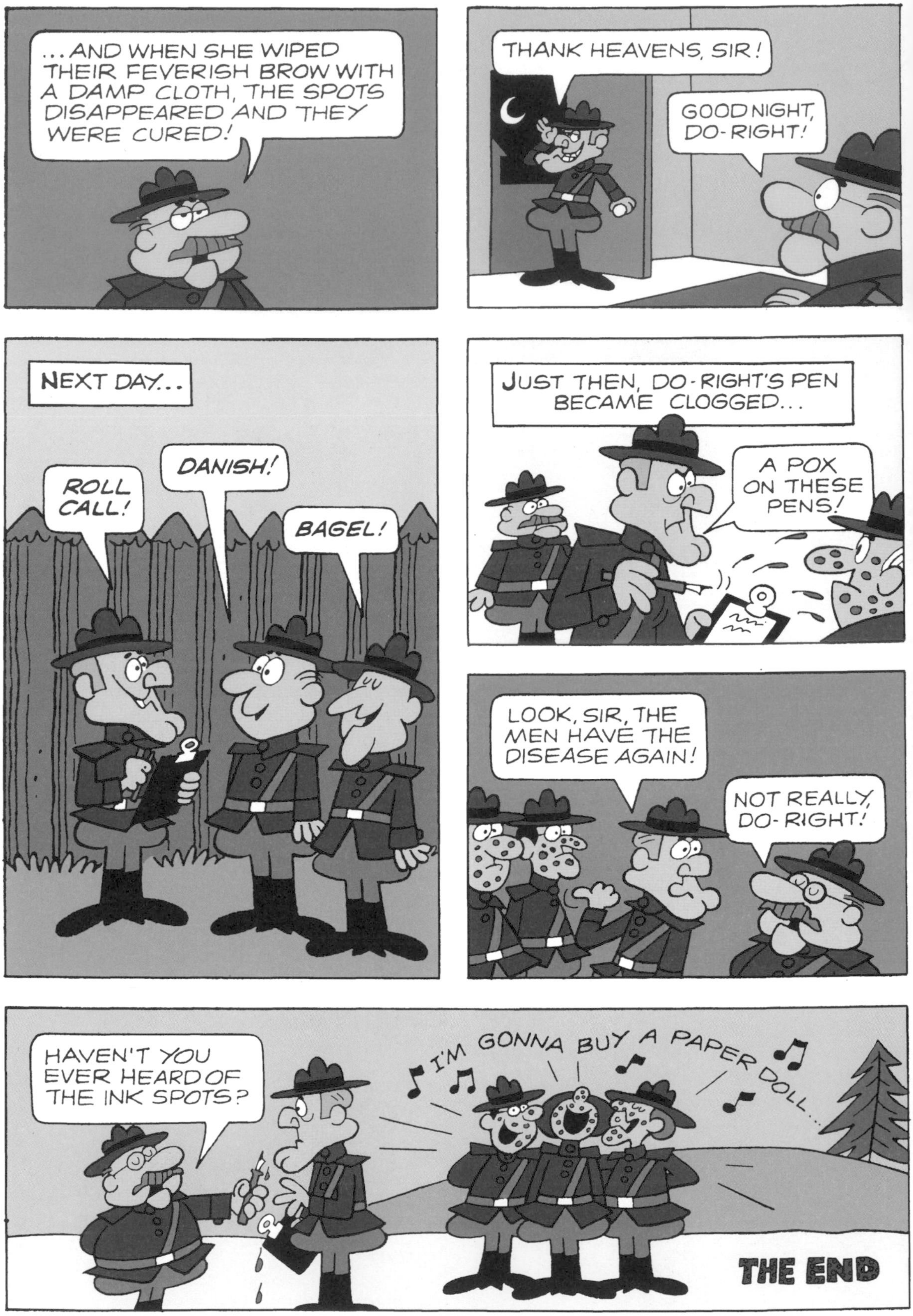
...AND WHEN SHE WIPED THEIR FEVERISH BROW WITH A DAMP CLOTH, THE SPOTS DISAPPEARED AND THEY WERE CURED!
THANK HEAVENS, SIR!
GOOD NIGHT, DO-RIGHT!
NEXT DAY...
ROLL CALL!
DANISH!
BAGEL!
JUST THEN, DO-RIGHT'S PEN BECAME CLOGGED...
A POX ON THESE PENS!
LOOK, SIR, THE MEN HAVE THE DISEASE AGAIN!
NOT REALLY, DO-RIGHT!
HAVEN'T YOU EVER HEARD OF THE INK SPOTS?
I'M GONNA BUY A PAPER DOLL...
THE END

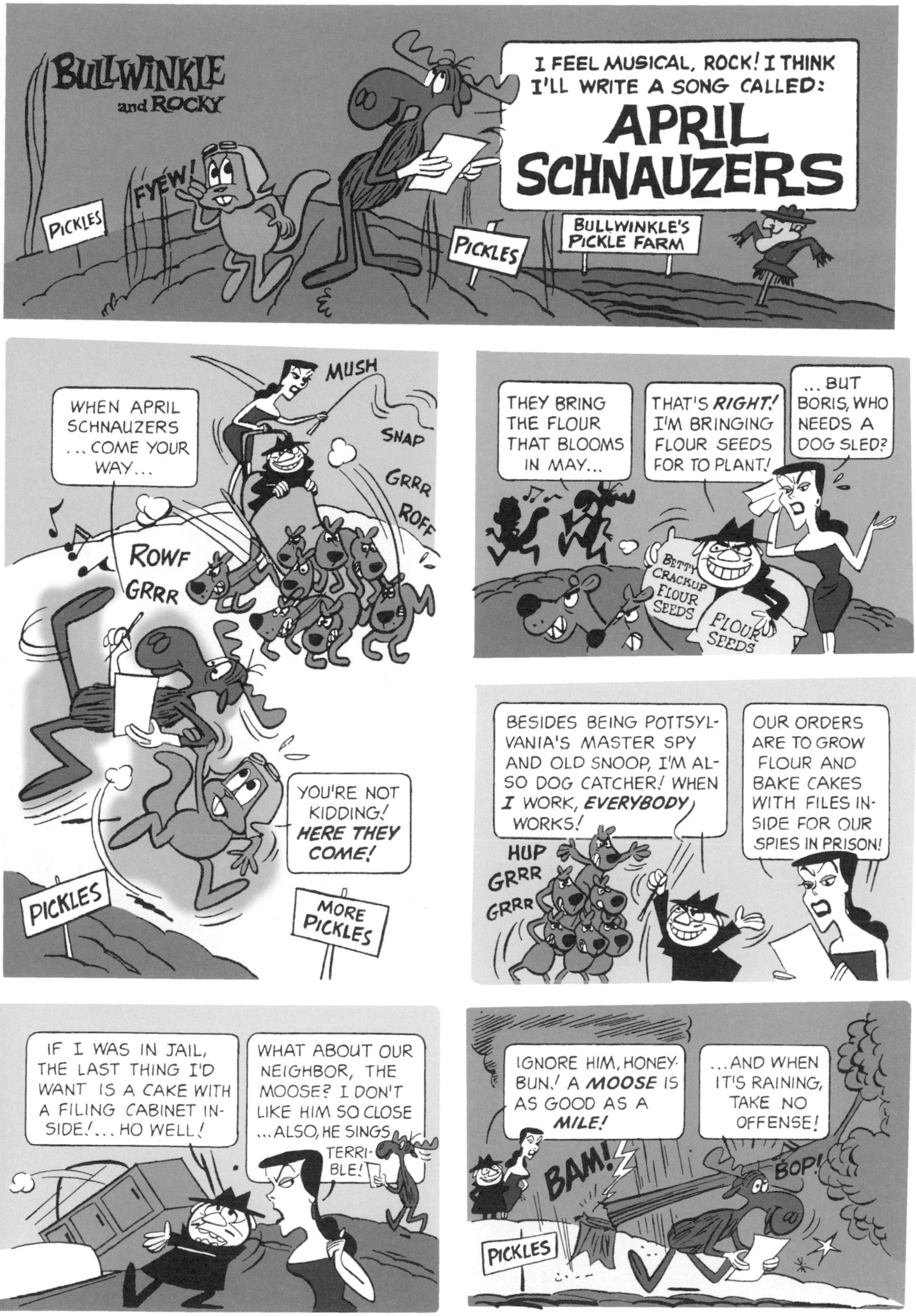
BULLWINKLE and ROCKY
I FEEL MUSICAL, ROCK! I THINK I'LL WRITE A SONG CALLED:
APRIL SCHNAUZERS
FYEW!
PICKLES
PICKLES
BULLWINKLE'S PICKLE FARM
WHEN APRIL SCHNAUZERS ...COME YOUR WAY...
MUSH
SNAP
GRRR
ROFF
ROWF
GRRR
YOU'RE NOT KIDDING! HERE THEY COME!
PICKLES
MORE PICKLES
THEY BRING THE FLOUR THAT BLOOMS IN MAY...
THAT'S RIGHT! I'M BRINGING FLOUR SEEDS FOR TO PLANT!
...BUT BORIS, WHO NEEDS A DOG SLED?
BETTY CRACKUP FLOUR SEEDS
FLOUR SEEDS
BESIDES BEING POTTSYL-VANIA'S MASTER SPY AND OLD SNOOP, I'M AL-SO DOG CATCHER! WHEN I WORK, EVERYBODY WORKS!
OUR ORDERS ARE TO GROW FLOUR AND BAKE CAKES WITH FILES IN-SIDE FOR OUR SPIES IN PRISON!
HUP
GRRR
GRRR
IF I WAS IN JAIL, THE LAST THING I'D WANT IS A CAKE WITH A FILING CABINET IN-SIDE!... HO WELL!
WHAT ABOUT OUR NEIGHBOR, THE MOOSE? I DON'T LIKE HIM SO CLOSE ...ALSO, HE SINGS TERRI-BLE!
IGNORE HIM, HONEY-BUN! A MOOSE IS AS GOOD AS A MILE!
...AND WHEN IT'S RAINING, TAKE NO OFFENSE!
BAM!
BOP!
PICKLES

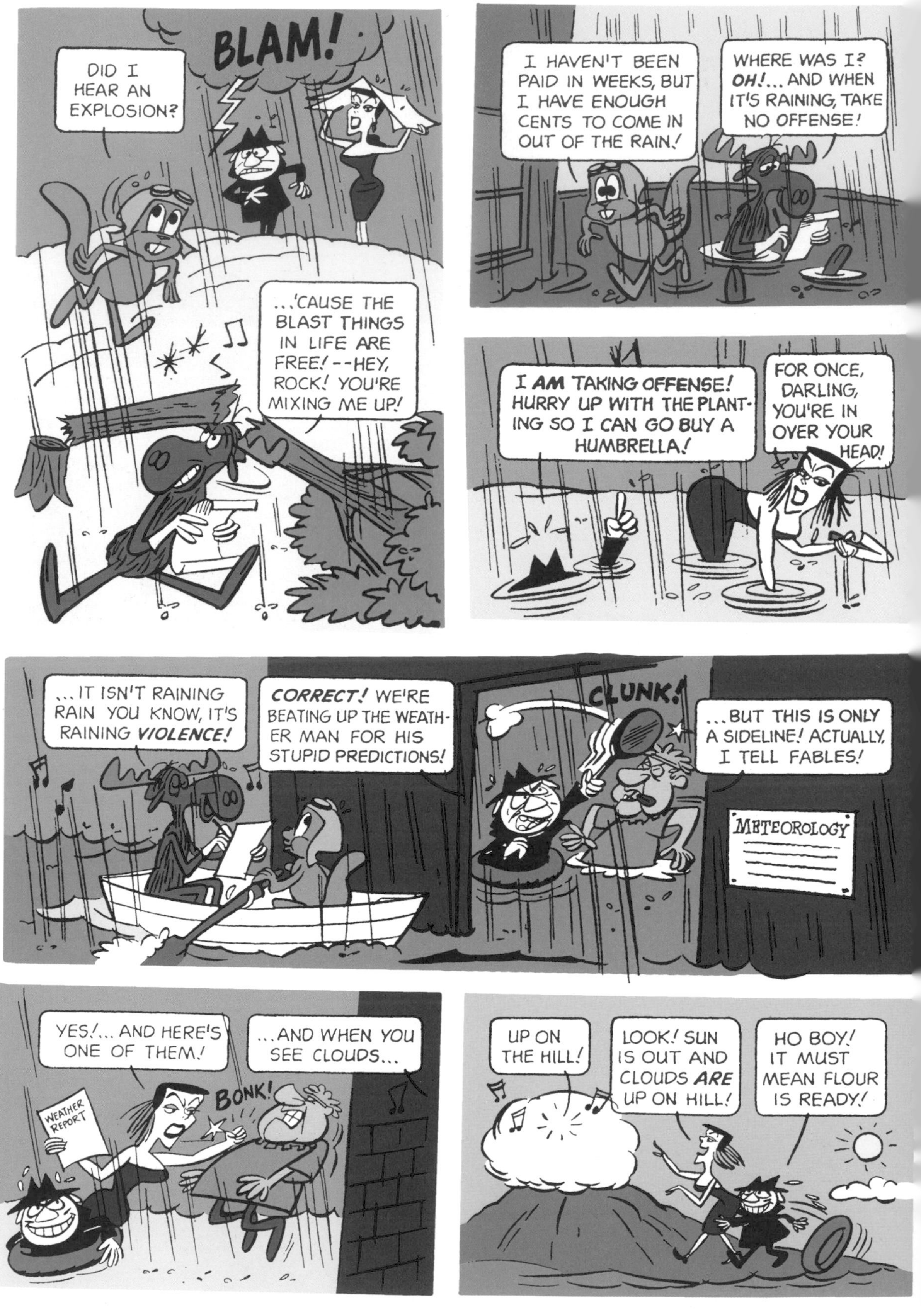
BLAM!
DID I HEAR AN EXPLOSION?
...'CAUSE THE BLAST THINGS IN LIFE ARE FREE! --HEY, ROCK! YOU'RE MIXING ME UP!
I HAVEN'T BEEN PAID IN WEEKS, BUT I HAVE ENOUGH CENTS TO COME IN OUT OF THE RAIN!
WHERE WAS I? OH!... AND WHEN IT'S RAINING, TAKE NO OFFENSE!
I AM TAKING OFFENSE! HURRY UP WITH THE PLANTING SO I CAN GO BUY A HUMBRELLA!
FOR ONCE, DARLING, YOU'RE IN OVER YOUR HEAD!
...IT ISN'T RAINING RAIN YOU KNOW, IT'S RAINING VIOLENCE!
CORRECT! WE'RE BEATING UP THE WEATHER MAN FOR HIS STUPID PREDICTIONS!
CLUNK!
...BUT THIS IS ONLY A SIDELINE! ACTUALLY, I TELL FABLES!
METEOROLOGY
YES!... AND HERE'S ONE OF THEM!
WEATHER REPORT
BONK!
...AND WHEN YOU SEE CLOUDS...
UP ON THE HILL!
LOOK! SUN IS OUT AND CLOUDS ARE UP ON HILL!
HO BOY! IT MUST MEAN FLOUR IS READY!

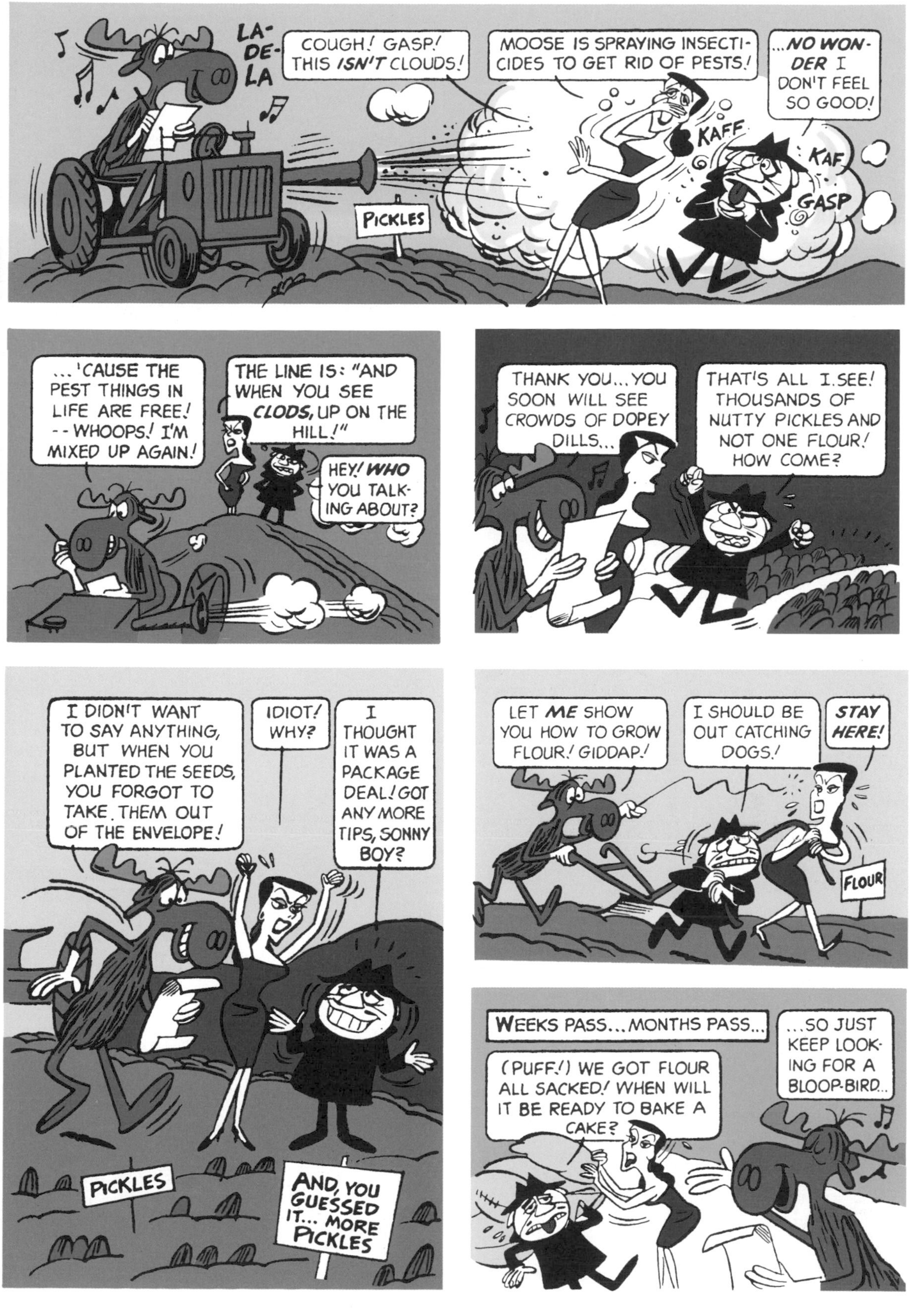
LA-DE-LA
COUGH! GASP! THIS ISN'T CLOUDS!
MOOSE IS SPRAYING INSECTICIDES TO GET RID OF PESTS!
...NO WONDER I DON'T FEEL SO GOOD!
KAFF
KAF
GASP
PICKLES
...'CAUSE THE PEST THINGS IN LIFE ARE FREE! --WHOOPS! I'M MIXED UP AGAIN!
THE LINE IS: "AND WHEN YOU SEE CLODS, UP ON THE HILL!"
HEY! WHO YOU TALKING ABOUT?
THANK YOU... YOU SOON WILL SEE CROWDS OF DOPEY DILLS...
THAT'S ALL I SEE! THOUSANDS OF NUTTY PICKLES AND NOT ONE FLOUR! HOW COME?
I DIDN'T WANT TO SAY ANYTHING, BUT WHEN YOU PLANTED THE SEEDS, YOU FORGOT TO TAKE THEM OUT OF THE ENVELOPE!
IDIOT! WHY?
I THOUGHT IT WAS A PACKAGE DEAL! GOT ANY MORE TIPS, SONNY BOY?
PICKLES
AND, YOU GUESSED IT... MORE PICKLES
LET ME SHOW YOU HOW TO GROW FLOUR! GIDDAP!
I SHOULD BE OUT CATCHING DOGS!
STAY HERE!
FLOUR
WEEKS PASS... MONTHS PASS...
...SO JUST KEEP LOOKING FOR A BLOOP-BIRD...
(PUFF!) WE GOT FLOUR ALL SACKED! WHEN WILL IT BE READY TO BAKE A CAKE?

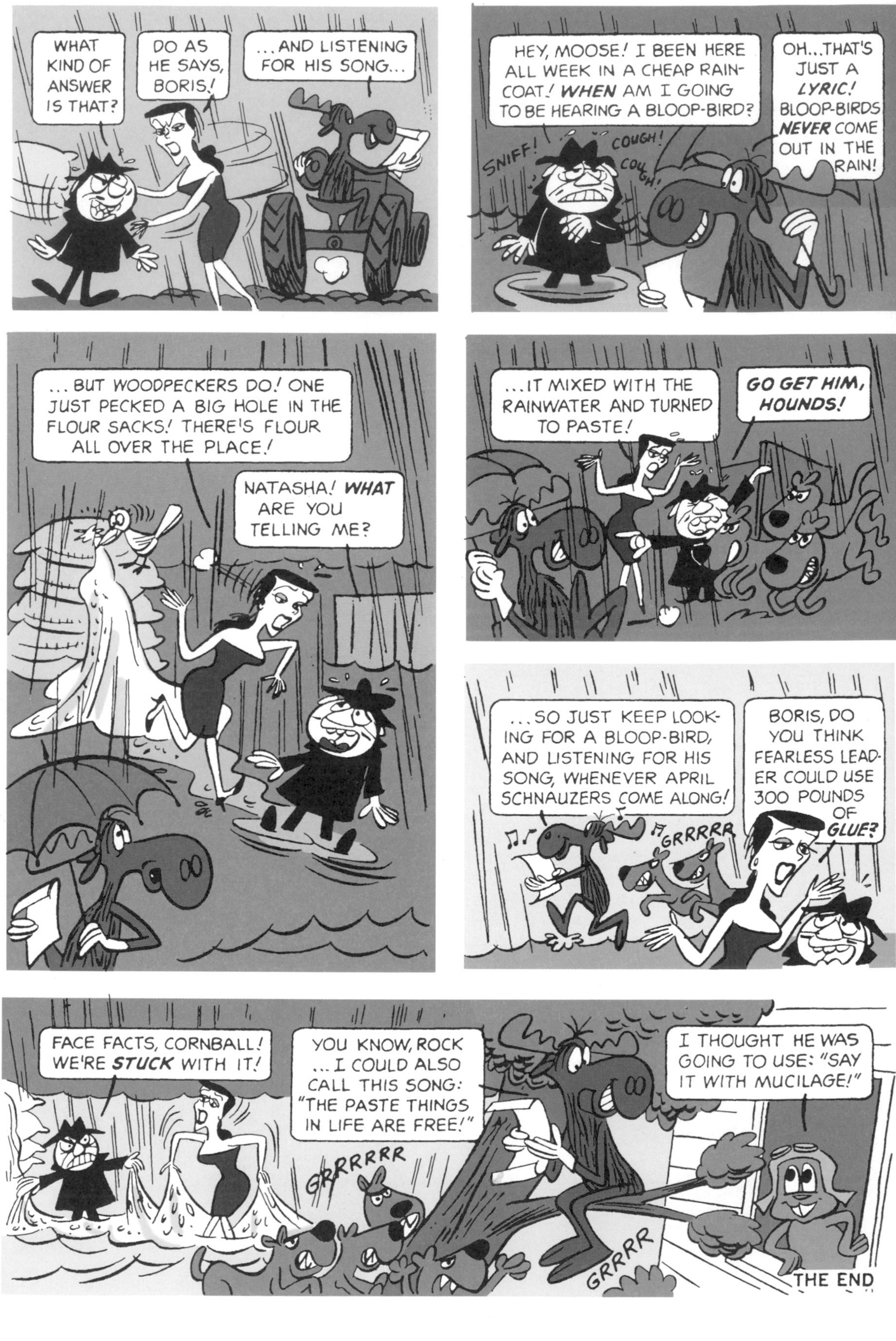
WHAT KIND OF ANSWER IS THAT?
DO AS HE SAYS, BORIS!
...AND LISTENING FOR HIS SONG...
HEY, MOOSE! I BEEN HERE ALL WEEK IN A CHEAP RAIN-COAT! WHEN AM I GOING TO BE HEARING A BLOOP-BIRD?
SNIFF!
COUGH!
COUGH!
OH...THAT'S JUST A LYRIC! BLOOP-BIRDS NEVER COME OUT IN THE RAIN!
...BUT WOODPECKERS DO! ONE JUST PECKED A BIG HOLE IN THE FLOUR SACKS! THERE'S FLOUR ALL OVER THE PLACE!
NATASHA! WHAT ARE YOU TELLING ME?
...IT MIXED WITH THE RAINWATER AND TURNED TO PASTE!
GO GET HIM, HOUNDS!
...SO JUST KEEP LOOK-ING FOR A BLOOP-BIRD, AND LISTENING FOR HIS SONG, WHENEVER APRIL SCHNAUZERS COME ALONG!
GRRRRR
BORIS, DO YOU THINK FEARLESS LEAD-ER COULD USE 300 POUNDS OF GLUE?
FACE FACTS, CORNBALL! WE'RE STUCK WITH IT!
YOU KNOW, ROCK ...I COULD ALSO CALL THIS SONG: "THE PASTE THINGS IN LIFE ARE FREE!"
I THOUGHT HE WAS GOING TO USE: "SAY IT WITH MUCILAGE!"
GRRRRRR
GRRRR
THE END

BULLWINKLE and ROCKY

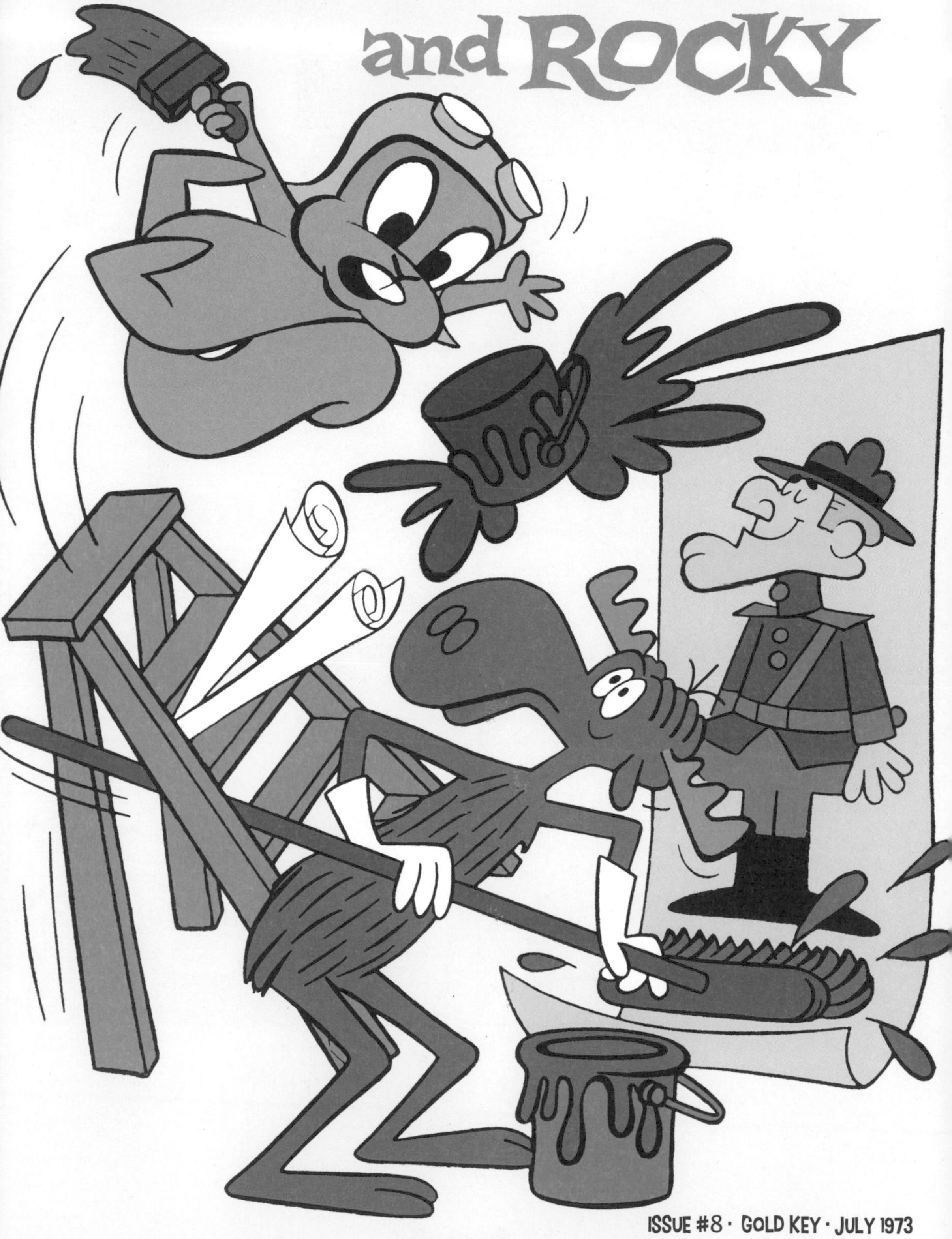

ISSUE #8 · GOLD KEY · JULY 1973

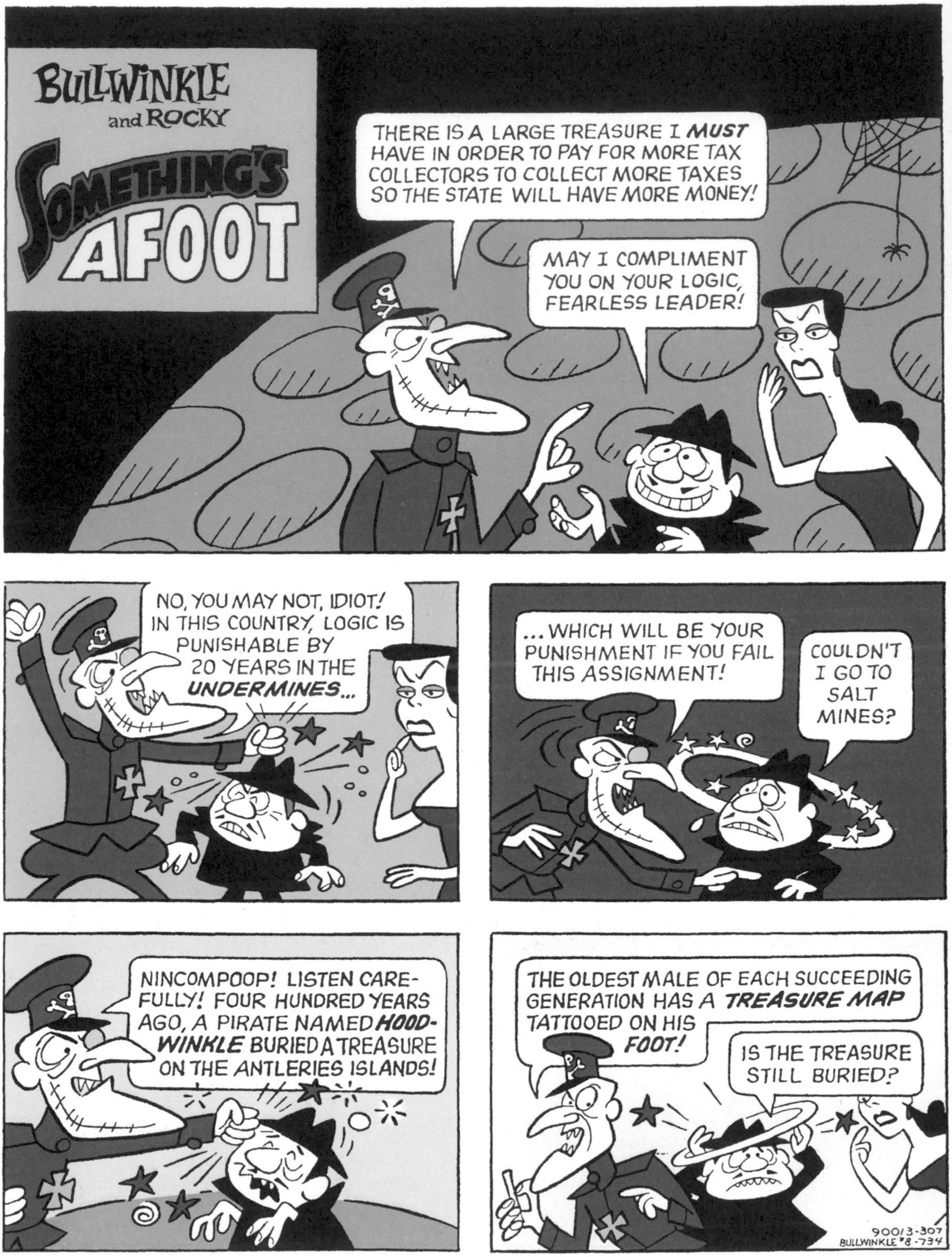
BULLWINKLE and ROCKY
SOMETHING'S AFOOT
THERE IS A LARGE TREASURE I MUST HAVE IN ORDER TO PAY FOR MORE TAX COLLECTORS TO COLLECT MORE TAXES SO THE STATE WILL HAVE MORE MONEY!
MAY I COMPLIMENT YOU ON YOUR LOGIC, FEARLESS LEADER!
NO, YOU MAY NOT, IDIOT! IN THIS COUNTRY, LOGIC IS PUNISHABLE BY 20 YEARS IN THE UNDERMINES...
...WHICH WILL BE YOUR PUNISHMENT IF YOU FAIL THIS ASSIGNMENT!
COULDN'T I GO TO SALT MINES?
NINCOMPOOP! LISTEN CAREFULLY! FOUR HUNDRED YEARS AGO, A PIRATE NAMED HOODWINKLE BURIED A TREASURE ON THE ANTLERIES ISLANDS!
THE OLDEST MALE OF EACH SUCCEEDING GENERATION HAS A TREASURE MAP TATTOOED ON HIS FOOT!
IS THE TREASURE STILL BURIED?
90013-307
BULLWINKLE #8-734

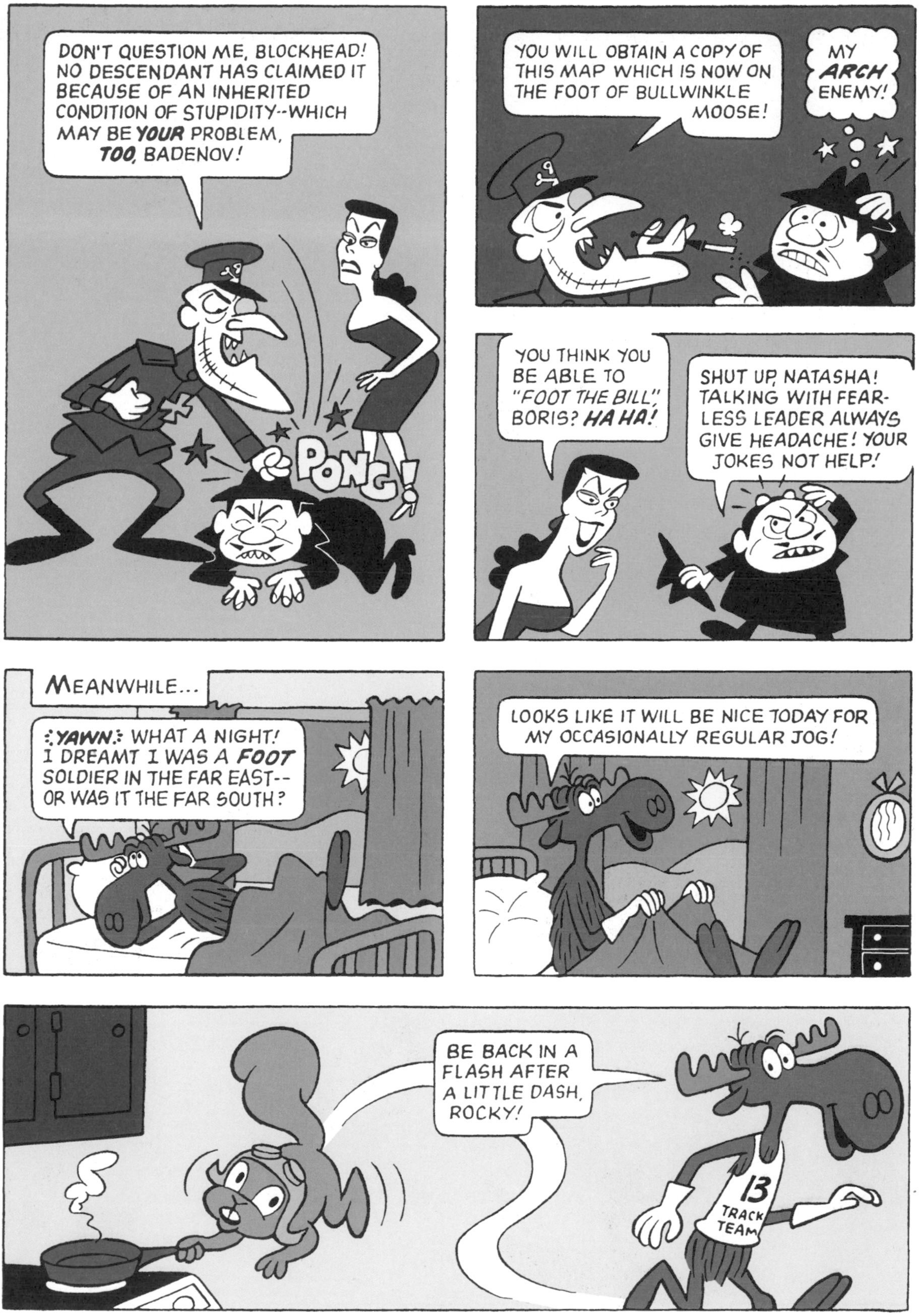
DON'T QUESTION ME, BLOCKHEAD! NO DESCENDANT HAS CLAIMED IT BECAUSE OF AN INHERITED CONDITION OF STUPIDITY--WHICH MAY BE YOUR PROBLEM, TOO, BADENOV!
PONG!
YOU WILL OBTAIN A COPY OF THIS MAP WHICH IS NOW ON THE FOOT OF BULLWINKLE MOOSE!
MY ARCH ENEMY!
YOU THINK YOU BE ABLE TO "FOOT THE BILL", BORIS? HA HA!
SHUT UP, NATASHA! TALKING WITH FEARLESS LEADER ALWAYS GIVE HEADACHE! YOUR JOKES NOT HELP!
MEANWHILE...
YAWN! WHAT A NIGHT! I DREAMT I WAS A FOOT SOLDIER IN THE FAR EAST--OR WAS IT THE FAR SOUTH?
LOOKS LIKE IT WILL BE NICE TODAY FOR MY OCCASIONALLY REGULAR JOG!
BE BACK IN A FLASH AFTER A LITTLE DASH, ROCKY!
13
TRACK TEAM

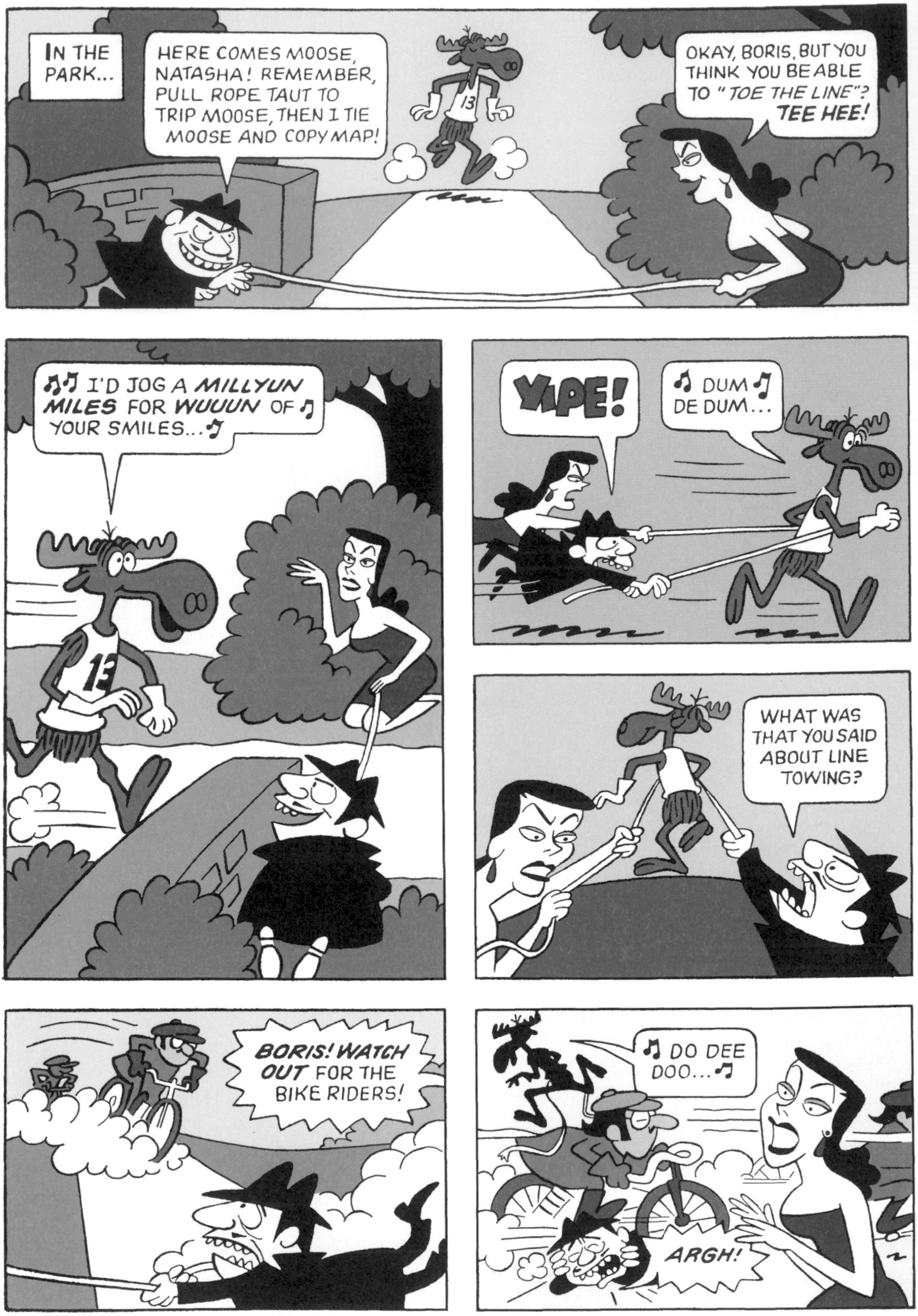
IN THE PARK...
HERE COMES MOOSE, NATASHA! REMEMBER, PULL ROPE TAUT TO TRIP MOOSE, THEN I TIE MOOSE AND COPY MAP!
OKAY, BORIS, BUT YOU THINK YOU BE ABLE TO "TOE THE LINE"? TEE HEE!
♫ I'D JOG A MILLYUN MILES FOR WUUUN OF ♪ YOUR SMILES... ♫
YIPE!
♪ DUM ♫ DE DUM...
WHAT WAS THAT YOU SAID ABOUT LINE TOWING?
BORIS! WATCH OUT FOR THE BIKE RIDERS!
♪ DO DEE DOO... ♫
ARGH!

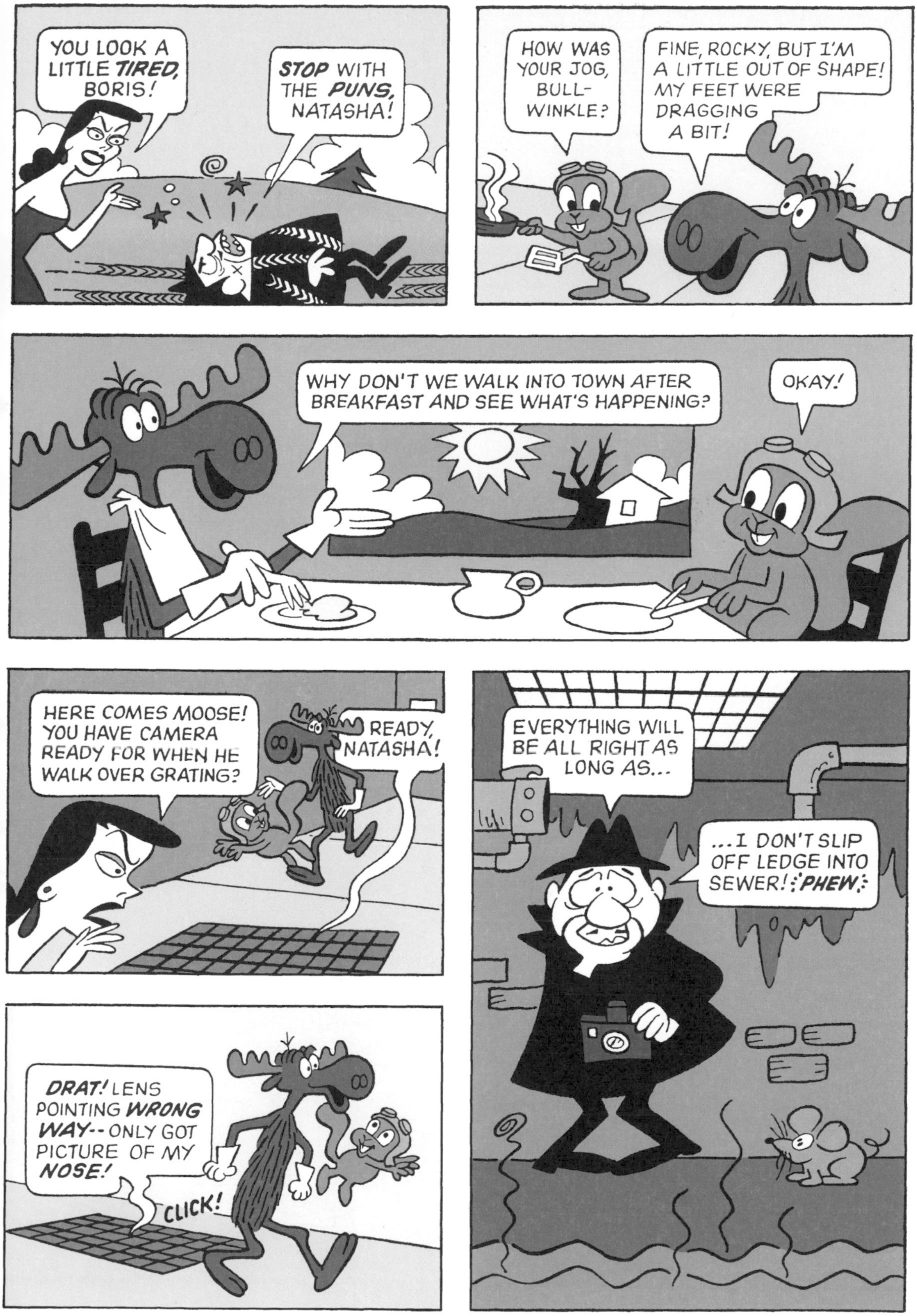
YOU LOOK A LITTLE TIRED, BORIS!
STOP WITH THE PUNS, NATASHA!
HOW WAS YOUR JOG, BULL-WINKLE?
FINE, ROCKY, BUT I'M A LITTLE OUT OF SHAPE! MY FEET WERE DRAGGING A BIT!
WHY DON'T WE WALK INTO TOWN AFTER BREAKFAST AND SEE WHAT'S HAPPENING?
OKAY!
HERE COMES MOOSE! YOU HAVE CAMERA READY FOR WHEN HE WALK OVER GRATING?
READY, NATASHA!
EVERYTHING WILL BE ALL RIGHT AS LONG AS...
...I DON'T SLIP OFF LEDGE INTO SEWER! PHEW
DRAT! LENS POINTING WRONG WAY-- ONLY GOT PICTURE OF MY NOSE!
CLICK!

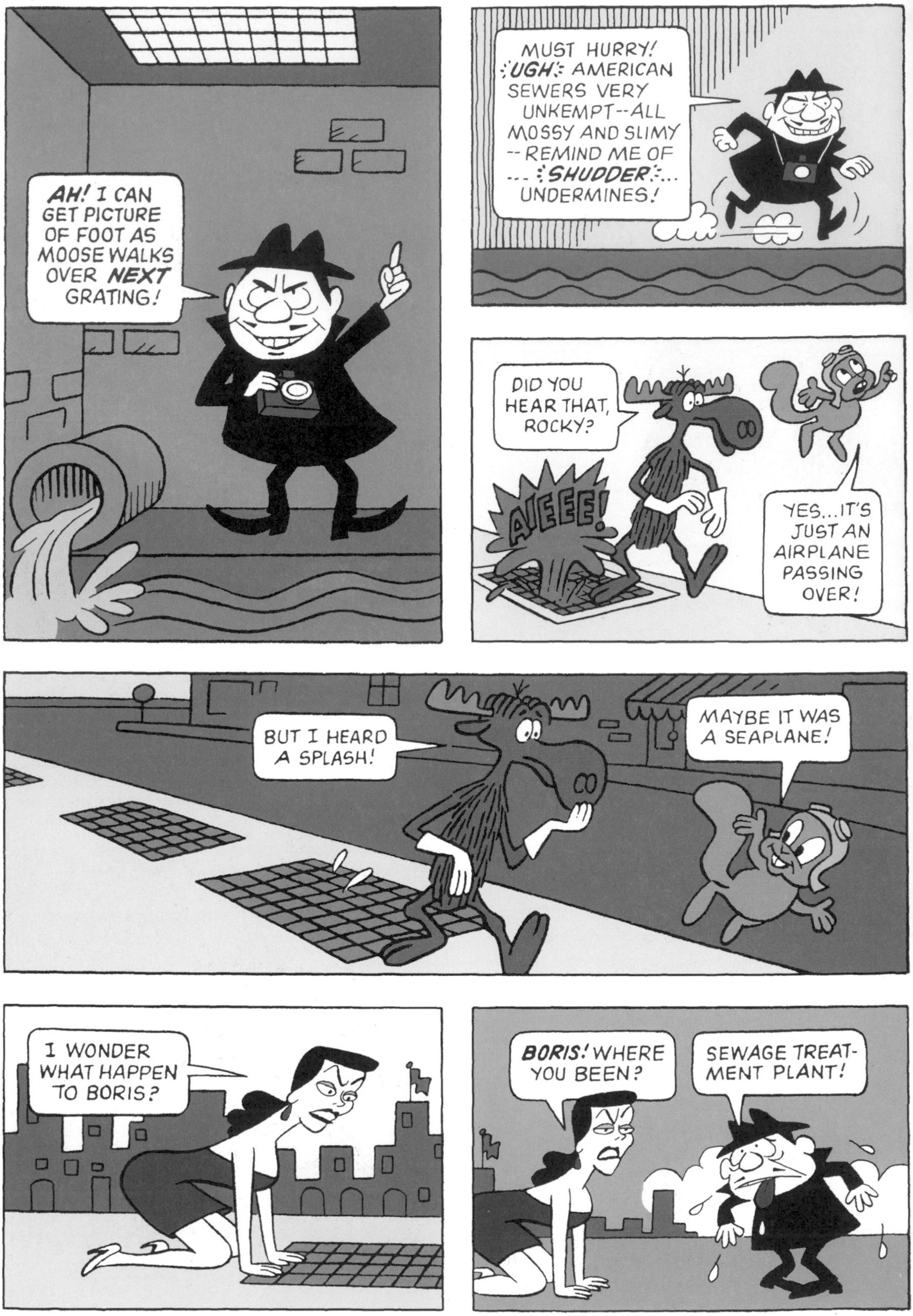
AH! I CAN GET PICTURE OF FOOT AS MOOSE WALKS OVER NEXT GRATING!
MUST HURRY! UGH AMERICAN SEWERS VERY UNKEMPT--ALL MOSSY AND SLIMY --REMIND ME OF ... SHUDDER... UNDERMINES!
DID YOU HEAR THAT, ROCKY?
AIEEE!
YES...IT'S JUST AN AIRPLANE PASSING OVER!
BUT I HEARD A SPLASH!
MAYBE IT WAS A SEAPLANE!
I WONDER WHAT HAPPEN TO BORIS?
BORIS! WHERE YOU BEEN?
SEWAGE TREATMENT PLANT!

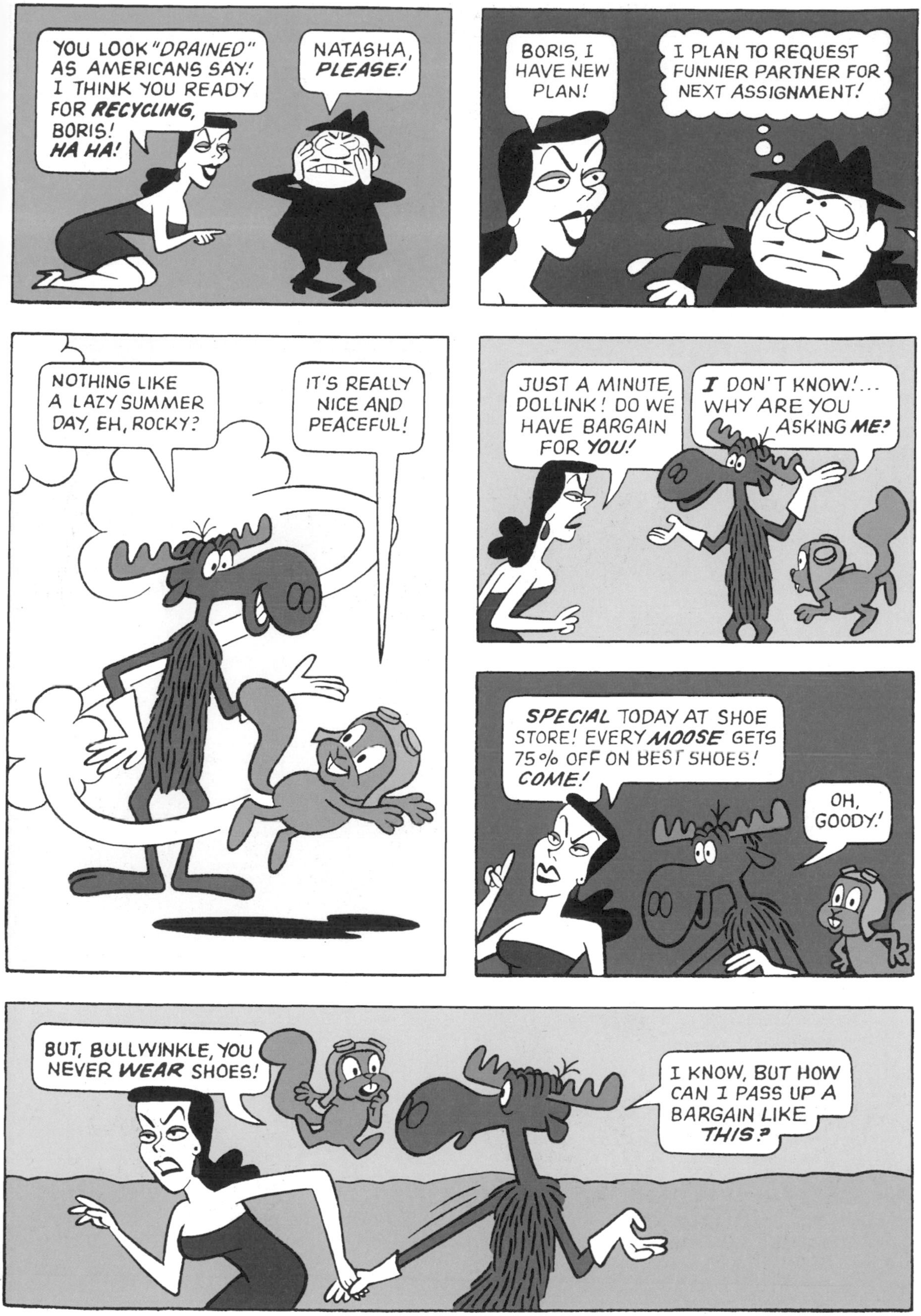
YOU LOOK "DRAINED" AS AMERICANS SAY! I THINK YOU READY FOR RECYCLING, BORIS! HA HA!
NATASHA, PLEASE!
BORIS, I HAVE NEW PLAN!
I PLAN TO REQUEST FUNNIER PARTNER FOR NEXT ASSIGNMENT!
NOTHING LIKE A LAZY SUMMER DAY, EH, ROCKY?
IT'S REALLY NICE AND PEACEFUL!
JUST A MINUTE, DOLLINK! DO WE HAVE BARGAIN FOR YOU!
I DON'T KNOW!... WHY ARE YOU ASKING ME?
SPECIAL TODAY AT SHOE STORE! EVERY MOOSE GETS 75% OFF ON BEST SHOES! COME!
OH, GOODY!
BUT, BULLWINKLE, YOU NEVER WEAR SHOES!
I KNOW, BUT HOW CAN I PASS UP A BARGAIN LIKE THIS?

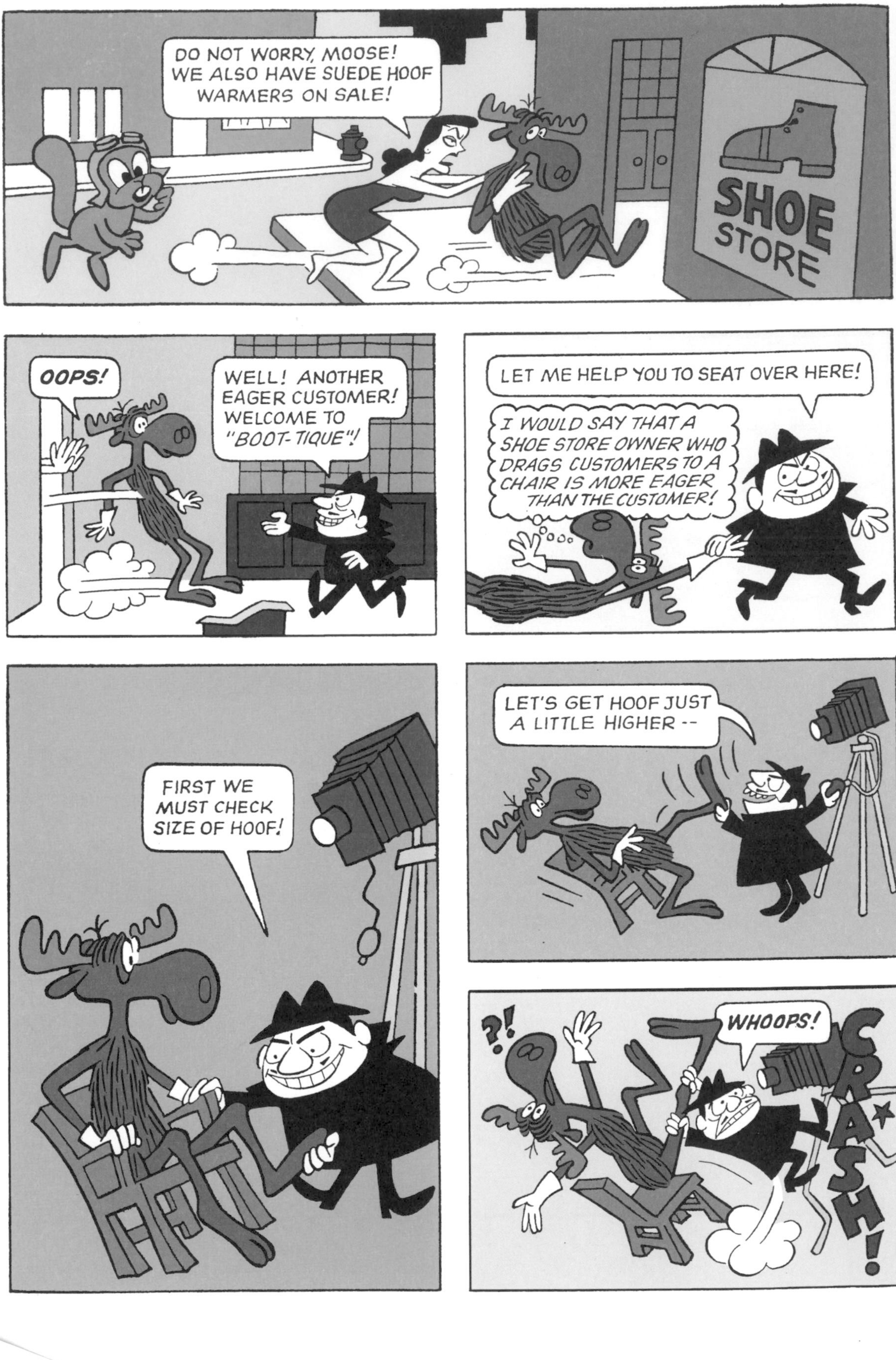
DO NOT WORRY, MOOSE! WE ALSO HAVE SUEDE HOOF WARMERS ON SALE!
SHOE STORE
OOPS!
WELL! ANOTHER EAGER CUSTOMER! WELCOME TO "BOOT-TIQUE"!
LET ME HELP YOU TO SEAT OVER HERE!
I WOULD SAY THAT A SHOE STORE OWNER WHO DRAGS CUSTOMERS TO A CHAIR IS MORE EAGER THAN THE CUSTOMER!
FIRST WE MUST CHECK SIZE OF HOOF!
LET'S GET HOOF JUST A LITTLE HIGHER --
?!
WHOOPS!
CRASH!

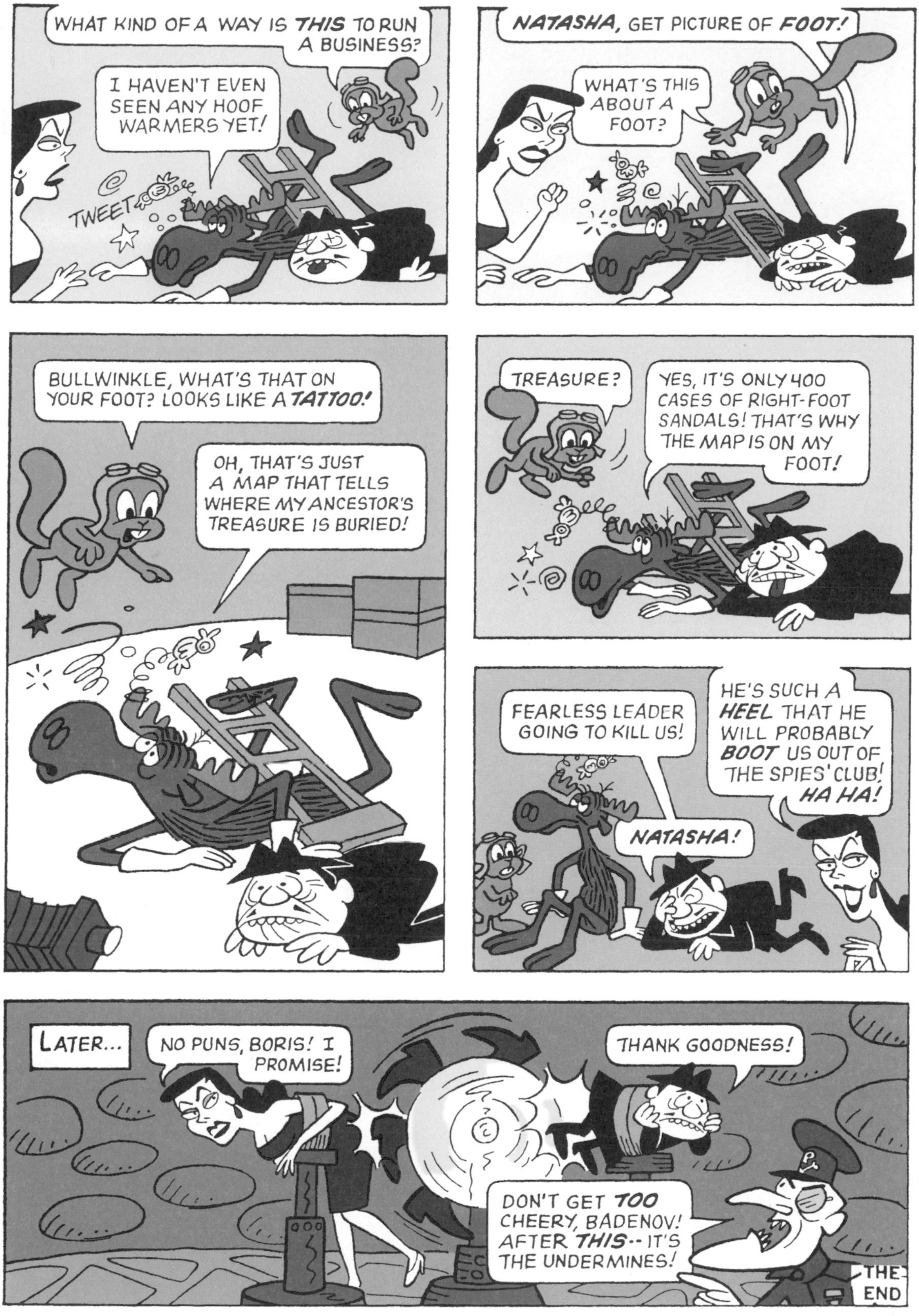
WHAT KIND OF A WAY IS THIS TO RUN A BUSINESS?
I HAVEN'T EVEN SEEN ANY HOOF WARMERS YET!
TWEET
NATASHA, GET PICTURE OF FOOT!
WHAT'S THIS ABOUT A FOOT?
BULLWINKLE, WHAT'S THAT ON YOUR FOOT? LOOKS LIKE A TATTOO!
OH, THAT'S JUST A MAP THAT TELLS WHERE MY ANCESTOR'S TREASURE IS BURIED!
TREASURE?
YES, IT'S ONLY 400 CASES OF RIGHT-FOOT SANDALS! THAT'S WHY THE MAP IS ON MY FOOT!
FEARLESS LEADER GOING TO KILL US!
HE'S SUCH A HEEL THAT HE WILL PROBABLY BOOT US OUT OF THE SPIES' CLUB! HA HA!
NATASHA!
LATER...
NO PUNS, BORIS! I PROMISE!
THANK GOODNESS!
DON'T GET TOO CHEERY, BADENOV! AFTER THIS-- IT'S THE UNDERMINES!
THE END

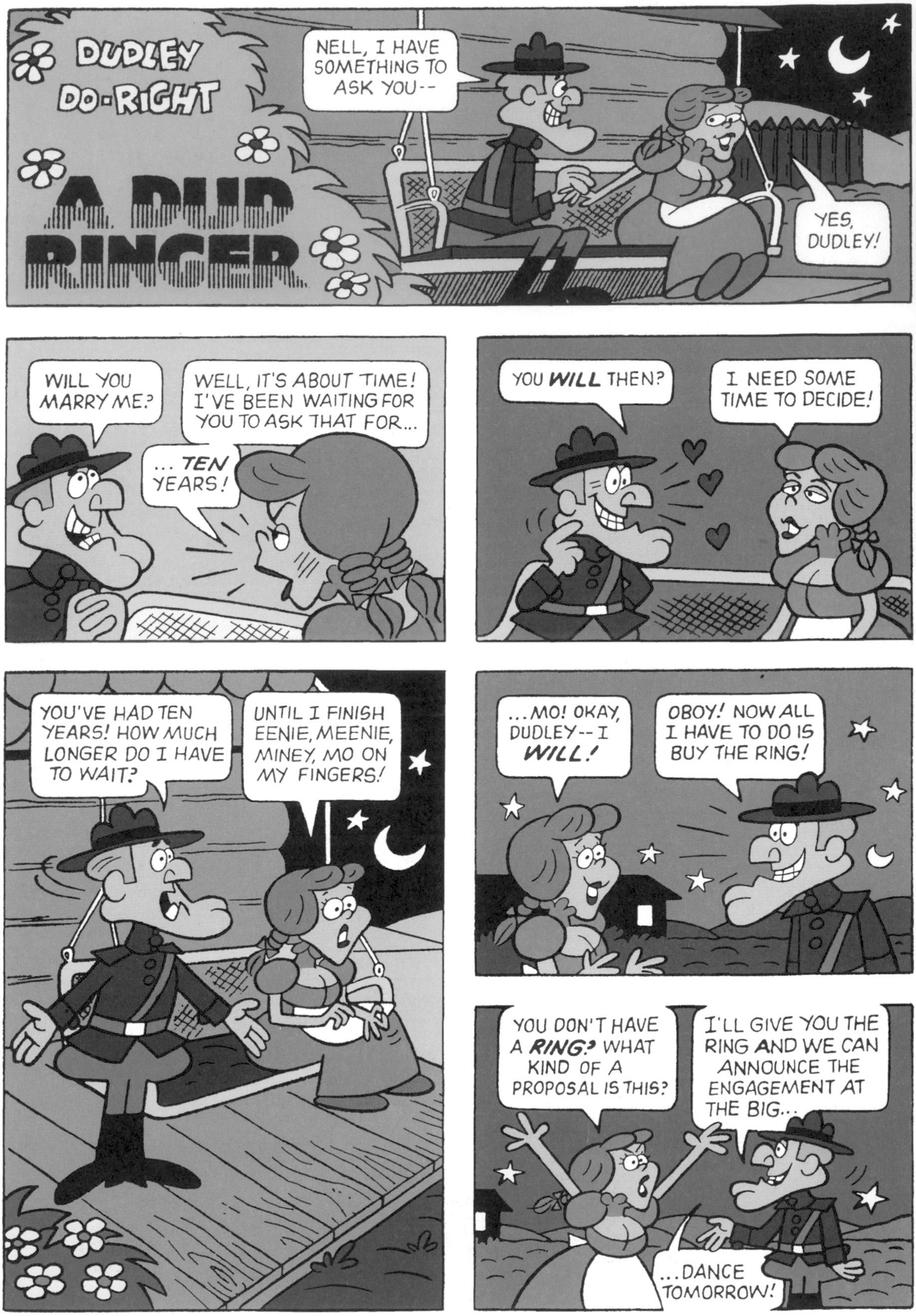
DUDLEY DO-RIGHT
A DUD RINGER
NELL, I HAVE SOMETHING TO ASK YOU--
YES, DUDLEY!
WILL YOU MARRY ME?
WELL, IT'S ABOUT TIME! I'VE BEEN WAITING FOR YOU TO ASK THAT FOR...
... TEN YEARS!
YOU WILL THEN?
I NEED SOME TIME TO DECIDE!
YOU'VE HAD TEN YEARS! HOW MUCH LONGER DO I HAVE TO WAIT?
UNTIL I FINISH EENIE, MEENIE, MINEY, MO ON MY FINGERS!
...MO! OKAY, DUDLEY-- I WILL!
OBOY! NOW ALL I HAVE TO DO IS BUY THE RING!
YOU DON'T HAVE A RING? WHAT KIND OF A PROPOSAL IS THIS?
I'LL GIVE YOU THE RING AND WE CAN ANNOUNCE THE ENGAGEMENT AT THE BIG...
...DANCE TOMORROW!

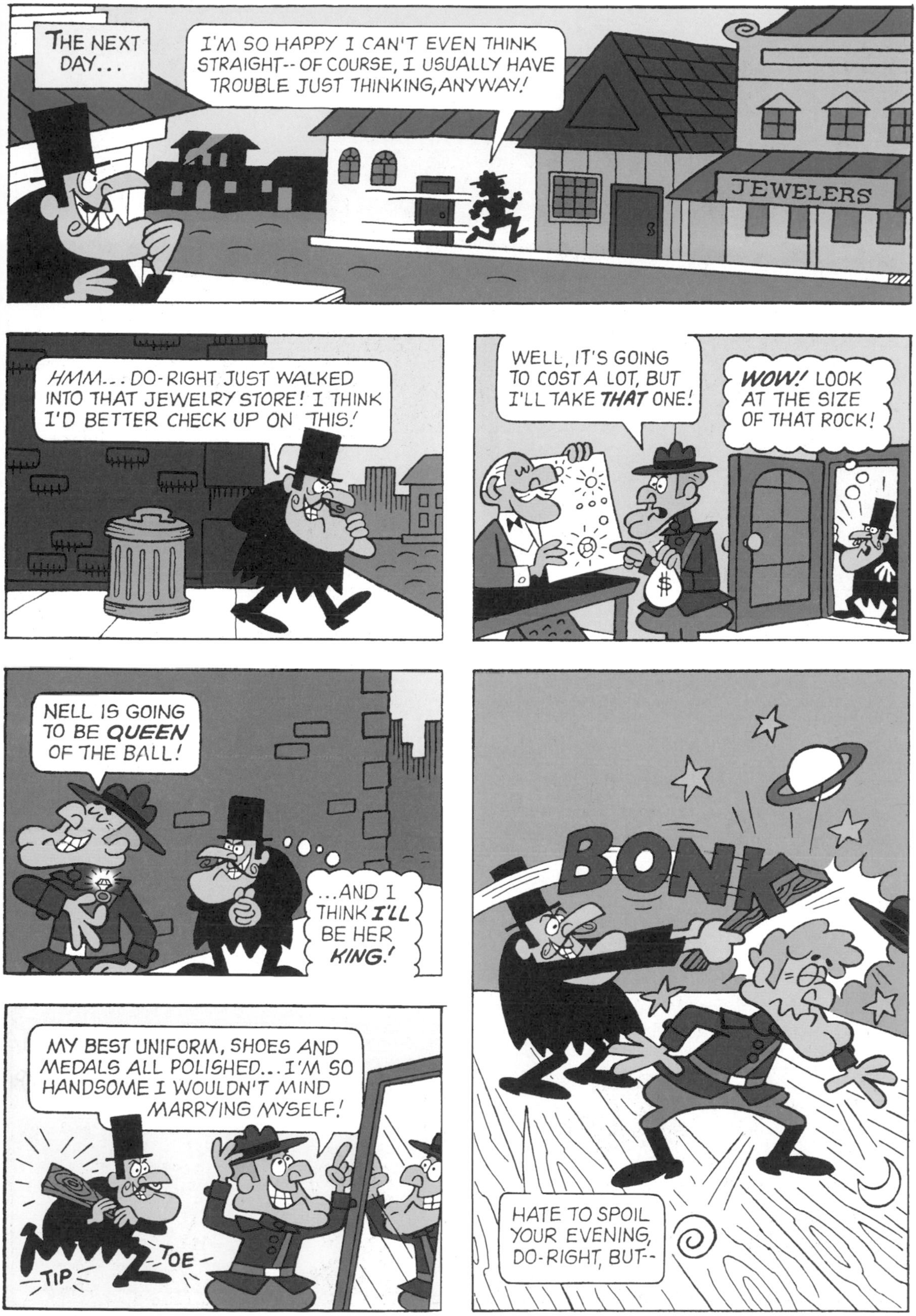
THE NEXT DAY...
I'M SO HAPPY I CAN'T EVEN THINK STRAIGHT-- OF COURSE, I USUALLY HAVE TROUBLE JUST THINKING, ANYWAY!
JEWELERS
HMM... DO-RIGHT JUST WALKED INTO THAT JEWELRY STORE! I THINK I'D BETTER CHECK UP ON THIS!
WELL, IT'S GOING TO COST A LOT, BUT I'LL TAKE THAT ONE!
WOW! LOOK AT THE SIZE OF THAT ROCK!
NELL IS GOING TO BE QUEEN OF THE BALL!
...AND I THINK I'LL BE HER KING!
BONK
HATE TO SPOIL YOUR EVENING, DO-RIGHT, BUT--
MY BEST UNIFORM, SHOES AND MEDALS ALL POLISHED... I'M SO HANDSOME I WOULDN'T MIND MARRYING MYSELF!
TIP
TOE

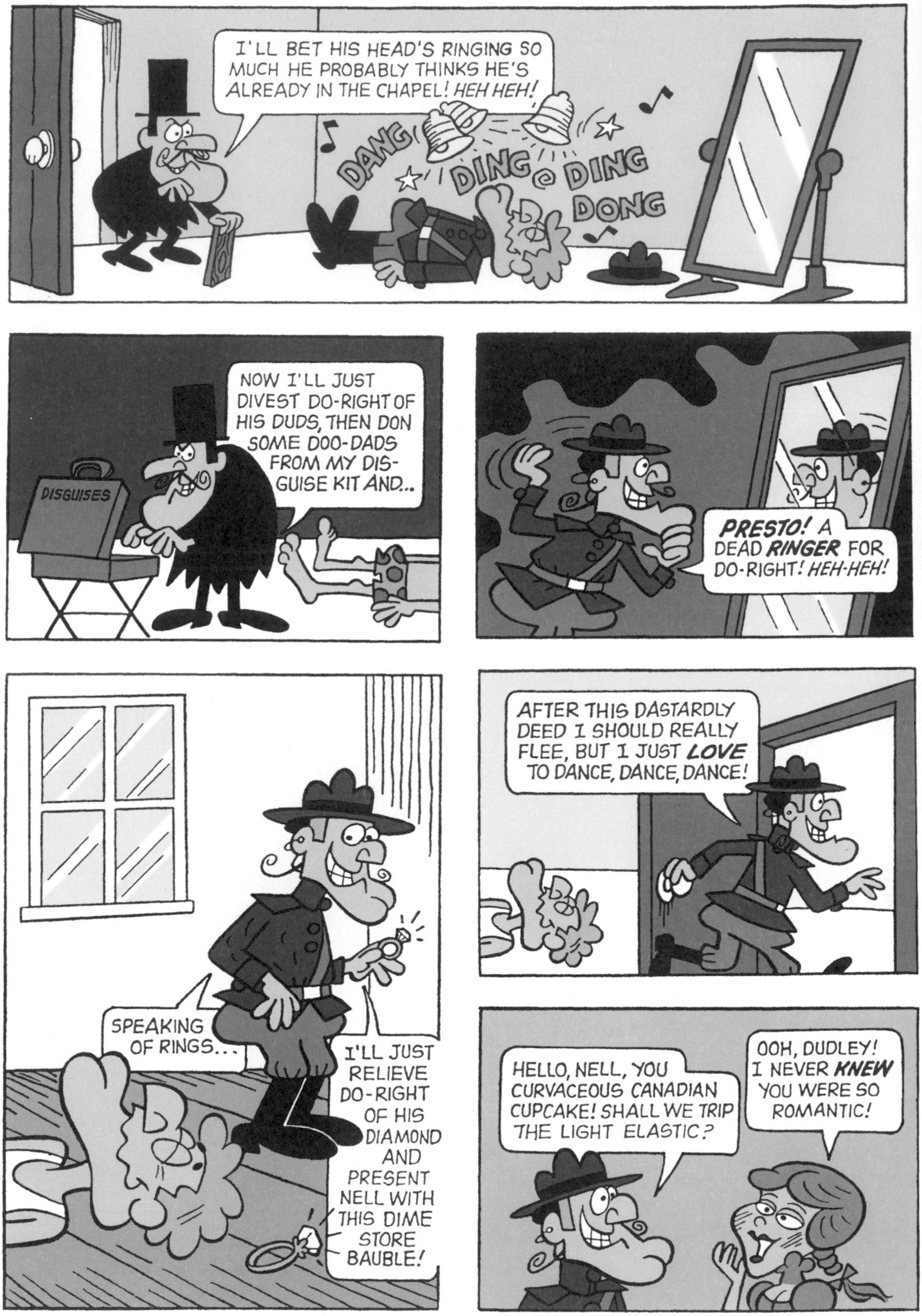
I'LL BET HIS HEAD'S RINGING SO MUCH HE PROBABLY THINKS HE'S ALREADY IN THE CHAPEL! HEH HEH!
DANG
DING
DING
DING
DONG
NOW I'LL JUST DIVEST DO-RIGHT OF HIS DUDS, THEN DON SOME DOO-DADS FROM MY DISGUISE KIT AND...
DISGUISES
PRESTO! A DEAD RINGER FOR DO-RIGHT! HEH-HEH!
SPEAKING OF RINGS...
I'LL JUST RELIEVE DO-RIGHT OF HIS DIAMOND AND PRESENT NELL WITH THIS DIME STORE BAUBLE!
AFTER THIS DASTARDLY DEED I SHOULD REALLY FLEE, BUT I JUST LOVE TO DANCE, DANCE, DANCE!
HELLO, NELL, YOU CURVACEOUS CANADIAN CUPCAKE! SHALL WE TRIP THE LIGHT ELASTIC?
OOH, DUDLEY! I NEVER KNEW YOU WERE SO ROMANTIC!

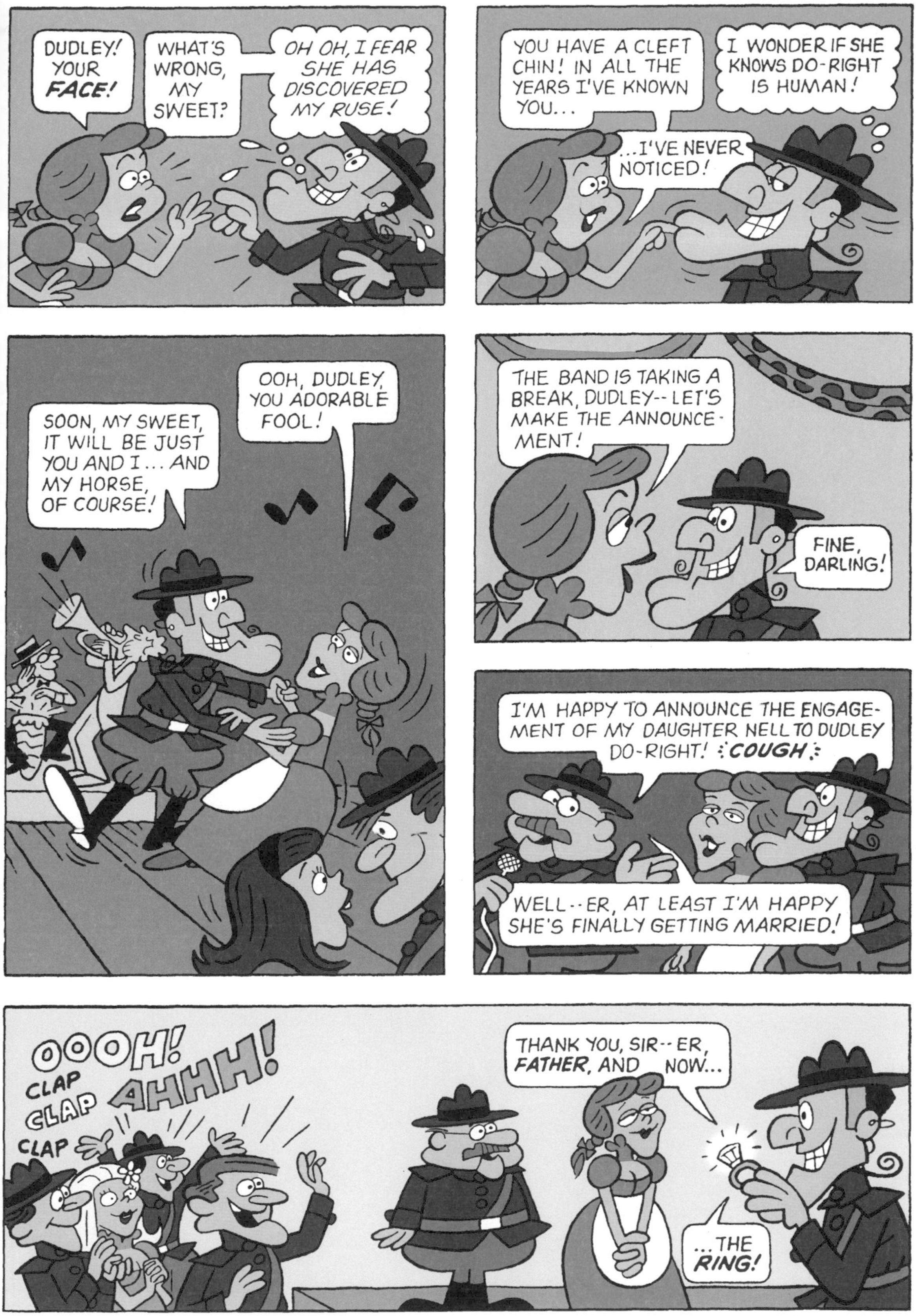
DUDLEY! YOUR FACE!
WHAT'S WRONG, MY SWEET?
OH OH, I FEAR SHE HAS DISCOVERED MY RUSE!
YOU HAVE A CLEFT CHIN! IN ALL THE YEARS I'VE KNOWN YOU...
...I'VE NEVER NOTICED!
I WONDER IF SHE KNOWS DO-RIGHT IS HUMAN!
SOON, MY SWEET, IT WILL BE JUST YOU AND I... AND MY HORSE, OF COURSE!
OOH, DUDLEY, YOU ADORABLE FOOL!
THE BAND IS TAKING A BREAK, DUDLEY-- LET'S MAKE THE ANNOUNCE-MENT!
FINE, DARLING!
I'M HAPPY TO ANNOUNCE THE ENGAGE-MENT OF MY DAUGHTER NELL TO DUDLEY DO-RIGHT! COUGH
WELL--ER, AT LEAST I'M HAPPY SHE'S FINALLY GETTING MARRIED!
OOOH!
CLAP
CLAP
CLAP
AHHH!
THANK YOU, SIR-- ER, FATHER, AND NOW...
...THE RING!

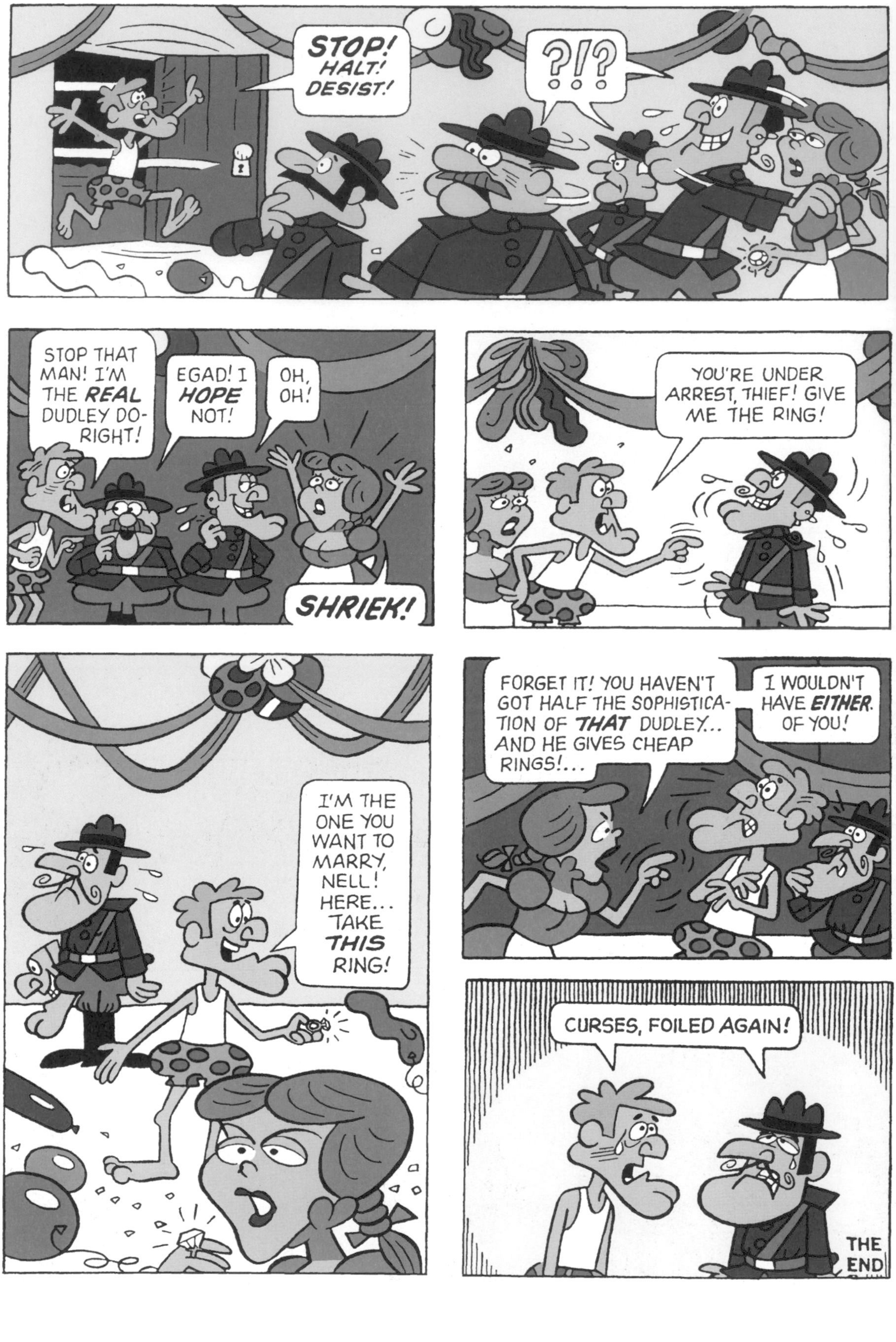
STOP! HALT! DESIST!
?!?
STOP THAT MAN! I'M THE REAL DUDLEY DO-RIGHT!
EGAD! I HOPE NOT!
OH, OH!
SHRIEK!
YOU'RE UNDER ARREST, THIEF! GIVE ME THE RING!
I'M THE ONE YOU WANT TO MARRY, NELL! HERE... TAKE THIS RING!
FORGET IT! YOU HAVEN'T GOT HALF THE SOPHISTICATION OF THAT DUDLEY... AND HE GIVES CHEAP RINGS!...
I WOULDN'T HAVE EITHER OF YOU!
CURSES, FOILED AGAIN!
THE END

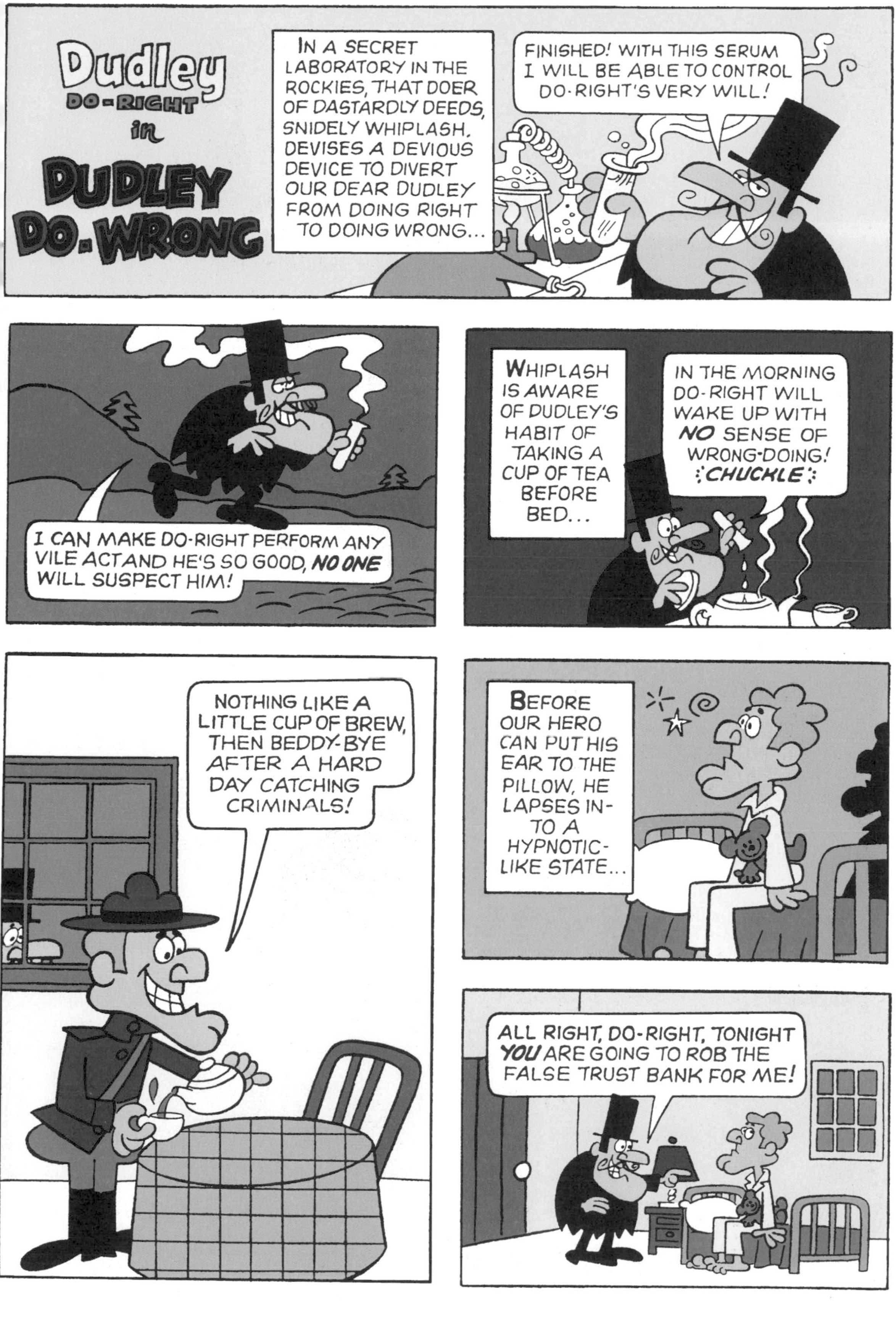
Dudley DO-RIGHT in DUDLEY DO-WRONG
IN A SECRET LABORATORY IN THE ROCKIES, THAT DOER OF DASTARDLY DEEDS, SNIDELY WHIPLASH, DEVISES A DEVIOUS DEVICE TO DIVERT OUR DEAR DUDLEY FROM DOING RIGHT TO DOING WRONG...
FINISHED! WITH THIS SERUM I WILL BE ABLE TO CONTROL DO-RIGHT'S VERY WILL!
I CAN MAKE DO-RIGHT PERFORM ANY VILE ACT AND HE'S SO GOOD, NO ONE WILL SUSPECT HIM!
WHIPLASH IS AWARE OF DUDLEY'S HABIT OF TAKING A CUP OF TEA BEFORE BED...
IN THE MORNING DO-RIGHT WILL WAKE UP WITH NO SENSE OF WRONG-DOING! CHUCKLE
NOTHING LIKE A LITTLE CUP OF BREW, THEN BEDDY-BYE AFTER A HARD DAY CATCHING CRIMINALS!
BEFORE OUR HERO CAN PUT HIS EAR TO THE PILLOW, HE LAPSES IN-TO A HYPNOTIC-LIKE STATE...
ALL RIGHT, DO-RIGHT, TONIGHT YOU ARE GOING TO ROB THE FALSE TRUST BANK FOR ME!

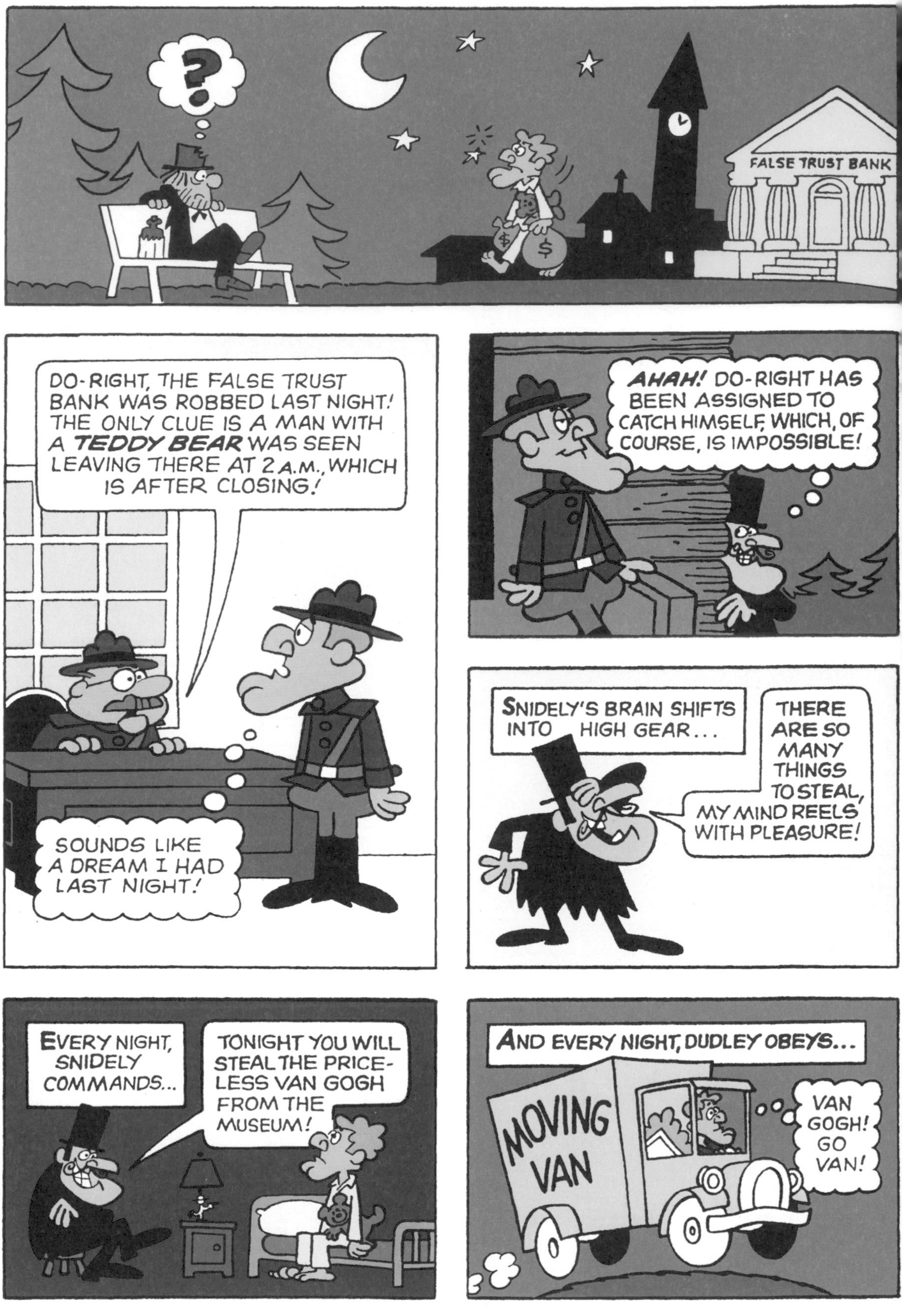
FALSE TRUST BANK
DO-RIGHT, THE FALSE TRUST BANK WAS ROBBED LAST NIGHT! THE ONLY CLUE IS A MAN WITH A TEDDY BEAR WAS SEEN LEAVING THERE AT 2 A.M., WHICH IS AFTER CLOSING!
SOUNDS LIKE A DREAM I HAD LAST NIGHT!
AHAH! DO-RIGHT HAS BEEN ASSIGNED TO CATCH HIMSELF, WHICH, OF COURSE, IS IMPOSSIBLE!
SNIDELY'S BRAIN SHIFTS INTO HIGH GEAR...
THERE ARE SO MANY THINGS TO STEAL, MY MIND REELS WITH PLEASURE!
EVERY NIGHT, SNIDELY COMMANDS...
TONIGHT YOU WILL STEAL THE PRICELESS VAN GOGH FROM THE MUSEUM!
AND EVERY NIGHT, DUDLEY OBEYS...
MOVING VAN
VAN GOGH! GO VAN!

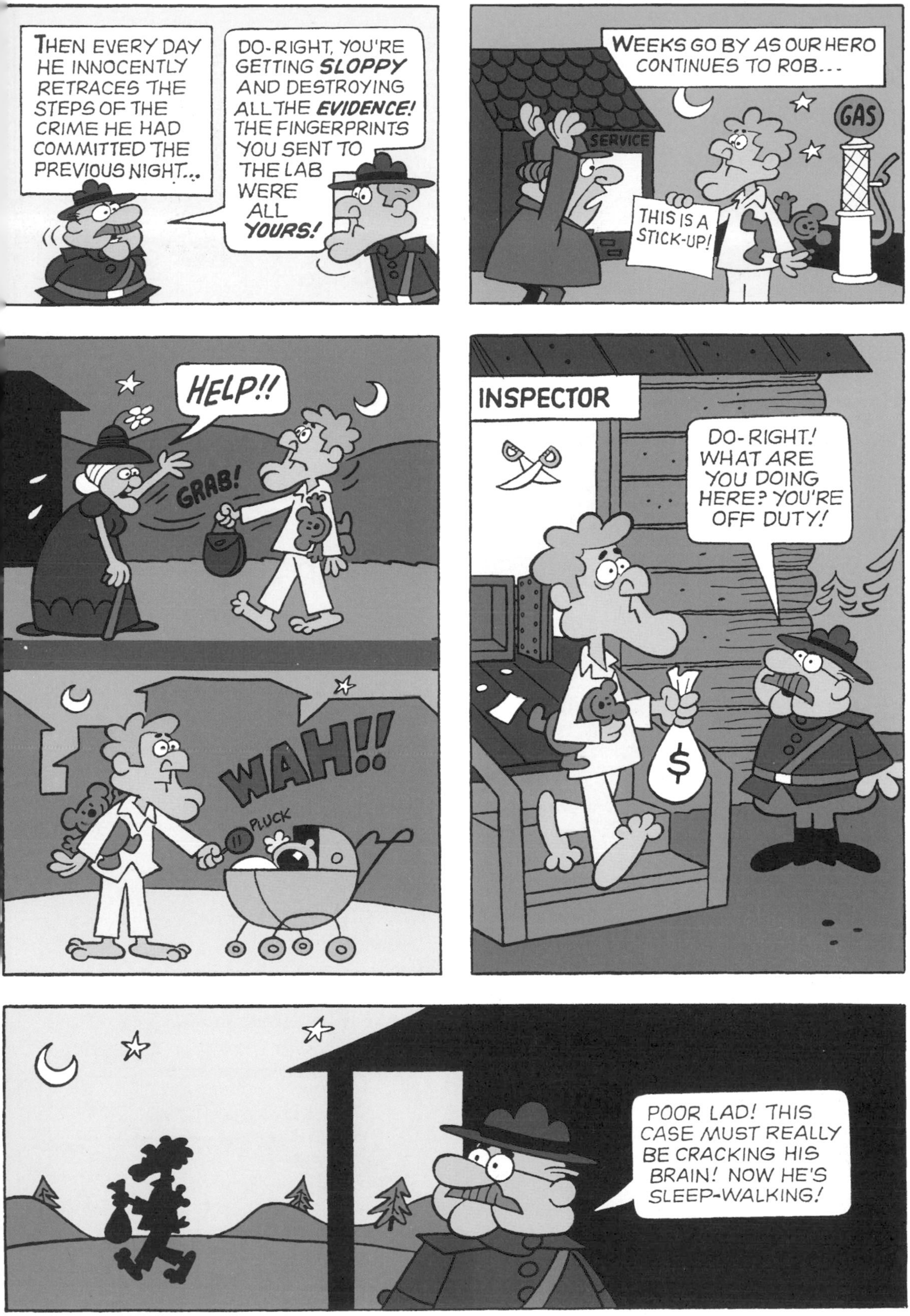
THEN EVERY DAY HE INNOCENTLY RETRACES THE STEPS OF THE CRIME HE HAD COMMITTED THE PREVIOUS NIGHT...
DO-RIGHT, YOU'RE GETTING SLOPPY AND DESTROYING ALL THE EVIDENCE! THE FINGERPRINTS YOU SENT TO THE LAB WERE ALL YOURS!
WEEKS GO BY AS OUR HERO CONTINUES TO ROB...
SERVICE
GAS
THIS IS A STICK-UP!
HELP!!
GRAB!
WAH!!
PLUCK
INSPECTOR
DO-RIGHT! WHAT ARE YOU DOING HERE? YOU'RE OFF DUTY!
$
POOR LAD! THIS CASE MUST REALLY BE CRACKING HIS BRAIN! NOW HE'S SLEEP-WALKING!

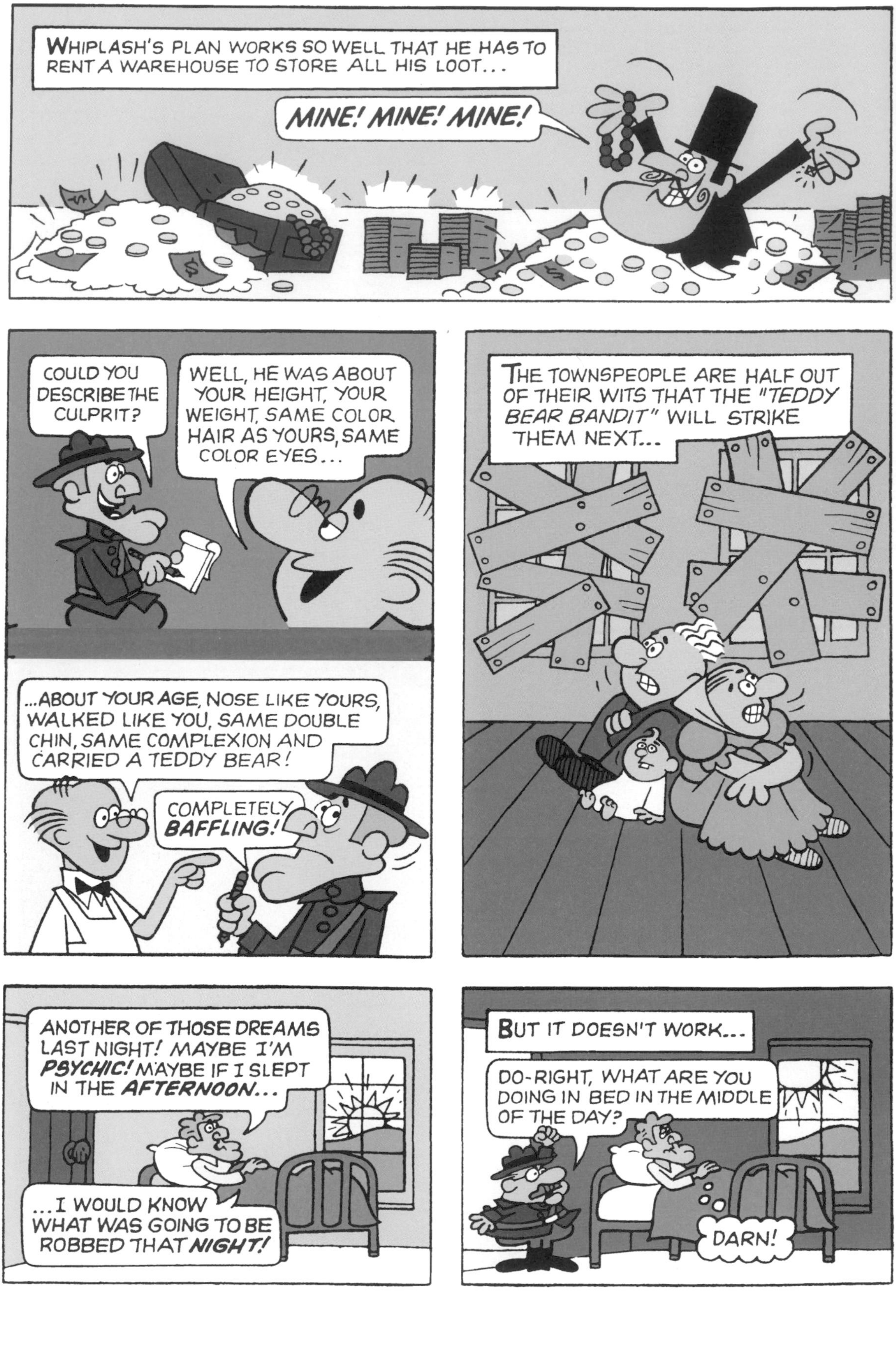
WHIPLASH'S PLAN WORKS SO WELL THAT HE HAS TO RENT A WAREHOUSE TO STORE ALL HIS LOOT...
MINE! MINE! MINE!
COULD YOU DESCRIBE THE CULPRIT?
WELL, HE WAS ABOUT YOUR HEIGHT, YOUR WEIGHT, SAME COLOR HAIR AS YOURS, SAME COLOR EYES...
...ABOUT YOUR AGE, NOSE LIKE YOURS, WALKED LIKE YOU, SAME DOUBLE CHIN, SAME COMPLEXION AND CARRIED A TEDDY BEAR!
COMPLETELY BAFFLING!
THE TOWNSPEOPLE ARE HALF OUT OF THEIR WITS THAT THE "TEDDY BEAR BANDIT" WILL STRIKE THEM NEXT...
ANOTHER OF THOSE DREAMS LAST NIGHT! MAYBE I'M PSYCHIC! MAYBE IF I SLEPT IN THE AFTERNOON...
...I WOULD KNOW WHAT WAS GOING TO BE ROBBED THAT NIGHT!
BUT IT DOESN'T WORK...
DO-RIGHT, WHAT ARE YOU DOING IN BED IN THE MIDDLE OF THE DAY?
DARN!

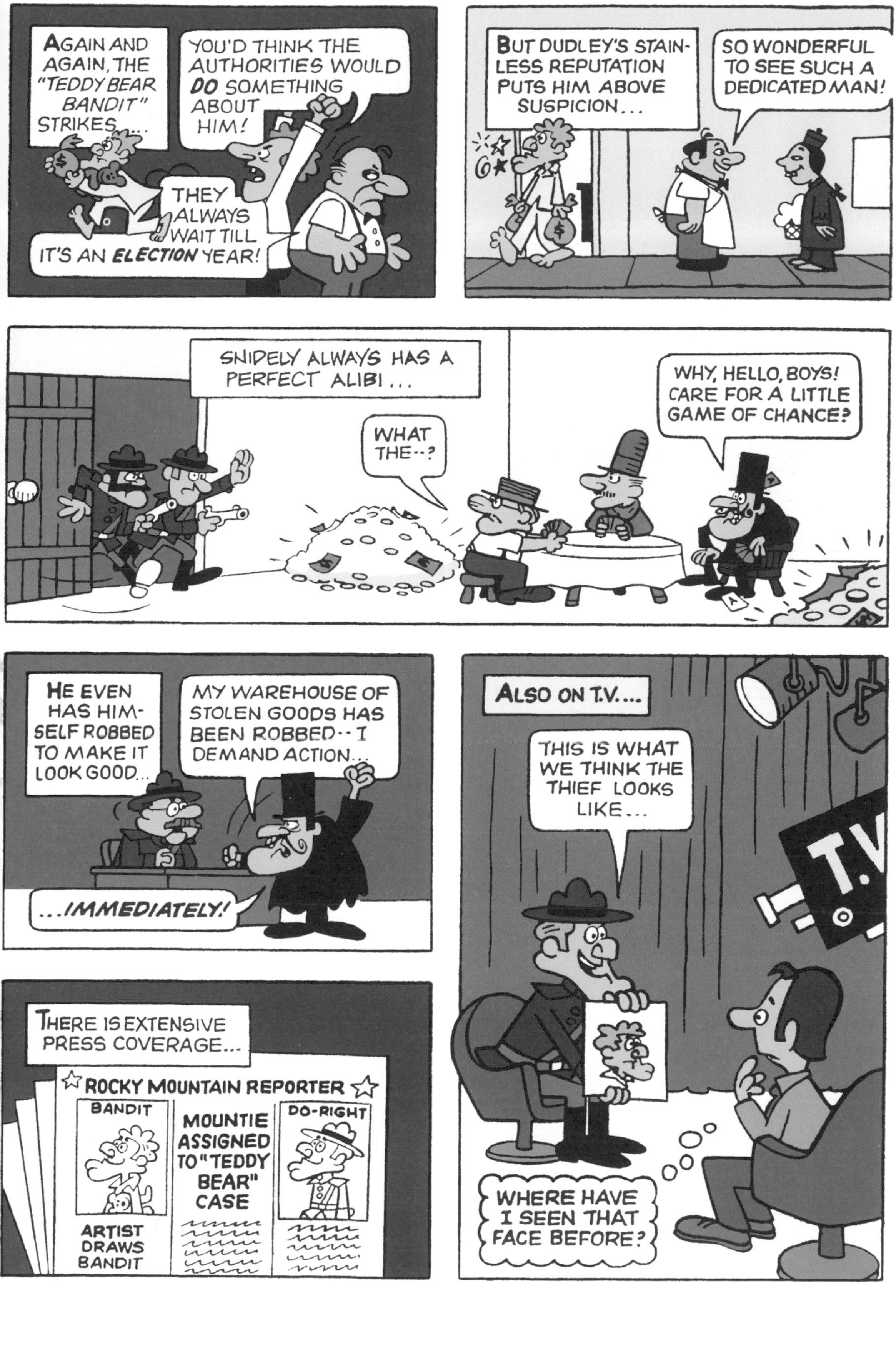
AGAIN AND AGAIN, THE "TEDDY BEAR BANDIT" STRIKES...
YOU'D THINK THE AUTHORITIES WOULD **DO** SOMETHING ABOUT HIM!
THEY ALWAYS WAIT TILL IT'S AN **ELECTION** YEAR!
BUT DUDLEY'S STAINLESS REPUTATION PUTS HIM ABOVE SUSPICION...
SO WONDERFUL TO SEE SUCH A DEDICATED MAN!
SNIDELY ALWAYS HAS A PERFECT ALIBI...
WHAT THE--?
WHY, HELLO, BOYS! CARE FOR A LITTLE GAME OF CHANCE?
HE EVEN HAS HIMSELF ROBBED TO MAKE IT LOOK GOOD...
MY WAREHOUSE OF STOLEN GOODS HAS BEEN ROBBED-- I DEMAND ACTION...
...**IMMEDIATELY!**
THERE IS EXTENSIVE PRESS COVERAGE...
ROCKY MOUNTAIN REPORTER
BANDIT
ARTIST DRAWS BANDIT
MOUNTIE ASSIGNED TO "TEDDY BEAR" CASE
DO-RIGHT
ALSO ON T.V....
THIS IS WHAT WE THINK THE THIEF LOOKS LIKE...
T.V
WHERE HAVE I SEEN THAT FACE BEFORE?

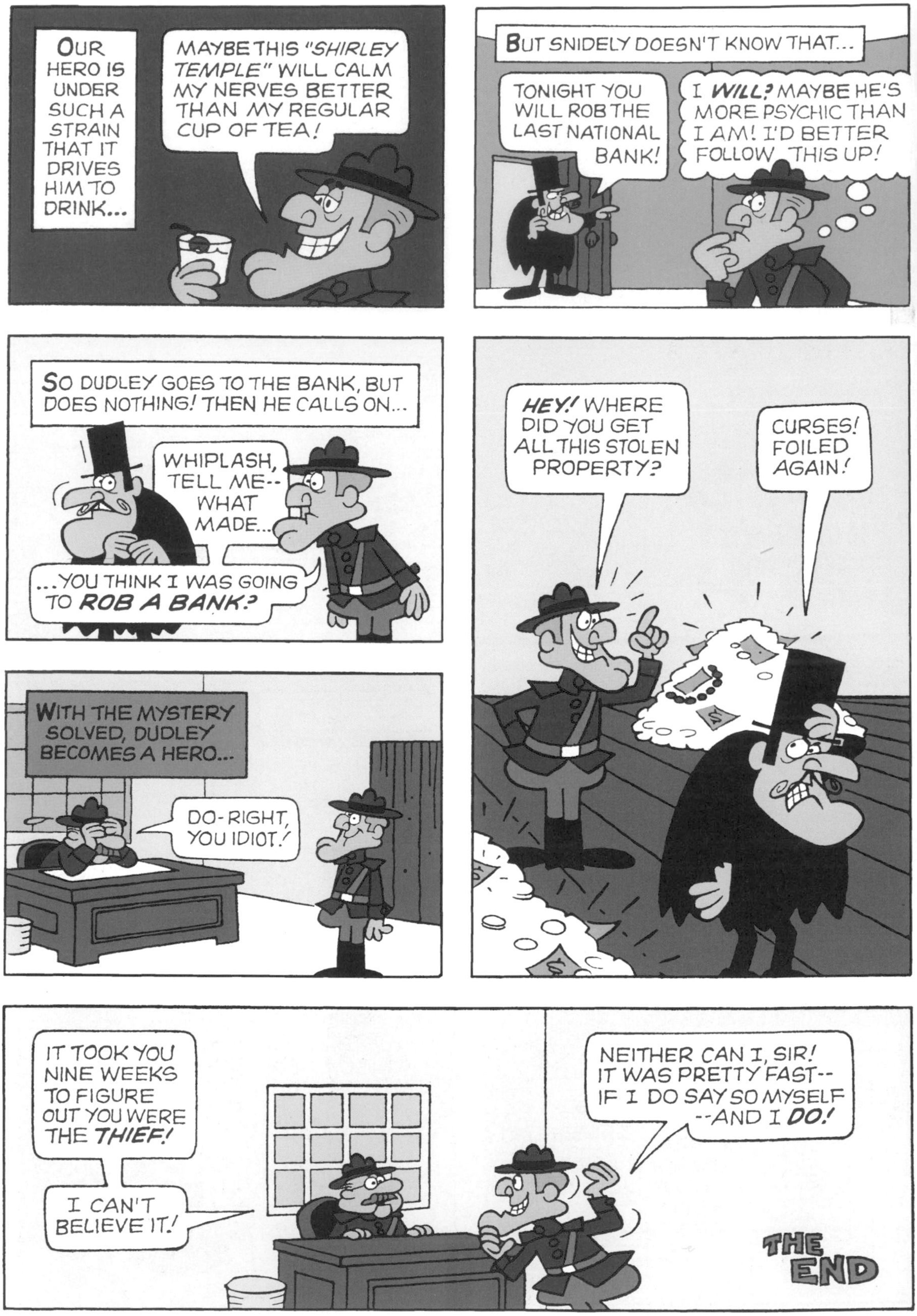
OUR HERO IS UNDER SUCH A STRAIN THAT IT DRIVES HIM TO DRINK...
MAYBE THIS "SHIRLEY TEMPLE" WILL CALM MY NERVES BETTER THAN MY REGULAR CUP OF TEA!
BUT SNIDELY DOESN'T KNOW THAT...
TONIGHT YOU WILL ROB THE LAST NATIONAL BANK!
I WILL? MAYBE HE'S MORE PSYCHIC THAN I AM! I'D BETTER FOLLOW THIS UP!
SO DUDLEY GOES TO THE BANK, BUT DOES NOTHING! THEN HE CALLS ON...
WHIPLASH, TELL ME-- WHAT MADE...
...YOU THINK I WAS GOING TO ROB A BANK?
HEY! WHERE DID YOU GET ALL THIS STOLEN PROPERTY?
CURSES! FOILED AGAIN!
WITH THE MYSTERY SOLVED, DUDLEY BECOMES A HERO...
DO-RIGHT, YOU IDIOT!
IT TOOK YOU NINE WEEKS TO FIGURE OUT YOU WERE THE THIEF!
I CAN'T BELIEVE IT!
NEITHER CAN I, SIR! IT WAS PRETTY FAST-- IF I DO SAY SO MYSELF --AND I DO!
THE END

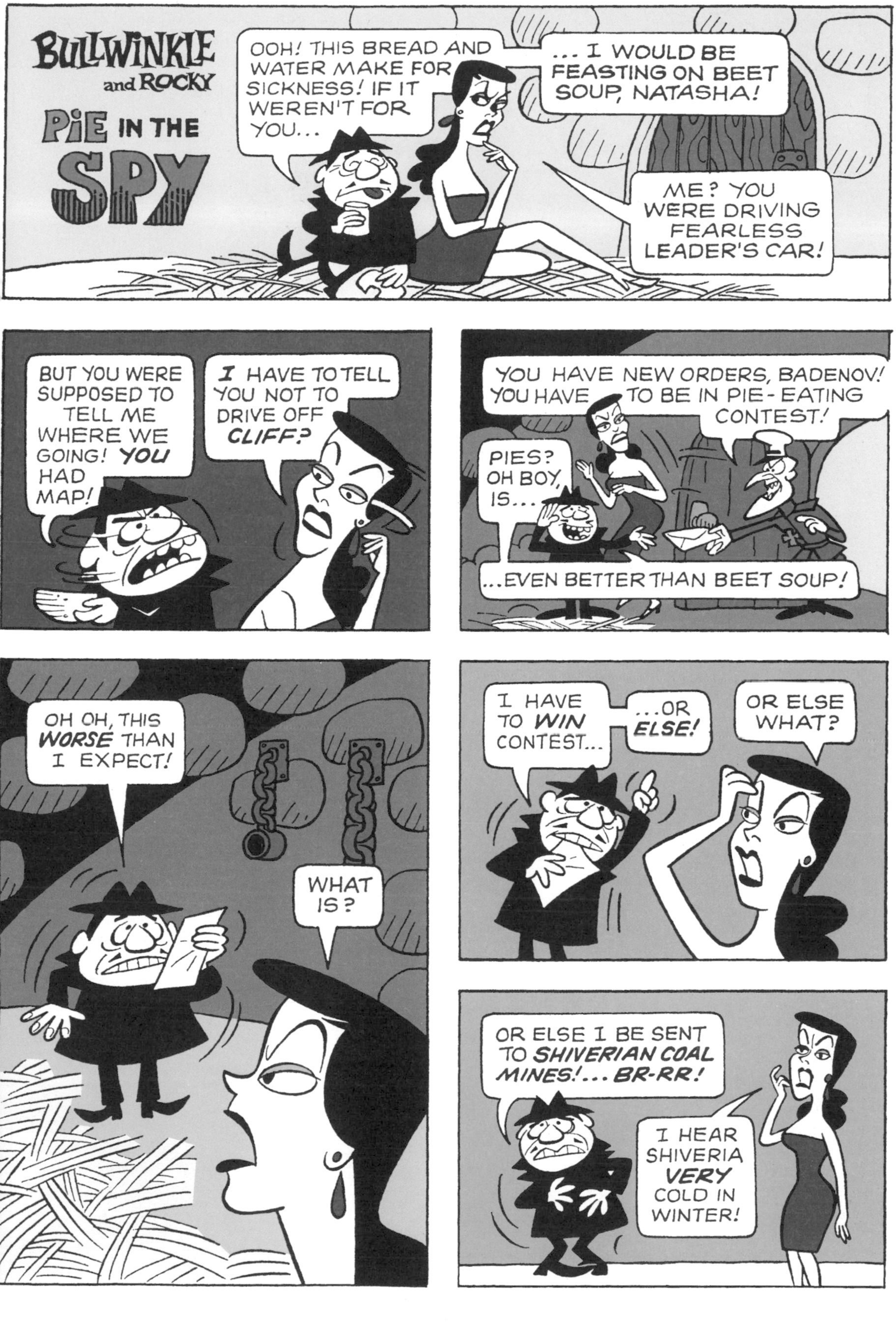
BULLWINKLE and ROCKY
PIE IN THE SPY
OOH! THIS BREAD AND WATER MAKE FOR SICKNESS! IF IT WEREN'T FOR YOU...
... I WOULD BE FEASTING ON BEET SOUP, NATASHA!
ME? YOU WERE DRIVING FEARLESS LEADER'S CAR!
BUT YOU WERE SUPPOSED TO TELL ME WHERE WE GOING! YOU HAD MAP!
I HAVE TO TELL YOU NOT TO DRIVE OFF CLIFF?
YOU HAVE NEW ORDERS, BADENOV! YOU HAVE TO BE IN PIE-EATING CONTEST!
PIES? OH BOY, IS...
...EVEN BETTER THAN BEET SOUP!
OH OH, THIS WORSE THAN I EXPECT!
WHAT IS?
I HAVE TO WIN CONTEST...
...OR ELSE!
OR ELSE WHAT?
OR ELSE I BE SENT TO SHIVERIAN COAL MINES!... BR-RR!
I HEAR SHIVERIA VERY COLD IN WINTER!

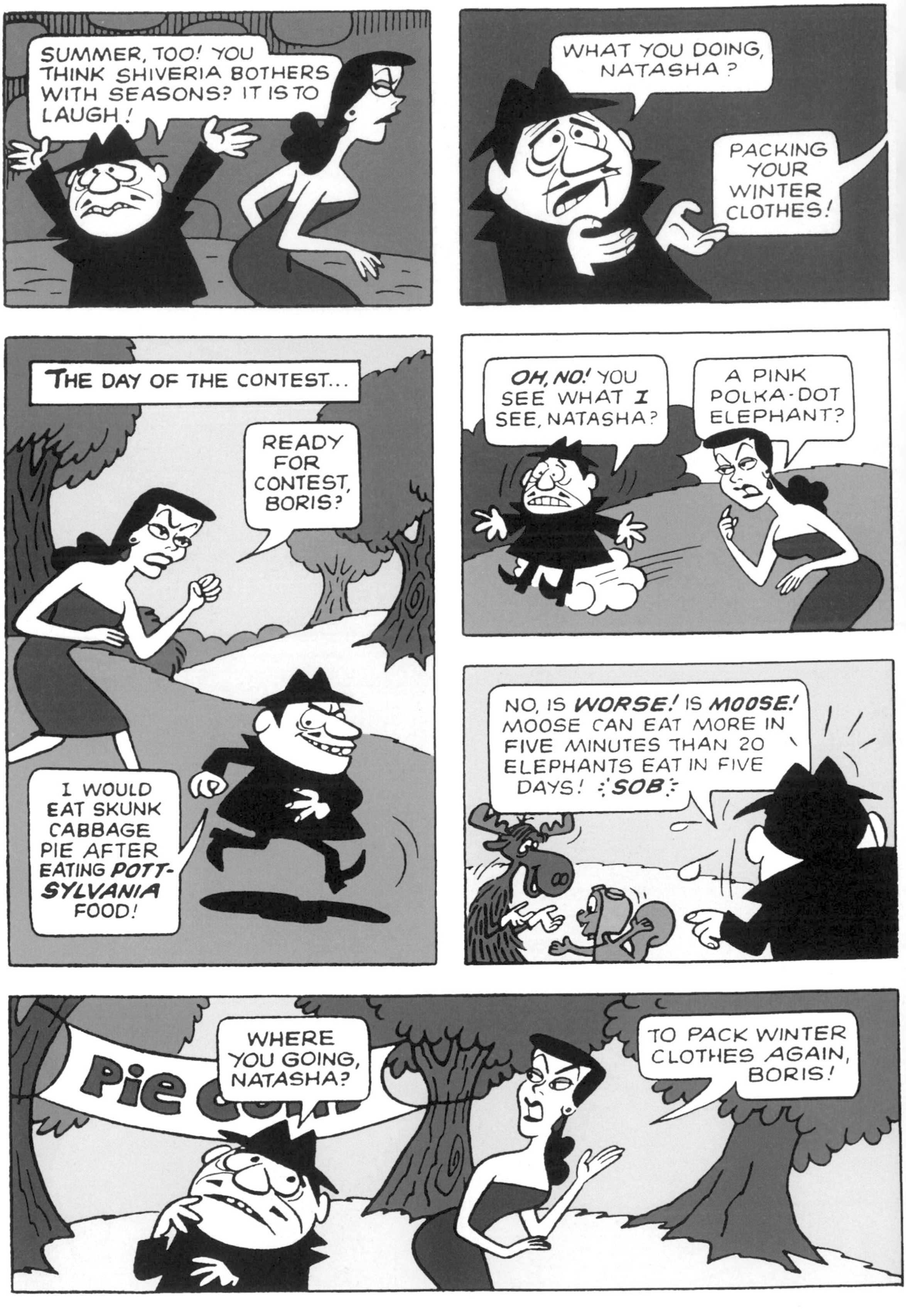
SUMMER, TOO! YOU THINK SHIVERIA BOTHERS WITH SEASONS? IT IS TO LAUGH!
WHAT YOU DOING, NATASHA?
PACKING YOUR WINTER CLOTHES!
THE DAY OF THE CONTEST...
READY FOR CONTEST, BORIS?
I WOULD EAT SKUNK CABBAGE PIE AFTER EATING POTT-SYLVANIA FOOD!
OH, NO! YOU SEE WHAT I SEE, NATASHA?
A PINK POLKA-DOT ELEPHANT?
NO, IS WORSE! IS MOOSE! MOOSE CAN EAT MORE IN FIVE MINUTES THAN 20 ELEPHANTS EAT IN FIVE DAYS! SOB
Pie
WHERE YOU GOING, NATASHA?
TO PACK WINTER CLOTHES AGAIN, BORIS!

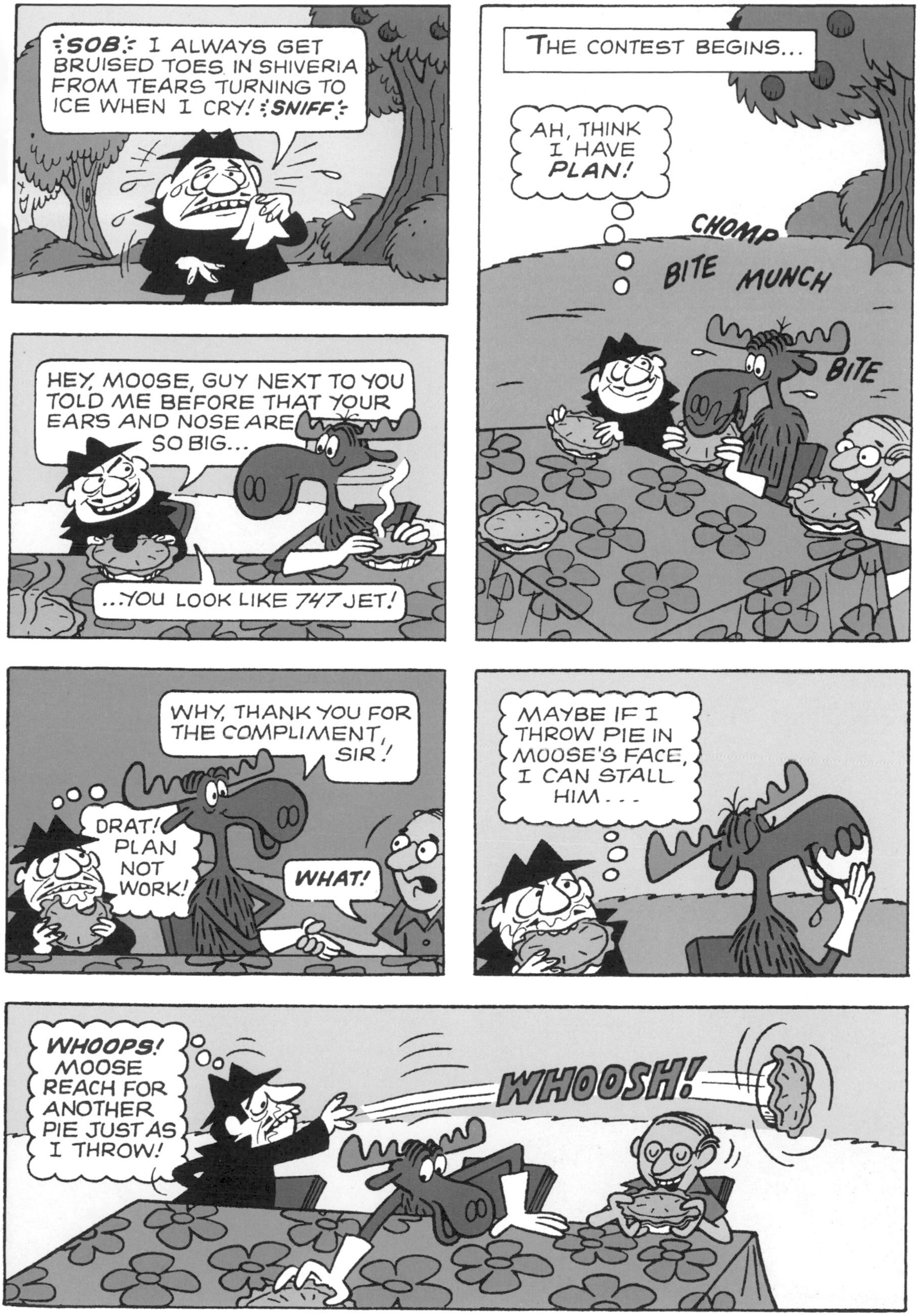

:SOB: I ALWAYS GET BRUISED TOES IN SHIVERIA FROM TEARS TURNING TO ICE WHEN I CRY! :SNIFF:
THE CONTEST BEGINS...
AH, THINK I HAVE PLAN!
CHOMP
BITE
MUNCH
BITE
HEY, MOOSE, GUY NEXT TO YOU TOLD ME BEFORE THAT YOUR EARS AND NOSE ARE SO BIG...
...YOU LOOK LIKE 747 JET!
WHY, THANK YOU FOR THE COMPLIMENT, SIR!
DRAT! PLAN NOT WORK!
WHAT!
MAYBE IF I THROW PIE IN MOOSE'S FACE, I CAN STALL HIM...
WHOOPS! MOOSE REACH FOR ANOTHER PIE JUST AS I THROW!
WHOOSH!

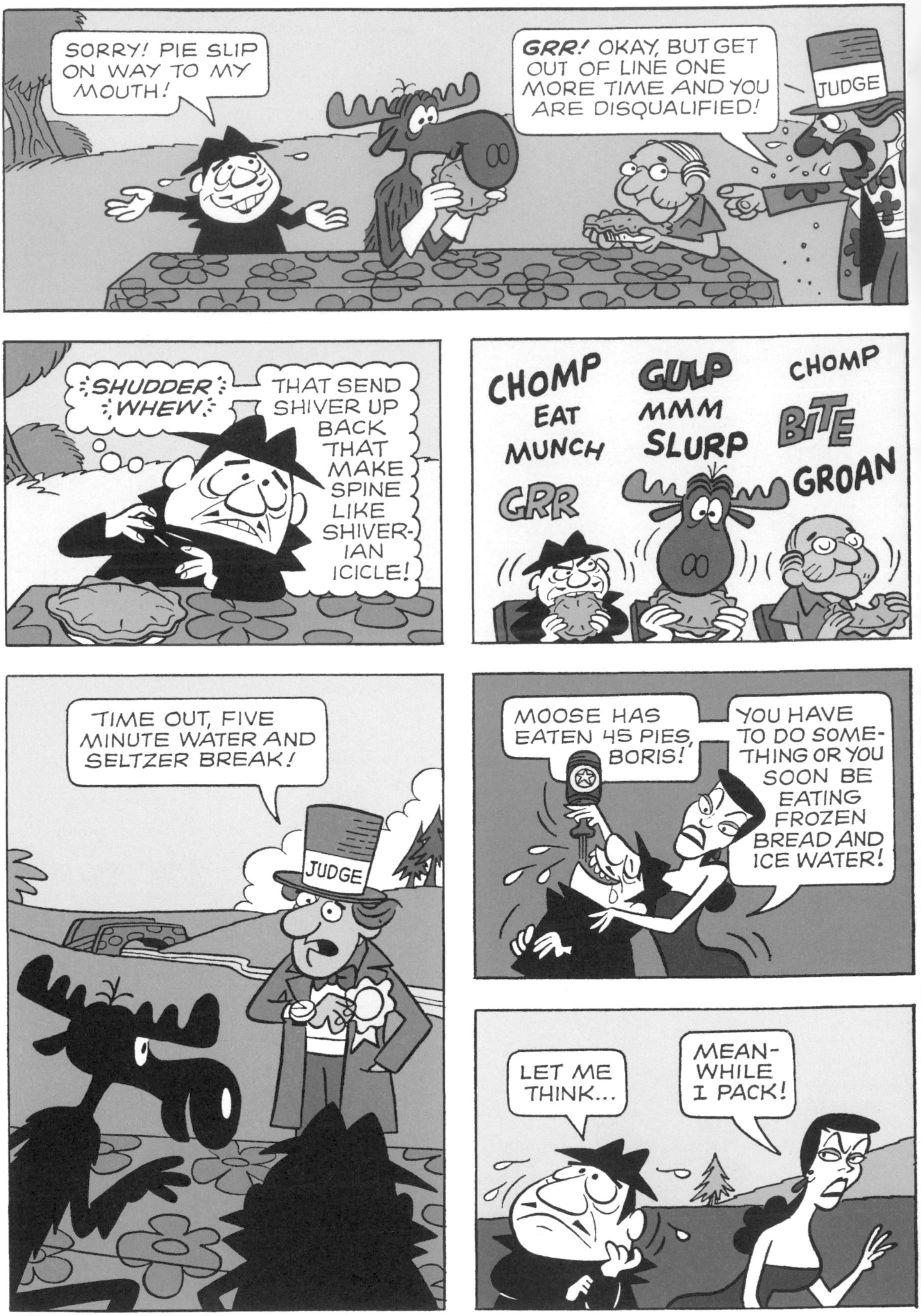
SORRY! PIE SLIP ON WAY TO MY MOUTH!
GRR! OKAY, BUT GET OUT OF LINE ONE MORE TIME AND YOU ARE DISQUALIFIED!
JUDGE
SHUDDER WHEW
THAT SEND SHIVER UP BACK THAT MAKE SPINE LIKE SHIVER-IAN ICICLE!
CHOMP
GULP
CHOMP
EAT
MMM
MUNCH
SLURP
BITE
GRR
GROAN
TIME OUT, FIVE MINUTE WATER AND SELTZER BREAK!
JUDGE
MOOSE HAS EATEN 45 PIES, BORIS!
YOU HAVE TO DO SOME-THING OR YOU SOON BE EATING FROZEN BREAD AND ICE WATER!
LET ME THINK...
MEAN-WHILE I PACK!

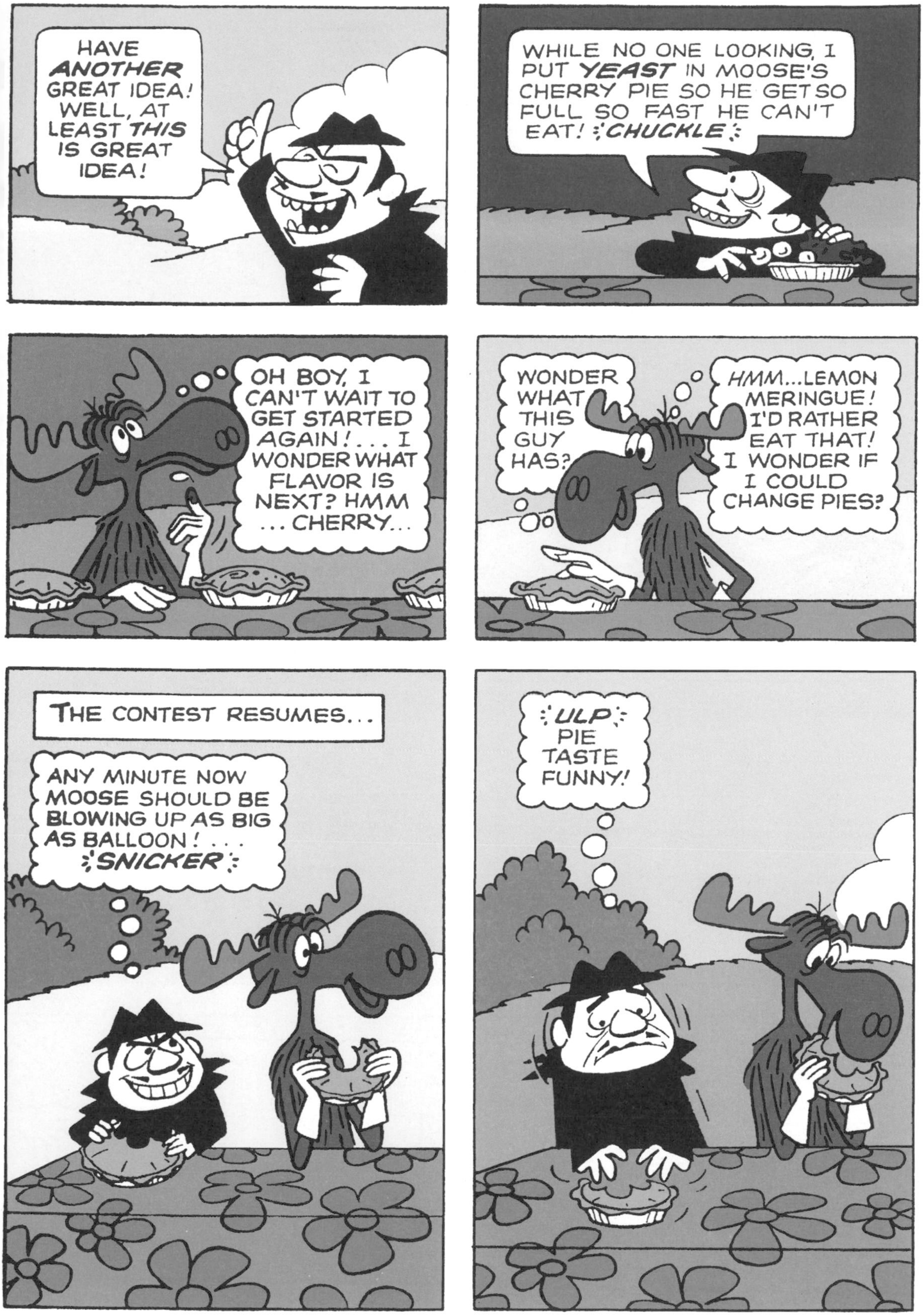
HAVE ANOTHER GREAT IDEA! WELL, AT LEAST THIS IS GREAT IDEA!
WHILE NO ONE LOOKING, I PUT YEAST IN MOOSE'S CHERRY PIE SO HE GET SO FULL SO FAST HE CAN'T EAT! CHUCKLE
OH BOY, I CAN'T WAIT TO GET STARTED AGAIN! . . . I WONDER WHAT FLAVOR IS NEXT? HMM . . . CHERRY . . .
WONDER WHAT THIS GUY HAS?
HMM...LEMON MERINGUE! I'D RATHER EAT THAT! I WONDER IF I COULD CHANGE PIES?
THE CONTEST RESUMES . . .
ANY MINUTE NOW MOOSE SHOULD BE BLOWING UP AS BIG AS BALLOON! . . . SNICKER
ULP PIE TASTE FUNNY!

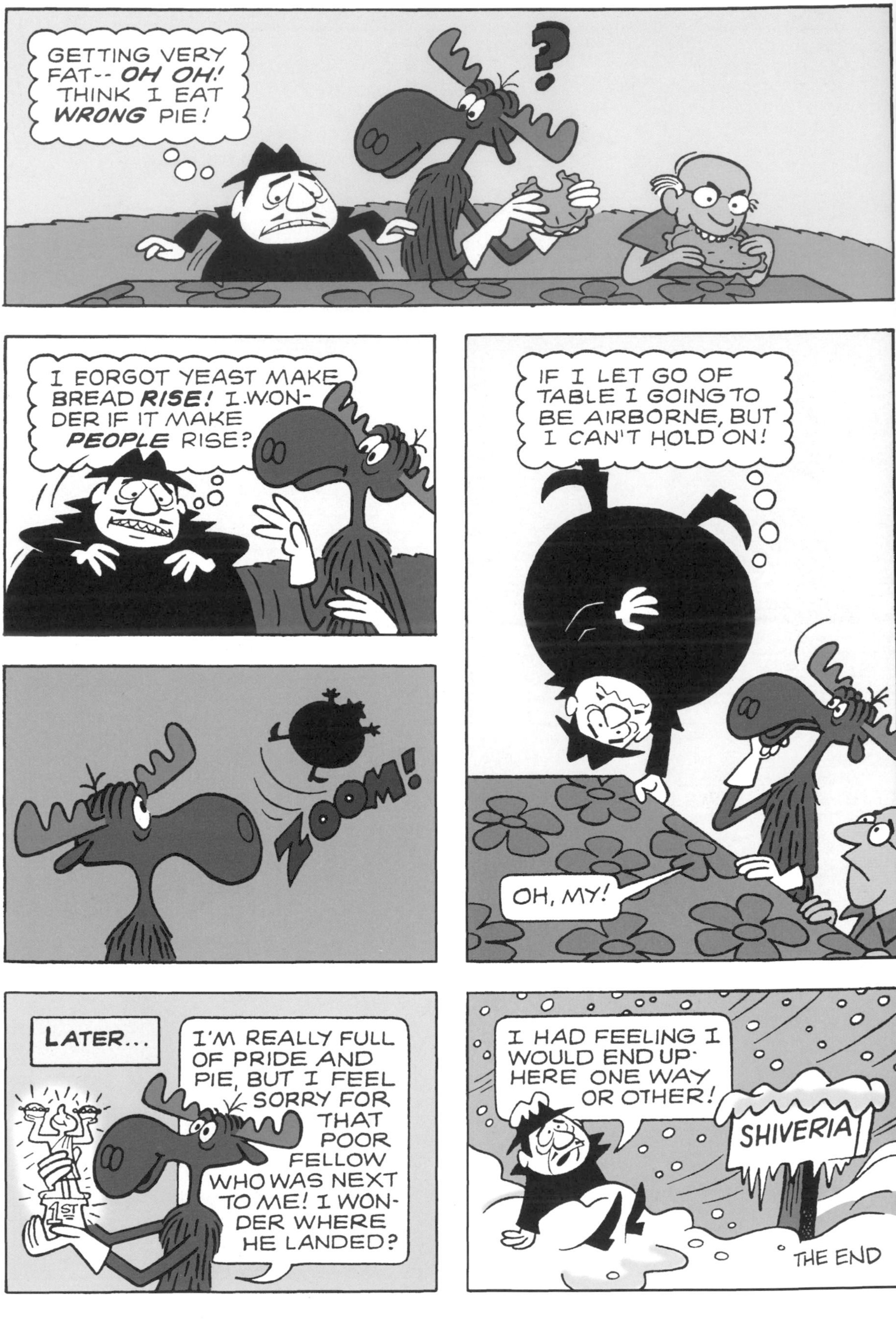
GETTING VERY FAT-- OH OH! THINK I EAT WRONG PIE!
I FORGOT YEAST MAKE BREAD RISE! I WONDER IF IT MAKE PEOPLE RISE?
ZOOM!
IF I LET GO OF TABLE I GOING TO BE AIRBORNE, BUT I CAN'T HOLD ON!
OH, MY!
LATER...
I'M REALLY FULL OF PRIDE AND PIE, BUT I FEEL SORRY FOR THAT POOR FELLOW WHO WAS NEXT TO ME! I WONDER WHERE HE LANDED?
1ST
I HAD FEELING I WOULD END UP HERE ONE WAY OR OTHER!
SHIVERIA
THE END

ROCKY & BULLWINKLE™
CLASSICS
VOLUME 2

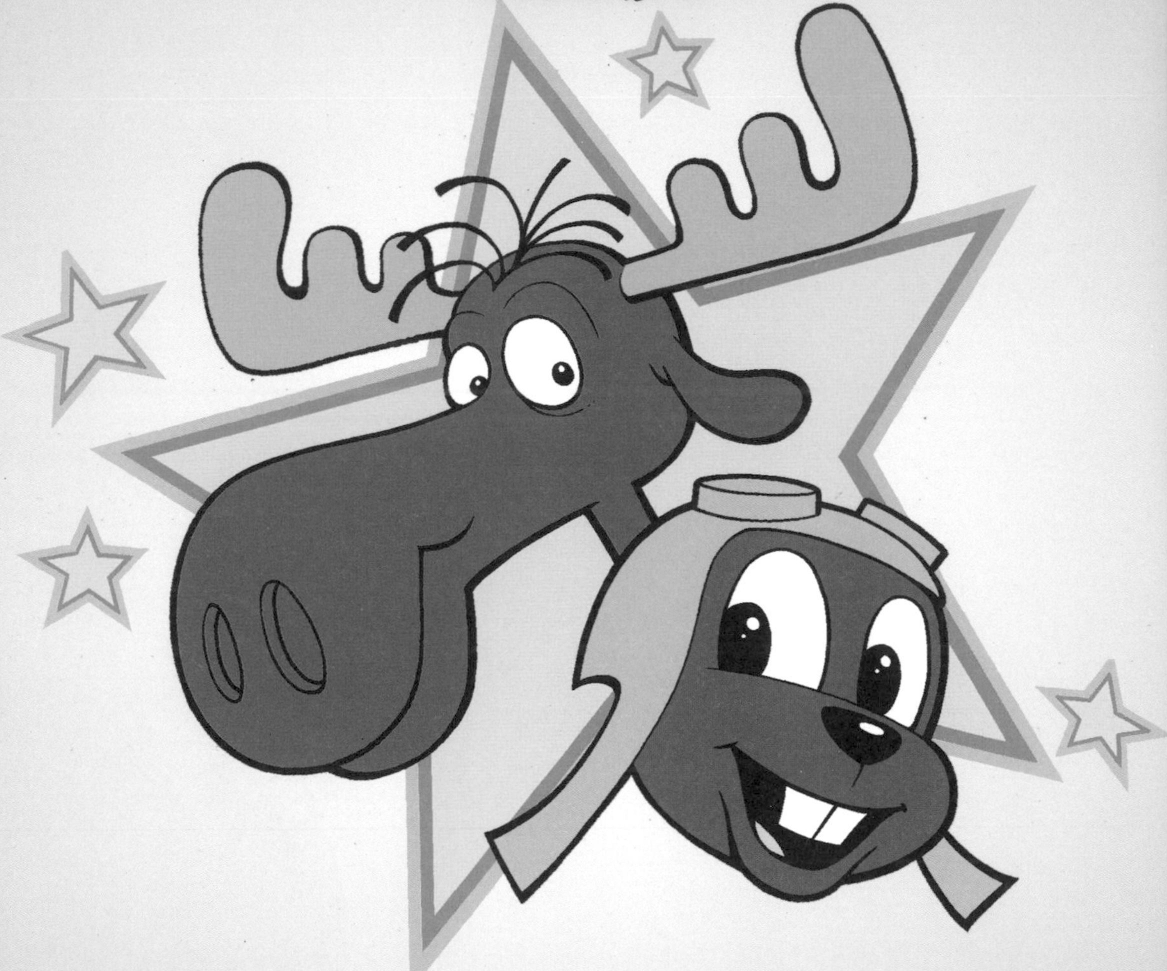